CW00741270

INDUSTRIAL LIGHT & MAGIC

INDUSTRIAL LIGHT & MAGIC
The Art of Innovation

Contents

PREVIOUS SPREAD

Akira Kurosawa's *Dreams* (1990), with a matte painting
by Yusei Uesegi

OPPOSITE

Terminator Salvation (2009)

Foreword

WHAT IS ILM? Is it a company? For sure. It's the first of its kind. It was a company long before digital effects even existed. Is it a place? Indeed. From the moment you set eyes on the bronze Yoda in the courtyard fountain, you know you've arrived. Even if you knew nothing of ILM's storied history, the memorabilia alone would make it an exhilarating destination for any film fan. You should probably also lump in its historical love-children—Pixar, Kerner Optical, and the mythical Skywalker Ranch—and the archives to get an accurate sense of its "place." Is ILM an idea? A concept? A dream? To me, this is the most accurate description.

ILM was a twinkle in the eye of a young George Lucas as he set out to convince his financiers that he could actually translate what he'd written on the page into celluloid for the allotted amount of cash earmarked for *Star Wars*. And ILM has been dancing on the head of the pin that separates art and commerce ever since.

ILM, the "idea," is indeed the most compelling aspect of this institution. Accounts of its early days are only hearsay to my generation of filmmaker. They are the artifacts I pass in the halls: the ancient optical printer that was the workhorse of the early years; the miniatures hanging in the stairwells and sealed in lucite*; photos of the first computers used by ILM to record and repeat camera moves, as well as TIE Fighter choreography; the Lucas/Spielberg nameplate on one of the offices that suggests countless conversations regarding whips and fedoras. It is this mosaic of disparate images that conjures the "idea" of ILM.

The Big Bang of modern technical filmmaking happened between George Lucas's ears and it was shared and compounded by peers like Steven Spielberg who continued to stretch ILM's platoon of pioneering craftsmen to their limits by challenging the constantly expanding-boundaries of what can and can't be done in a movie. From the stained-glass villain in *Young Sherlock Holmes*, to the first CG skeleton tests coming out of "the pit" for *Jurassic Park*, ILM's collaboration with George Lucas's groundbreaking peers added the grist of imagination to the mill of innovation.

At this point, it is incumbent upon me to clarify an important point that is often overlooked. Filmmakers who task ILM with challenges do just that. They present a seemingly unsolvable problem.

Unsolvable because it's never been done before. And it falls upon the visual effects supervisors, artists, coordinators, animators, producers, and technicians to make the impossible possible. Filmmakers provide vision, challenges, and, hopefully, inspiration. But it falls upon the magic elves to bake the cookies.

The name may have seemed folly when it was first conceived (and illustrated by Struzan and Pangrazio) but it has somehow lived up to its flippant promise and the magic spread. Not just to the offshoots of George's sprawling empire of sound, gaming, and animation, but also in the fruits that took root in other orchards like Pixar, Photoshop, Pro-Tools, and the Avid editing system. The magic continues to spread to myriad effects houses around the globe that have been formed around both the talent forged in the crucible of ILM as well as the conceit that this work could be done at all.

For my generation of filmmaker, ILM represents something different. It is a means by which we can both touch history and, if we're lucky enough, make history. George and those of his generation broke the rules and, by default, wrote the rules. No longer renegades, these filmmakers and technicians are now the giants on whose shoulders we stand.

The movie business has always been about talent. ILM and institutions like it are the backbone of the new generation of cinema. A nonlinear scattergun of ideas can meld into a fully realized, cohesive vision that can be shared around the globe thanks to the ever growing pool of technically minded storytellers that make up the rank and file of the digital age. As barriers fall, new possibilities open. And, like the Force, CGI has both a light and a dark side. When used as a tool to continue the chain of inspiring and thoughtful archetypal storytelling from the cave walls of Lascaux to movie screens, phones, and tablets around the world, it brings out the best in us. When used as a puerile distraction from rushed, shoddy filmmaking it brings out our worst. Either way, it's here to stay. And, living up to its original promise, ILM allows the medium of Film to be limited only by what can be imagined.

Jon Favreau

Director of *Iron Man* (2008), *Iron Man 2* (2010), and *Cowboys & Aliens* (2011)

---

* I would be remiss if I didn't point out that I am an astronaut in one of those miniatures: the *Messiah* from *Deep Impact*.

RIGHT

Iron Man 2 (2010)

Preface: A Place Called Home

ASKING INDUSTRIAL LIGHT & MAGIC to execute a shot depicting the celestial music of the spheres would be a fitting challenge. ILM has had the gravitational pull of a planet on directors and craftspeople since George Lucas first threw down the gauntlet several decades ago—"How are we going to do *Star Wars?*" The answer to his question brought the first group of expert players under his conductor's baton. Soon, more like-minded virtuosos were brought into this orbit and they formed other great symphonies. As Richard Edlund put it, "The people who have ideas to do things should be allowed to do them." For a dreamer like me, it is essential to have "a place" where this simple edict rings true: If you can imagine it, magic can happen.

Today, ILM exerts an influence on the most daring storytellers. It's our job as directors to feed ILM what George fed them—the elixir of problem solving—to throw food at the appetite that defines them. And as we continue to bring challenges to ILM and witness that sparkle in the eyes of the artists who work there, we are in a way preserving a place for those who will follow. I enjoy presenting puzzles that they haven't quite seen before—"We need to get back to you on that. It's going to be . . . tricky." I get to see the gears beginning to turn, excitement and trepidation migrating through the halls. As a director I get exponential creative returns by presenting a challenge to the explorers who silently beg, "Dare us. Dare us to do something that can't be done. Because nothing's impossible." This symbiotic relationship facilitates a core reaction, making Industrial Light & Magic the proverbial dream factory.

When I work with ILM at that level, at that threshold of the unknown, there are sometimes failures, but also daily epiphanies. I provide the intent, and then we collectively go to a place where there is no data on how something is going to look or feel or work. That's the spirit of the unknown. The recipe book is fluid.

To an outsider, a studio executive, or a producer, ILM may appear to be a bit of an enigma, a massive box that one plugs into, with completed shots emerging from the other end. But, for me, spending thousands of hours working there, it is a family, a thriving ecosystem, my crew. And just as I cast a film, from a large pool of actors, I seek out specific talents for specific responsibilities when working at ILM. I want the best cloth-simulation guy and the best lighting technician. I demand a direct dialogue with the artists, and I will confide in them the deepest hidden intentions so that they become vested and passionate in the pursuit of the singularity I desire. ILM has always been about the people. It's an assemblage of artisans who, in a strange way, are protected from all the insanity that we deal with here in Hollywood. It remains a sanctuary where they can focus on how to execute a shot. And there is an essential purity in that.

More than ever, audiences are demanding something new. They want to discover and champion new stories. As animation, interactive entertainment, and film continue to collide and influence one another, whole new forms of narrative are waiting to be born. We are presently at a threshold. Visual effects are on a celestial par with dreams, and narrative may not always adhere to the confines of traditional cinematic language. As we slip from the known into a logic of dreams, I am glad that there remains "a place" where stories can be told by a group of craftspeople who are ready to meet that challenge. Who knows where it may take us . . .

Gore Verbinski

Director of *Pirates of the Caribbean: The Curse of the Black Pearl* (2003), *Dead Man's Chest* (2006), *At World's End* (2007), and *Rango* (2011)

LEFT
Rango (2011)

Introduction

INDUSTRIAL LIGHT & MAGIC has created visual effects for hundreds of films, many of which are cultural and cinematic landmarks. From the fantastic creatures and otherworldly environments of the *Star Wars* galaxy to the astounding dinosaurs of *Jurassic Park*, from the raging waters of *The Perfect Storm* and the dramatic power of *Twister* to the extraordinary characters of *Pirates of the Caribbean* and *Iron Man*, the imagery created by ILM has fundamentally changed the face of filmmaking, making it possible to tell stories and create visual experiences that could only have been dreamed of in the past. The goal for those who work at ILM has always been to find the most creative and effective way to realize the vision of a filmmaker—to bring to the screen an accurate representation of what the director has imagined. At ILM, pushing the envelope of what is possible, both creatively and technologically, is a way of life.

For three years, from 2001 through 2003, I was the producer of the Lucasfilm History Project. In the course of conducting 135 interviews to create this oral-history archive, I had the privilege of speaking to thirty ILM employees, past and present. The stories they had to tell, of their own experiences and of the very unique creative environment at ILM, were captivating. I was pleased, therefore, when I was asked to write this book on the history of ILM from 1995 to 2011. The experience would clearly provide an opportunity to explore not only the tremendous technological accomplishments of the company during that period, but also to hear more from the individuals who have been the creative force behind ILM's memorable imagery. At the outset of this project, I suggested, and my Lucasfilm editor J. W. Rinzler agreed, that the primary voice of the book should come from the unique community of individuals who work at ILM—the people who, on a daily basis, are exercising the highest level of creative problem-solving. The emphasis in the chapters is therefore on the people of ILM telling their own stories of working on the films.

In the interviews I conducted for this book, members of the ILM team for each production discussed not only the technological innovations, but also their experience in creating the imagery and discovering new capabilities that have ultimately had a significant impact on the visual effects industry as a whole. The secret of ILM's success is an amazing group of people—those who have worked there in the past and those who work there today. They are the true heroes of the art form that is visual effects—the creative minds behind the technological innovations.

As George Lucas has said, "ILM was designed to do the impossible." I hope that after exploring these pages you'll agree—that is *exactly* what the individuals who make up ILM have done, and what they will continue to do as they move into the company's fourth decade.

Pamela Glintenkamp

RIGHT

Ghostbusters 2 (1989)

FOLLOWING SPEAD

Star Trek IV: The Voyage Home (1986)

THE FILMS

The First Two Decades

1975–1994

George Lucas, chairman of the board, Lucasfilm Ltd.:

"Right from the beginning, ILM was designed to do the impossible. So even on the first *Star Wars*, things were accomplished that had never been done before, which was exciting. Every time I make a movie with ILM, we're pushing the envelope. I'm able to open my imagination and go places that I couldn't go *without* ILM. So I'm very pleased, as a filmmaker, that I can tell the stories I want to tell and that ILM can bring them forth better than I can even imagine them."

VISUAL EFFECTS HAVE BEEN an important part of filmmaking for more than one hundred years now. In fact, some of the earliest experiments in the art of cinema, such as George Méliès's *A Trip to the Moon* (1902), were dependent on visual effects for the thrill they offered audiences.

For more than thirty-five years, Industrial Light & Magic has had an extraordinary history as one of the premiere visual effects companies in the world. This book explores some of the major challenges, innovations, and industry-changing accomplishments at ILM, concentrating on the period from 1995 to the company's first full-length animated film, *Rango*, in 2011.

Two previous books have covered the history of this extraordinary visual effects company: Thomas G. Smith's *Industrial Light & Magic: The Art of Special Effects*, which presented ILM's landmark achievements from 1975 to 1985, and Mark Cotta Vaz and Patricia Rose Duignan's *Industrial Light & Magic: Into the Digital Realm*, which picked up the story of ILM's innovative work from 1986 to 1996. Each of these publications provides detailed information and insights into the accomplishments of ILM during its first and second decades.

The first chapter of this book provides a brief summary of some of the accomplishments in the periods covered by the first two volumes. It's a prelude to the later chapters' exploration of an extraordinary fifteen-year period in ILM's history—a period that is clearly just another remarkable era in an ongoing story of achievement.

To understand and appreciate what ILM does, it's best to start with an impression of what makes this company unique. This is the lens through which we can best understand the history that follows.

PREVIOUS SPREAD

Star Wars: Episode IV *A New Hope* (1977)

ABOVE

At its first facility, a warehouse in Van Nuys, California, the ILM crew shot for *Star Wars*

George Lucas:

"Visual effects are an art form. It's just like painting, where there's a very high level of talent and technical expertise. You need the technical and creative sides of things, and you need the best people in order to make it work. You also have to be able to keep the company going over a period of time so that they can profit from the experience. And that's the thing that ILM brings to the table more than anyone else: They have the *most* experience and, I think, the *most* talented people—and we've been around for the *longest* amount of time."

Scott Farrar, visual effects supervisor:

"It's very collegial at ILM. A lot of us work out these problems together, so you have a body of knowledge and pain that you share from all of these different things that you've tried through the years. And you can always phone somebody up and say, 'Hey, remember when we did this?' and 'Here's my problem now.' It's like a think tank."

Jeff White, associate visual effects supervisor:

"The consistency and the high level of work that ILM creates are thanks to the people and the relationships they have. It's really the heart of the work that we do. All of the innovation that happens here, both on the artistic front and the technology front, is solely based on the people that we have. Anytime you're faced with a challenge or have a shot where it's like, 'Hmmm, what's the best approach on this?' there's a good chance that somebody else has already had to do something like it. So you've got this incredible library of knowledge of visual effects and filmmaking to draw upon when you're trying to solve these problems."

Each project that ILM undertakes brings a new set of challenges, and typically, new breakthrough accomplishments. ILM thus drives its own capabilities, and those of the effects industry overall, forward.

George Lucas:

"We're always on the leading edge of technology. That's because ILM is able to put a lot of money into research and development. That, combined with super-talented people and

the technical backup, makes it a facility and an organization like no other."

Roger Guyett, visual effects supervisor:

"We're overachievers. It's always been this way, and I think this is part of ILM's history. The fascinating thing about working here is we're doing things that we're not totally convinced we're actually going to succeed at. You're always riding the knife edge. A lot of the stuff we do is very innovative, and, quite often, you have failure staring you in the face. But that's what makes the job interesting and brings everyone in here every day, because it's a process of discovery and creation— and it's an immense challenge."

Inspired by just these sorts of challenges, in the first thirty years of the company, the ILM team has earned fifteen Academy Awards for Best Visual Effects, twenty-four additional nominations in that category, and twenty-four Scientific and Technical Achievement Awards from the Academy in recognition of the critical role the company's advances in technology have played in the industry. ILM is also the only entertainment company to date to be recognized with the National Medal of Technology and Innovation, the highest honor for technological achievement bestowed by the president of the United States.

Lynwen Brennan, president, ILM:

"For a large of percentage of the movies that we work on, we're developing technology on the fly. We're also asking for innovation from the artists and the visual effects supervisors. Sometimes our innovation comes from an idea that's more about shot composition, so it's also about that collaboration and that partnership with the director—but it's exciting to work on something where you're not sure how you're going to do it, and at the end, you see it really gel and come to fruition."

Chrissie England, former president, ILM (2004–2010):

"To do groundbreaking work, we have to build new software or hardware in order to meet the challenges of the filmmakers. And when you take on innovative work like that, it's not exactly the easiest place to make money. So we've been very lucky through the years to have George, who believes in us, is proud to share us with the filmmaking community, and, at times, has subsidized us, because there were years where we weren't a money-making business."

George Lucas:

"Now, more than 90 percent of ILM's work is done for outside filmmakers. It was born out of me in the first few years; I was the one that used the place almost exclusively, and then I let Steven [Spielberg] use it, and then, eventually, they turned into a visual effects company and did a lot of outside work."

Chrissie England:

"There are so many iconic moments that we've created for people. When you think of the Star Destroyer coming overhead in *Star Wars*, or the first time you see the *Tyrannosaurus rex* in *Jurassic Park*, or the boys on their bikes flying in front of the moon in *E.T.*, or Davy Jones in *Pirates of the Caribbean*, those are memorable moments in film history that we're all really proud to have contributed to."

Lynwen Brennan:

"George is passionate about ILM's place in the visual effects industry. He's tireless in ensuring that we don't rest on our laurels. He wants to make sure we're constantly pushing that envelope in terms of what we can do. And that's infectious. It comes down from the top, from George. Every person here has that passion, has that drive to do something new, to do something better, to continually amaze both the people we're working with, the directors, and ultimately the audiences. In order to be here, you have to live and breathe what we do. No one gets into this business to make a fortune. They get into it because they have that passion and enthusiasm, and they want to amaze audiences."

Jim Morris, former president, ILM (1994–2004):

"ILM is an incredibly creative company that is fundamentally responsible for not only the modern age of visual effects in motion pictures, but also, in many ways, for having fundamentally changed the art of cinema. When George established ILM in the 1970s, it was to create effects for the original *Star Wars* films. He had a vision for creating visual effects that was very different from what had happened in the past. He wanted to have volumes and volumes of effects so that he could completely immerse the audience in a world they'd never been in before. He accomplished that, and *Star Wars* and ILM became milestones in terms of the cinema of spectacle. Over the years, ILM has pioneered photographic and digital visual effects and animation for film that have fundamentally changed the kinds of stories that can be told and how these movies can be made. It really has given filmmakers phenomenal tools to get their dreams up on the screen."

LEFT
The original ILM logo by Drew Struzan, based on an illustration by Michael Pangrazio

Stop-motion animation was used for the tauntaun and rider in *Star Wars*: Episode V *The Empire Strikes Back* (1980).

TIMELINE: THE EARLY YEARS

1975 to 1977

Star Wars: Episode IV *A New Hope*

In 1975, ILM is established to produce visual effects for *Star Wars*. The company's original location is in an industrial warehouse in Van Nuys, California, just ten miles from the heart of Hollywood. The new company is made up of young, inexperienced, and extraordinarily enthusiastic creative people. They are funded with a million dollars to build equipment to create visual effects, most of which have never been attempted before on such a vast scale.

The creative minds of the young ILM develop new tools and adapt existing techniques to produce jaw-dropping visual effects. The innovations include an electronic motion control camera system, called the Dykstraflex, which makes it possible to program and repeat specific camera moves to photograph models. Using the new motion control system facilitates compositing within a single film frame numerous elements that are photographed on separate motion control "passes."

ILM's astounding technological advances in the making of *Star Wars* also include the development of new blue-screen matting procedures. And in a prelude to future technology, early computer graphics work is featured in a scene revealing the Death Star on a monitor display.

Academy Award®: Best Visual Effects

John Stears, John Dykstra, Richard Edlund, Grant McCune, Robert Blalack

1978 to 1980

Star Wars: Episode V *The Empire Strikes Back*

ILM begins work on *The Empire Strikes Back* and moves to San Rafael in Northern California. As with ILM's original Los Angeles location during the production of *Star Wars*, a series of large spaces is once again transformed into a visual effects facility. A second story is built over the heads of the ILM crew, who dodge plaster and wood chips as they work—without heat or air-conditioning. Despite the lack of creature comforts, the ILM team develops a new high-speed VistaVision camera, as well as a four-projector-head optical printer for compositing. The new Quad printer, along with an increased sophistication in blue-screen techniques, results in matte shots for *The Empire Strikes Back* being far superior to those in *Star Wars*.

A stop-motion department is established at ILM to work on the tauntaun creatures and snow walkers featured in the *Empire* battle sequence. By combining motion control and standard stop-motion techniques, the creation of the tauntaun shots lays the groundwork for a new technology the company will later develop, called Go-Motion.

Academy Award®: Special Achievement Award for Visual Effects

Brian Johnson, Richard Edlund, Dennis Muren, Bruce Nicholson

1981

Dragonslayer

ILM's first non-Lucasfilm production, *Dragonslayer*, inspires the full development of the Go-Motion process, in which motion control technology is adapted to stop-motion-style puppet animation. Go-Motion creates realistic motion blur and smooth character articulation. Dragon rod puppets are mounted on a programmable model mover and photographed in front of miniature sets or a blue screen.

Academy Award® Nomination: Best Visual Effects

Dennis Muren, Phil Tippett, Ken Ralston, Brian Johnson

Raiders of the Lost Ark

Visual effects are especially prominent in the climactic ending of *Raiders of the Lost Ark*, in which the unsealing of the Ark of the Covenant results in a supernatural event. Live-action footage that had been shot on stage by Spielberg's main unit is enhanced with opticals and matte paintings, including the creation of the massive warehouse in which the Ark is stored. Cel animation and water-tank photography are used to create

ghostly images. In some cases, more than fifty in-camera passes are made to maintain the image quality.

Academy Award®: Best Visual Effects

Richard Edlund, Kit West, Bruce Nicholson, Joe Johnston

1982

E.T.: The Extra-Terrestrial

The now iconic image of *E.T.* and his human friends on flying bicycles crossing the face of the moon is created by ILM using Go-Motion miniatures. The figures are shot as blue-screen elements and then inserted optically into live-action plates. ILM's Model Shop is responsible for building a forced-perspective suburban neighborhood, miniature forests, and *E.T.*'s mother ship.

Academy Award®: Best Visual Effects

Carlo Rambaldi, Dennis Muren, Kenneth Smith

Poltergeist

ILM's work necessitates the establishment of a twenty-person animation department to create the poltergeists. Animated smoke shapes are shot in multiple passes to create generic spirits. Other, more defined spirit forms are created using high-speed photography of an actress draped in fabric, and flown against black. The optical department enhances shots of actors on a black set with lights attached to their chests, in order to create apparitions that were barely visible.

Academy Award® Nomination: Best Visual Effects

Richard Edlund, Michael Wood, Bruce Nicholson

RIGHT

For *Young Sherlock Holmes*, John Lasseter painstakingly hand-animated the motion of the stained-glass knight, while new rendering technology was created to realize the final image.

Star Trek II: The Wrath of Khan

ILM works with another group at Lucasfilm, the Computer Division, to create the "Genesis Effect" for this film. The sequence features CG images of a projectile striking a planet's surface, the firestorm that follows, and the rapid evolution of greenery, mountains, and oceans against a CG star field. The final image of the sequence showing an earthlike planet was ILM's first digital matte painting. The Genesis Effect was the first completely computer-generated sequence in film production.

1983

Star Wars: Episode VI Return of the Jedi

More than two thousand visual effects storyboards are drawn for the more than nine hundred shots that ILM produces. The work on *Return of the Jedi* involves more than five hundred composites. This is estimated as the most complicated and largest visual effects job undertaken for a motion picture at that time. All in all, *Return of the Jedi* requires 25 percent more effects shots and photographic elements than *The Empire Strikes Back*. The scenes are filled with Go-Motion creatures and machines, space shots that look like World War I air

battle sequences, as well as the typical imaginative places and characters that make up the *Star Wars* universe; ILM's Creature Shop assigns fourteen creature makers to the project, to make more than fifty new aliens. Thirty-nine matte paintings are created for *Return of the Jedi*. This is the most complex and challenging matte painting assignment ILM had attempted to date.

Academy Award®: Special Achievement Award for Visual Effects

Richard Edlund, Dennis Muren, Ken Ralston, Phil Tippett

1984

Indiana Jones and the Temple of Doom

ILM creates 140 visual effects shots for this film. The sequences featuring ILM's creative solutions include racing mine cars, bubbling lava, crashing aircraft, bursting cliff faces, and a swarm of bugs. The mine-car chase takes four months to complete and includes more than a third of all of the effects shots in the film. Lava effects are generated by shooting a mixture of red-tinted glycerin and water, illuminated from below.

Academy Award®: Best Visual Effects

Dennis Muren, Michael J. McAlister, Lorne Peterson, George Gibbs

The Ewok Adventure

The impressive effects incorporated in Lucasfilm's first prime-time television production include a latent-image matte painting displaying views of an alien landscape. Blue-screen photography is used for process shots of human characters and Ewoks interacting with the enormous Gorax.

Primetime Emmy Award: Outstanding Special Visual Effects

Michael Pangrazio, Dennis Muren, Phil Tippett, Jon Berg, Harley Jessup,
John Ellis, Christopher Evans

1985

Young Sherlock Holmes

ILM's Computer Graphics Division is established to work on this film. A breakthrough in computer graphics is achieved with the first three-dimensional, fully computer-generated character to be featured in a full-length film, the "stained-glass man." Final composites, composed of the CG knight, animated shadows, and a stained-glass window matte painting, are printed out directly onto film by a revolutionary laser scanner. This was also the first ILM project to use numerous blue-screen puppets.

Academy Award® Nomination: Best Visual Effects

Dennis Muren, Kit West, John Ellis, Dave Allen

Cocoon

Effects shots, including the alien mother ship, stormy turbulence, and a scene of alien lovemaking, are created using miniatures, matte paintings, and optical effects.

Academy Award®: Best Visual Effects

Ken Ralston, Ralph McQuarrie, Scott Farrar, David Berry

Back to the Future

The handful of visual effects shots for this film includes the time-travel effect itself—a dynamic display of light and color that is created by the animation department.

Ewoks: The Battle for Endor

ILM's work on this Ewoks television special includes matte paintings along with sequences involving stop-motion animation.

Primetime Emmy Award: Outstanding Special Visual Effects

Michael J. McAlister

Mishima: A Life in Four Chapters

For this joint Lucasfilm, Zoetrope, and Filmlink project, ILM creates ritualistic suicide imagery of blood on paper, composited with the film's titles.

Out of Africa

ILM provides an effects solution when the live-action train continually breaks down on location. A miniature train setup is constructed and photographed against blue-screen. This is then composited with plates shot in Kenya.

Amazing Stories

ILM provides a shot for the recurring end credits of this television anthology, produced by Spielberg's Amblin Entertainment. A forced-perspective street miniature is shot on a stage to show a suburban neighborhood transitioning from day to night. Two computer-controlled lighting setups are used to create the lighting transition.

ABOVE LEFT

Eddie Murphy (Chandler Jarrell) at ILM during the making of *The Golden Child*.

ABOVE MIDDLE

Lt. Tuck Pendleton (Dennis Quaid) in the cockpit of his ship (*Innerspace*).

ABOVE RIGHT

The angry Jack Nicholson puppet from *The Witches of Eastwick*. Constructed and puppeteered by Howie Weed, the puppet was used for a transformation sequence.

1986

Labyrinth

This *tour de force* of puppeteering by Jim Henson's team is supported by matte paintings created at ILM.

Howard the Duck

The character of Howard is realized by the ILM creature shop, which constructs suits and animatronic heads worn by performers. ILM creates electrical charges generated by the evil Dark Overlord, and matte paintings are used to extend large-scale sets depicting Howard's home planet.

Captain EO

This seventeen-minute, 3-D space adventure, directed by Francis Ford Coppola and produced by George Lucas, is created for Disneyland and Walt Disney World. ILM assists the Disney effects team in the completion of motion control photography for shots featured in the opening space sequence.

Star Trek IV: The Voyage Home

ILM's young computer graphics department creates a dream sequence that includes a series of images depicting bodies transforming from one character to another. Laser scanning is used to create digital representations of the characters. The scans are then fed into ILM's computers for manipulation. The ILM team also creates whales so realistic that few people realize they are puppets. This is the first time anyone has made free-swimming and remote-controlled underwater animals. Lastly, the heads of principal cast members are scanned to create a time-travel effect.

The Golden Child

To achieve the frenetic look of documentary footage, ILM devises a field-operable motion control system that can record camera-shake on location and then repeat that handheld-style movement during the blue-screen Go-Motion puppet photography. The transformation of a character into a demon is the longest effect produced by ILM to date (sixty seconds).

1987

Star Tours

This simulator ride at Disneyland includes the new longest visual effects shot: four and a half minutes of continuous effects footage simulating an uninterrupted view from the StarSpeeder passenger bay.

Innerspace

Miniature sets representing internal body organs and pathways are composited with blue-screen footage of rod-puppeted submersible pods. Miniatures are mostly shot in the ILM water tank to create the liquid look of the internal environment.

Academy Award®: Best Visual Effects

Dennis Muren, Bill George, Harley Jessup, Kenneth Smith

The Witches of Eastwick

During the film's most complex scene, twenty puppeteers manipulate an angry Jack Nicholson puppet. After being photographed, the puppet is composited by ILM. The head area is left mostly featureless, so that Nicholson's facial characteristics can be added by projecting the filmed image of the actor onto the puppet head. Matte paintings and latent image composites are created for establishing shots of the film's expansive mansion.

1988

Willow

ILM creates the first morphing sequence for motion pictures. The company subsequently wins a Technical Achievement Award for its development of Morf, a computer graphics program allowing the fluid, on-screen transformation of one object into another.

Academy Award® Nomination: Best Visual Effects

Dennis Muren, Michael J. McAlister, Phil Tippett, Christopher Evans

Who Framed Roger Rabbit?

The film requires more composite shots than all three *Star Wars* films put together: 1,065 shots are created, incorporating some 10,000 separate elements. More than 70 percent of the total film travels through ILM's optical printers, and more than a thousand opticals are ultimately completed for the film, amounting to fifty-seven minutes of screen time. Because of the unprecedented use of opticals, nearly all live action is shot using the high-quality VistaVision format. ILM's camera department builds specially designed horizontal-film-format cameras for the main unit and names them VistaFlex cameras.

Academy Award®: Best Visual Effects

Ken Ralston, Richard Williams, Ed Jones, George Gibbs

1989

Lucasfilm Commercial Productions (LCP) is established. The new division makes commercials based on concepts developed by ad agencies. The division is described as a sister company to ILM. Although ILM has done effects shots for commercials previously, the division has an exclusive arrangement with ILM. Projects for LCP include spots for Pepsi, Coke, McDonald's, Burger King, Nike, Kellogg's, Acura, GM, BMW, Intel, etc.

Indiana Jones and the Last Crusade

The imagery showing the character Donovan aging and turning to dust is conceived as one continuous shot. Three motion-controlled puppet heads reveal the character in various stages of decomposition. Morphing is then employed to blend the three-stage photography into what appears to be an uninterrupted process. This shot is the first-ever digital composite of a full-screen, live-action image. With this shot, ILM finally realizes a goal George Lucas set when the first Computer Graphics Group was established at Lucasfilm: All of the elements are scanned in, digitally composited, and scanned back out to film.

The Abyss

ILM is one of nine effects facilities working on this film. The company creates the first soft-surface computer-generated 3-D character with the "pseudo-pod." Production of effects for the film involves the first extensive use of Adobe Photoshop software. Designed to manipulate still pictures, Photoshop allows the artist to manipulate digitized photographic data of background plate sets and create a digital model in which to integrate a computer-generated water-creature. Photoshop will become a major digital tool, used in developing art department concepts, in digitally creating matte paintings, and in painting shots to completion. The software is a major breakthrough, originally developed by ILMer John Knoll and his brother Tom.

Academy Award®: Best Visual Effects

Hoyt Yeatman, Dennis Muren, John Bruno, Dennis Skotak

Ghostbusters II

The two hundred effects shot in this film are produced in a period of only six months. Along with ghosts, the impressive imagery includes a river of slime, smoke clouds, and a walking Statue of Liberty.

Back to the Future Part II

ILM's work includes extremely ambitious split-screen shots. To meet the demands of the script, the VistaGlide is developed: a portable motion control dolly system with video playback that enables the operator to record an "A" pass, then split it and have it available for review as the "B" pass is being filmed. A critical software program for digital wire and rod removal is also used for the first time on this film.

Academy Award® Nomination: Best Visual Effects

Ken Ralston, Michael Lantieri, John Bell, Steve Gawley

1990

Die Hard 2: Die Harder

ILM creates the first digitally manipulated matte painting. Effects also include flying and crashing aircraft models. Forty effects shots are completed in five months.

1991

Backdraft

ILM contributes five critical shots to this film, as other visuals are accomplished through the skill of the film's on-set special effects supervisor and cinematographer. Miniatures, a matte painting, and live-action elements are combined to create imagery of a burning, collapsing rooftop.

Academy Award® Nomination: Best Visual Effects

Mikael Salomon, Allen Hall, Clay Pinney, Scott Farrar

Hook

With 200,000 accumulated work hours, this film is second only to *Return of the Jedi* for the most time-intensive ILM production up to this point. Tinkerbell's fluttering wings are nine-inch plastic devices built by the Model Shop and photographed separately. Go-Motion animation creates their flapping movement.

Academy Award® Nomination: Best Visual Effects

Eric Brevig, Harley Jessup, Mark Sullivan, Michael Lantieri

Terminator 2: Judgment Day

ILM is one of four teams working on this ambitious effects-laden film. ILM applies new innovation in digital compositing and computer graphics to create the first CG-animated main character, the liquid metal T-1000. The work on this film requires a significant expansion of

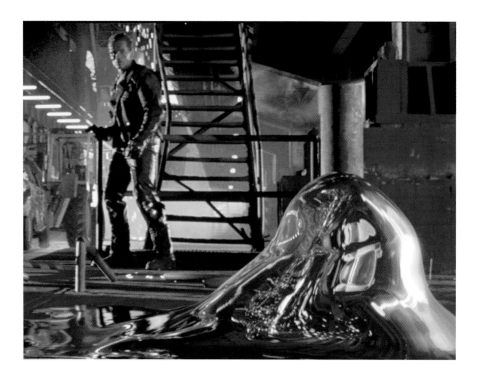

ILM's computer graphics department. Millions of dollars are invested in new hardware and software.

Academy Award®: Best Visual Effects

Dennis Muren, Stan Winston, Gene Warren Jr., Robert Skotak

1992

The Young Indiana Jones Chronicles

The Young Indiana Jones Chronicles is the first production to create completely digital matte paintings. Western Images provides digital effects for the series, while ILM's digital matte paintings are composited with live-action photography to create exotic environments. The series wins a Primetime Emmy Award for Outstanding Individual Achievement in Special Visual Effects.

Death Becomes Her

An experiment in the development of both commercial and proprietary software, much of the work on this film anticipates the effects breakthroughs of *Jurassic Park*. *Death Becomes Her* marks the first time human skin texture is computer generated, with the physical appearance of real-life actors altered digitally.

Academy Award®: Best Visual Effects

Ken Ralston, Doug Chiang, Douglas Smythe, Tom Woodruff Jr.

Memoirs of an Invisible Man

Seventy effects shots create the illusion of a wholly or partially invisible man interacting with his environment. Digital artists remove specific areas of the invisible man. Painting programs are used to fill in invisible areas with clean background plates.

1993

Jurassic Park

For the first time, digital technology is used to create a living, breathing character with skin, muscles, texture, and specific behavioral dispositions. The project marks a major advance in digitally simulating living organisms. The various software breakthroughs allow for unprecedented freedom in the digital compositing of CG creations and live-action film. For the first time in ILM's history, all restrictions on camera movement in background plates are removed, thanks to such software tools as Softimage. *Jurassic Park* is the first major film to use this commercial 3-D animation package. The film also pioneers work in the field of film input scanning.

Academy Award®: Best Visual Effects

Dennis Muren, Stan Winston, Phil Tippett, Michael Lantieri

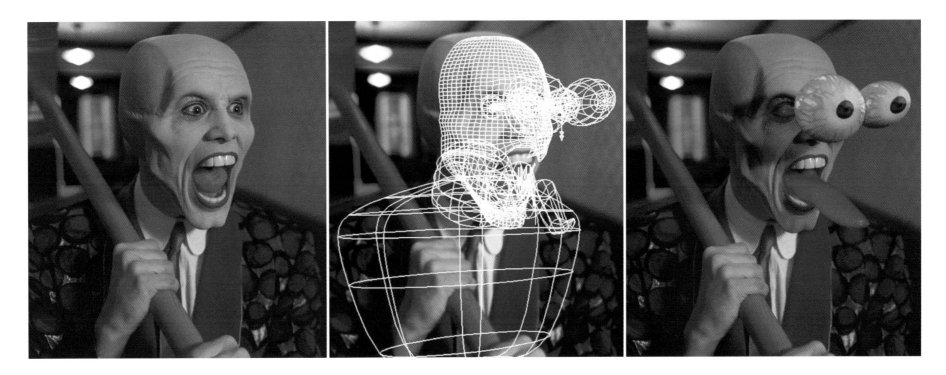

Schindler's List

ILM desaturates scenes featuring a young girl in red against stark surrounding footage, to match the black-and-white elements in the rest of the film. Complex rotoscoping is used to preserve the color image of the girl.

1994

Radioland Murders

The needs of this project provide the opportunity to use digital production tools developed for the *Young Indiana Jones* television series to create imagery for the higher-resolution format of a feature film. For the more than one hundred visual effects shots in this film, sets are built within the computer and miniatures are combined with digital matte paintings to create locations. Extras are cloned in the computer to create expansive crowds.

Baby's Day Out

Techniques developed for *Young Indiana Jones* are used to build sets or fill in missing walls and ceilings within the computer. Entire locations are created with digital matte paintings combined with miniatures.

Forrest Gump

ILM's work in the manipulation of archival footage breaks new ground. The film's characters interact seamlessly with historic figures. A variety of "invisible" effects are created, such as a falling feather (shot on blue screen and digitally composited), the transformation of a main character actor into a double amputee, and computer-generated jets, helicopters, birds, crowds, and ping-pong balls.

Academy Award®: Best Visual Effects

Ken Ralston, George Murphy, Stephen Rosenbaum, Allen Hall

The Hudsucker Proxy

Macintosh computer workstations are used to create matte paintings that are scanned out and then enlarged to sixty-feet-wide translight screens used as set backgrounds of the New York skyline.

The Mask

The ILM team uses computer graphics to seamlessly blend live action photography and Tex Avery style CG characters.

Academy Award® Nomination: Best Visual Effects

Scott Squires, Steve "Spaz" Williams, Tom Bertino, John Farhat

By 1995, ILM was ready to create the next generation of astounding imagery for films.

OPPOSITE

A one-fifth-scale miniature of the now-famous DeLorean DMC-12, originally constructed for the closing scene of *Back to the Future*, was extensively reworked for its more prominent role in *Back to the Future II*. More than twenty functions were built into the model, including working interior and exterior lights, a motorized steering wheel, wheels that rotated from standard to flying configurations, and opening doors.

RIGHT

Ken Ralston and Selwyn Eddy III at ILM, c. 1980

FOLLOWING SPREAD

Jurassic Park (1993). The T. rex targets his victim; just as the dinosaur grabs him, the live-action actor transitions into a full-body digital double.

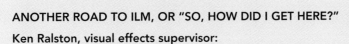

ANOTHER ROAD TO ILM, OR "SO, HOW DID I GET HERE?"
Ken Ralston, visual effects supervisor:

"I was always interested in visual effects. I have no explanation for it. When I was a little kid, I loved the films of Ray Harryhausen and fantasy and horror films, and I just had a very strangely clear vision of me doing that. When I was in the sixth grade, I was doing 8mm films.

"So through *Famous Monsters of Filmland* and Forrest J. Ackerman, I just wrote a fan letter. I didn't think much about it. I was invited to his home, which was basically a museum of all kinds of weird stuff. And through this process, I managed to meet Ray Harryhausen very briefly when I was a kid and I just kept getting more interested. I met a couple of guys who worked at a place called Cascade Pictures that did TV commercials. Dennis Muren was there, and Phil Tippett was there off and on.

"In high school, a friend of mine and I managed to make an 8mm movie called *The Bounds of Imagination*. We showed it to the guys at Cascade, and we got hired to do a strange little animated stop-motion puppet film that was seven minutes long, *Adventures in Underland*. That's how I got to Cascade, and I was there for years. Rick Baker would show up. So this young group of goofballs were there doing this work, and while we were there, Dennis got the script for *Star Wars*. We read it, and we thought it

was funny. I didn't think I was going to work on it. Dennis went off to work on it.

"But then I got a call from Dennis one night and was asked if I wanted to be a camera assistant on the film. Why not? And of course, no one knew about it, no one really had a clue what this thing was. I had never heard of ILM, because it didn't exist yet. Actually, the only movie of George's I'd ever seen was *THX*, which I loved, and I hadn't even seen *American Graffiti* at that time.

"So I went with Dennis to that place in Van Nuys and believe me, none of us knew we were making history, but that's what we ended up doing. Inadvertently, we created ILM. We just didn't know we were doing that, because we all worked in a business where typically, you finished the movie, you dismantled the whole thing, and you moved on to the next gig. And we had no idea, George included—*Star Wars* just did something none of us thought it would do. We had no clue. Even when Dennis and I were at the premiere, we didn't know what it was. In fact, we were worried about it because of our experiences on some of the film and things we had seen. We couldn't see the whole movie of course; we weren't as educated about looking at rough cuts back then as we are now. I know when it was over, we kind of looked at each other and the feeling was, *Who worked on this movie? Who did this? Because this is really great! And what the hell happened?*"

Casper

1995

Dennis Muren, digital character supervisor:

"The *Jurassic Park* dinosaurs had to be very natural, but it wasn't a performance. In *Casper*, it was completely different. The ghosts were supposed to be people who had passed away, which meant that the animation was unlike anything ILM had done in the past. Most of our animators back then were technical people; they could get spaceships to fly or even dinosaurs to move in certain ways, but to try to get an expression and a nuance in the face of a ghost was a completely new thing for us."

Director: Brad Silberling
Producer: Colin Wilson

ILM Show Leadership:
Digital Character Supervisor: Dennis Muren
Visual Effects Plate Supervisor: Scott Farrar
Visual Effects Producer: Janet Healy
Animation Directors: Eric Armstrong, Phil Nibbelink

DENNIS MUREN HAS DESCRIBED Casper's character as the "first digital performer ever." Casper talks, he shows emotion, and he has the full range of motion you'd expect of a "real" ghost.

Curt I. Miyashiro, digital effects artist:

"There was definitely a learning curve. We had to start looking at paradigms in the traditional animated world with facial animation and apply some of what had been done by Disney and others to see what might be applicable in the CG world."

Dennis Muren:

"It took quite a bit of looking at animated films and breaking down ways that a line of dialogue could be interpreted to teach the animators what we needed to do. I made a list of about two hundred attitudes, because many times, even within one line, the attitude of the character could change based on what word he said. Then we had to design the characters so you could see the attitudes that we were trying to express. That meant Casper had to have eyebrows—he had to have shape-changeable eyes with eyelids, top and bottom, and cheeks, so that you could see if he was smiling or frowning. He needed a little chin, because the chin expresses emotion when he's talking. But if you look at the Casper drawings in the comics, they didn't have those details developed very much. So we put them into our Casper, which helped give the expressions necessary to tell the story."

PREVIOUS SPREAD

A CG Casper gives an emotional performance alongside Kathleen Harvey (Christina Ricci).

ABOVE

An expressive Casper, a first in CG animation, as realized by ILM. *Casper* featured a whopping forty-seven minutes of CG animation. By comparision the groundbreaking *Jurassic Park*, released two years prior, had just six minutes.

GHOST OF A CHANCE

Dennis Muren:

"Contrary to popular belief, ILM doesn't get every Steven Spielberg project. We have to compete, just like everybody else. So we did a test in which Casper comes into a bedroom, looks in a mirror, winks at the camera, and then flies into the mirror and disappears. Another company did a test as well, but Spielberg [the executive producer] preferred ours. So we got the job.

"At that point, when we were competing for the job, we were still trying to be faithful to the original Casper design. And I think we didn't have the eyebrows, and the eyes were not as flexible as they eventually would become in production. We were trying to get an expression, but there was no way of doing it because of the design.

"But I guess we got the job because if you disregarded the performance part of it, Casper looked really ghost-y. We made sure his edges were soft and transparent. Yet we realized at that point how difficult the animation was going to be. In the test, there was a line of dialogue that just didn't come across very well in the performance because we were still thinking about animating objects, not thinking characters with an attitude and enthusiasm (and all of the expression that I'm using in my voice now). All of that would have to be in it. So we learned from the test that we had a lot more work to do on being able to create CG characters with a real sense of expression and emotion.

"All of this meant that the face couldn't be soft or transparent, because then you couldn't read the expression. If he's transparent, you can't see what his face is doing because you can see the background through him. So we ended up making the center of his face opaque, while the edges all around it were soft and magical and ghostly."

Stefen Fangmeier, digital character co-supervisor:

"There was just no way that you could do any of it with a puppet, because the quality of Casper with his transparency was really not a physical presence—although Stan Winston

ABOVE

Dr. James Harvey (Bill Pullman) is surrounded.

ABOVE, INSET

Wire frame of animated characters

actually did perform a test, which was pretty hilarious, where he had this sort of rubber Casper, this white, slightly transparent material, and moved it."

CALLING ALL CREW

The creation of the dinosaurs for *Jurassic Park* was rudimentary compared to creating the ghosts for *Casper*. The dinosaurs had six and a half minutes of screen time; *Casper*'s ghosts are on the screen for a full forty-seven minutes, almost half of the movie. ILM executed fifty-two shots for *Jurassic Park*. The facility created more than 350 shots for *Casper*, and they involved even more complex visual effects work.

The number of shots required ILM to advance its production pipeline. Much of the company's internal software was rewritten and upgraded so that it could be more easily employed by a greater number of people. More than sixty additional crew were hired for the project, many of whom came from commercial or industrial backgrounds.

Stefen Fangmeier:

"We made a huge effort to bring in traditionally trained paper-and-pencil animators and get them onto the computer. In traditional effects, you had animatronics and puppets. CG was much more in-between, having the three-dimensional reality of a puppet while also having the control of expression, fluidity, and performance that you have in traditional cell animation."

SPIRITED PERFORMANCES

Of course, director Brad Silberling had very specific ideas regarding the performances of the digital characters. He was involved throughout the nine months of postproduction directing the twenty-five ILM animators.

Dennis Muren:

"The CG characters were in almost an hour of the movie, and they carried whole dialogue scenes. They were also working alongside Bill Pullman and Christina Ricci in the same scene, so they had to be good actors. You could look on the other side of the frame to see if the CG characters were as realistic and as caring about something as the real actors."

For *Casper*, ILM developed tools that enabled animators to concentrate as much as possible on the artistic and performance side of the job, rather than the technical side. These included a library of facial expressions that the animators could employ as needed.

Curt Miyashiro:

"*Casper* set the foundations for what we needed to learn and the problems we would encounter as we undertook character animation in the future. We also saw what it would take, as we scaled up the facility to do bigger and bigger projects along the way—the sort of challenges we would face both from a technological point of view as well as just infrastructure and management of all of those people."

Dennis Muren:

"There's a wonderful scene were the camera moves in on Casper sitting next to Christina Ricci, and he's talking about what he was like as a young child. The camera moves into a close up of Casper, and there's so much feeling in his face; it's just like you're looking at a really good actor acting, and yet it's this transparent ghost. The moment showed me that this really could be done. You can create CG characters and put them right alongside real actors, and these animated characters will hold up."

Jumanji

1995

Stephen L. Price, visual effects supervisor:

"Joe Johnston offered Industrial Light & Magic the next greatest challenge of visual effects: the creation of very familiar, furry and non-furry animals, even if the design of those animals stretched into the imaginative world of the game of *Jumanji*."

Director: Joe Johnston
Producers: Scott Kroopf, William Teitler

ILM Show Leadership:
Visual Effects Supervisors: Stephen L. Price, Ken Ralston
Visual Effects Producer: Mark S. Miller
Animation Supervisor: Kyle Balda
Visual Effects Art Directors: Doug Chiang, George Hull,
  Claudia Mullaly

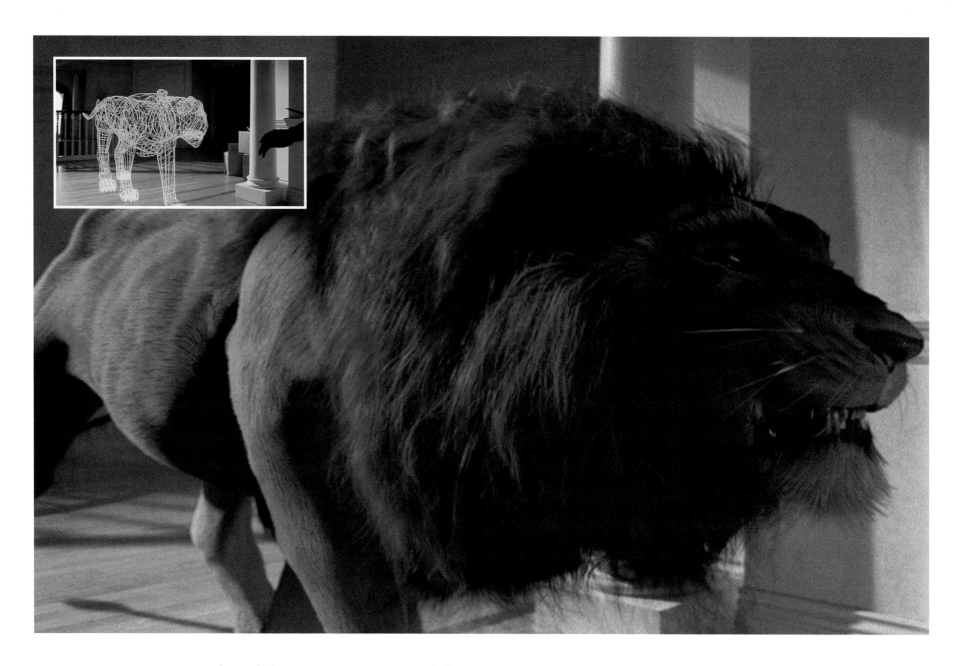

AS THE DIRECTOR OF *Jumanji*, Joe Johnston had a unique perspective: Not only was he the client, but he was also the former ILM art director who had started at the very beginning, on the original *Star Wars*. During *Jumanji*, Johnston was seen by the ILM team as "the whiz kid who had helped design the original *Star Wars* movies"—a rather unusual and intimidating reputation for a client. In addition, Johnston himself designed the visual effects sequences in *Jumanji*.

Habib Zargarpour, CG sequence supervisor:

"Joe Johnston would have an idea—he was always full of ideas, he had *lots* of ideas—and we'd have a meeting and he would say, 'The boy turns into plasma.' So we would spend a month doing research and development getting this boy to turn into plasma as he's getting sucked into the game. We'd show it to Johnston and he would say, 'Maybe it should be more like he turns into sand or dust.' There were these single words that would describe what Joe wanted and he probably wasn't aware that each one of those words was a month or two of doing R & D from scratch. These were the early days of computer graphics. There were still a lot of things we had never done before or hadn't yet discovered, but it certainly wasn't easy or intuitive. We were really creating effects no one had seen before."

ABOVE

In *Jumanji*, ILM's CG lion had to match the animatronic lion shot in principal photography, which involved using second-generation CG hair on the king of the jungle (the first-generation of CG hair had been created for *The Flintstones*, 1994).

ABOVE, INSET

Wire frame of the animation

ABOVE AND PREVIOUS SPREAD
To create the complex shot of
an elephant stomping on a car,
live-action footage (above left) of a
practical vehicle being crushed by
a special mechanical effects rig that
pulled the roof in was combined
with CG animation (wire frame,
above right); the final composite
shot is on the previous spread.

BAD HAIR DAY

ILM was called upon to help create the fantastic creatures and events that leap from the game board into "reality" as *Jumanji* is played. The creatures and events needed to be a seamless blend of fantasy and film reality, mimicking somewhat, but not completely, traditional animals. One of ILM's most important accomplishments on *Jumanji* was therefore the creation of photorealistic fur. The work to create the lion's mane was particularly challenging.

Ken Ralston, visual effects supervisor:

"Trying to do computer graphic hair back then—what a nightmare. The whole lion's mane was a painful process. It went on forever, and still at the end of the day you're looking at it and saying, 'I don't know, it's okay, but …' Yet, at the time, it was a huge stride forward trying to get that thing to look like hair.

"What made it difficult then, and to a certain degree still makes it difficult today, is the challenge of getting it to feel like individual hairs and to move like hairs. Shorthaired animals are easier to do than longhaired, so the lion's body wasn't the hard part. It was the mane that had to be animated in a way that looked like it was flowing. No tool had been built to do that at the time. So you were really fighting your way through it, trying to give it any look at all that made it seem like individual hairs. It took so much rendering power. It took weeks, I think, to make one of those shots pop out the other end just so we could look at it and go, 'That's no good, let's do it again.' The computer power just couldn't handle what we needed to get the hairs to look like hairs. So it sounds simple: 'Lion walks around, his hair is moving.' It's not even moving that much, just a little breeze on it, but at the time it was a very hard thing to do."

INTO THE VORTEX

Throughout ILM's history, the specific needs of individual projects have spurred forward the company's capabilities and associated technology. And inevitably, that forward movement ends up being critical to successfully meeting the *next* challenges of future films.

Ken Ralston:

"A film comes in—that's your challenge, and you fight your way through that one and learn an awful lot before you do the next one … you hope. The hair work on *Jumanji* was a big step forward. Some of the fluid dynamics work that went into doing the vortex at the end of the film was also important. For a long time, the weird stuff that was so hard for computers to do was anything that was supposed to look organic. It just fought you, so any step forward on that level helped."

For the vortex sequence, 3-D animation techniques were used to pull the animals through the walls and whip them into a tornado-like funnel.

Habib Zargarpour:

"We did a lot of particle work on *Jumanji* to achieve the effect of characters being sucked into the vortex and into

the board game. There was the aspect of creating photoreal animals, but more than that, the challenge was to distort them and suck them into a vortex. Distorting a creature was something that hadn't really been explored in 3-D before. It was very tricky, because the animals were built out of hundreds of individual pieces of what we call 'patches': square pieces of geometry that had to be stitched together. Every animal is actually like quilt-work, made of squares. There were hundreds of them, and the way that we had to work to harness the technology that existed back then made the work painful.

"We also had to create a dissolving effect where a character is actually coming apart and getting sucked into the game. The vortex and the game effects pushed the development of particle-system programs in new and innovative directions, which ultimately influenced important developments in particle effects for future projects."

MONKEY BUSINESS

Ken Ralston:

"We had to reanimate some of those monkeys so many times, because Joe had a very specific thing in mind, and I guess we weren't quite getting what he wanted.

"One sequence has a monkey that throws something, so to solve the problem, we set up a video camera in the ILM parking lot and filmed everyone throwing a ball. We were trying to get the action down."

Ultimately, the monkeys were 100 percent CG. Action was coordinated as if the work were being done with animals that could take direction. The design of the appearance of the monkeys went through thirty-four variations. A series of twenty monkey faces was sculpted by animator Geoff Campbell, and used in tandem with the new facial animation program, Caricature.

ANOTHER ROAD TO ILM, OR "SO, HOW DID I GET HERE?"

Roger Guyett, visual effects supervisor:

"Growing up in England, I never in a million years believed that I would ever be working in America and working on movies. It's literally like a dream come true. I had always been interested in films, and my father says that I just loved looking at movies and building things, but I never imagined I would get involved with this business.

"Strangely enough, I became really interested in graphic design—seeing people like Saul Bass and those kinds of funny paper cutout animations that he used to do at the beginning of movies, like *Man with the Golden Arm*. I wouldn't say I was specifically interested in visual effects, but I was very interested in graphics and animation, so I started trying to teach myself how to do some of that stuff. I saw an advertisement in *The Evening Standard* in London asking for somebody who might have some understanding of graphics and how they might be approached with a computer. It sounds mad because people didn't even know which words to use to describe the job at that point, so it was a very odd advertisement.

"I remember I was living with my girlfriend, and we were trying to pay the rent, and I applied for two jobs: One was drafting the gas pipelines through London's sewer system, which I knew I could do because I had done architectural drafting; the other one was this weird graphics job. It was really the early days in computer animation, and I basically lied about my ability to use a computer, but I really loved the people and I could see what they were trying to achieve. I went home and the gas board in London offered me the job. I decided to wait another day to see if I got offered the job in computer animation, rather than taking the gas board job. I did get the animation job, and I realized just how much I loved whatever this was.

"I think for anybody to suddenly discover something that that they feel so passionately about is so fortunate. Then I came to America at a time when the digital thing was just taking off, when ILM was making *Casper* (see pages 32–37). I wasn't sure whether it would be easy to find employment, but it was the easiest job I had ever walked into, because ILM was so desperate to find people; at that time there were just so few people that knew how to do that."

OPPOSITE

To create a sequence where rhinos burst through a door and stampede down a hallway, a plate of principal photography, in which a special mechanical rig pulled the wall away (above left), was combined with CG animation (wire frame, above right), for the final shots (below).

CHARGE OF THE CG LIGHT BRIGADE

Jumanji's stampede of rhinos, elephants, and zebras was quite different from the stampede of *Gallimimus* in *Jurassic Park*. In the case of *Jumanji*, ILM artists realized they were depicting animals the audience would know, so they couldn't "cheat" the representation to the same degree. For the stampede, run cycles were created. Dummy objects, called pawns, were used to block out the movement of the animals as they run through the streets. Painstaking animation was required to tie CG effects with practical effects for the exterior stampede shots. Work on enveloping for skin and muscle tissue was also undertaken, which involved addressing the apparent behavior of the animal's skin and muscles.

Ken Ralston:

"With CG elephants, we had to solve the problems involved in creating skin that looks like it's moving over muscles on top of a skeleton. All of that was in play on *Jumanji*. The further challenge was, 'How do you blend the CG work into the scene when you're lighting it to look like the location?' You have to create interactive elements to try to blend in the CG elements, like dust and bits of flying debris."

The destruction of the Parrish mansion involved adding layers of computer-generated debris. Some of the scenes have as many as thirty-five elements, color-corrected and repositioned to match the movement of the animals. The walls and floor were pristine in the original plate so the aftermath of the destruction was painted in.

The Only Constant Is Change—From Analog to Digital

THE TRANSITION TO THE DIGITAL AGE wasn't necessarily an easy one, nor did the shift occur overnight. The writing had been on the wall for some time, with computers promising a digital future even as ILM was establishing itself as the king of analog magic-making. Already a tool in fields such as architecture and design, computers had been in the background from the beginning, an obvious next step anticipated by those with the foresight to look to the horizon.

Of course, it could be argued that ILM had been in the digital age since its inception in 1975, when the young crew first interfaced its archaic motion picture cameras with custom-built computers to create the first motion control capabilities. It was not until the early 1980s, though, that the use of digital tools truly became a sign of things to come. What had begun on the shooting stage had inspired countless other innovations, touching virtually every aspect of visual effects.

Modeling, animation, roto-scoping, compositing and matte painting—these were all disciplines firmly rooted in the physical world. Foreseeing a streamlined digital future for even such traditionally tactile practices, George Lucas pushed his fledgling Computer Division to develop tools that would allow the lossless manipulation of sound and picture—and artists began to see limitless opportunities in the burgeoning technology. Though the

Stop-motion animator Phil Tippett uses traditional methods on a tauntaun and rider for *Star Wars: Episode V The Empire Strikes Back* (1980).

initially unwieldy tools fought the determined artists every step of the way, the rewards quickly came to those who persevered.

Of course, there were also those who opted out of the evolution—some initially and some entirely. Having worked so hard to stake their collective claim in what had proved to be a gold mine for the blockbuster film industry, they were protective of their established methods and of the aesthetics they were continuing to develop and perfect. Still fresh were the countless advances made by ILM during its effects renaissance and the architects of these developments were loath to see their revolutionary contributions outpaced.

Initial resistance was in fact heavy, with early digital adopters sometimes marginalized and ostracized by their analog peers. Fear and denial were common among those already established in practical and optical effects, with a pervading sense within the "shop" that those who embraced the new technologies were betraying the community. In the early days, before the real benefits of digital had been fully realized, it was viewed as a harbinger of the dark side—a phantom menace that could undermine a legacy hard won.

Some audiences, too, were resistant to the shift. The limitations of analog had long since established a polished comfort zone for cinemagoers—a safely constrained end result that could incrementally and consistently improve on what had come before, while at the same time remaining within the general limits of collective cultural expectations. The images and film-scapes generated by the effects vanguard were, in some cases, unlike anything audiences had seen before—and they were necessarily changing the way that films were made and viewed.

Despite hurdles and obstacles, the digital revolution represented immeasurable improvements for those willing to embrace it. Many of ILM's artists were generalists who could move easily from one creative discipline to the next. These hungry young wizards were problem solvers and innovators, adept at pioneering solutions in an uncharted field. And because of the frenetic pace, they were always looking for new ways to work their magic. Though computers did not at first have the processing power to support their endeavors, there was the potential for the nascent technology to revolutionize and streamline the art of cinema effects. People were—and still are—on the lookout for things the computer could do, and new ways to bring imagination to the screen.

Greg Grusby and Josh Kushins

Twister

1996

Henry LaBounta, digital tornado designer:

> "It was clear from the beginning that the visual effects on *Twister* would require us to rethink the way we did *everything* and come up with techniques that had never been used before."

Director: Jan de Bont
Producers: Ian Bryce, Michael Crichton, Kathleen Kennedy

ILM Show Leadership:
Visual Effects Supervisor: Stefen Fangmeier
Visual Effects Producer: Kim Bromley Carson
Visual Effects Art Director: Guy Hendrix Dyas

Academy Award® Nomination: Best Visual Effects
Stefen Fangmeier (ILM)
John Frazier
Habib Zargarpour (ILM)
Henry LaBounta (ILM)

BAFTA Film Award:
   Best Achievement in Special Visual Effects
Stefen Fangmeier (ILM)
John Frazier
Henry LaBounta (ILM)
Habib Zargarpour (ILM)

IN 1994, Steven Spielberg and Kathleen Kennedy commissioned a test from ILM to determine if it would be possible to use digital techniques to create realistic tornados. Dennis Muren supervised the experiment, working with a team that included Habib Zargarpour.

Habib Zargarpour, digital tornado designer:

"We got a fax from Spielberg that went to Dennis Muren. It basically said, 'We want to make this movie about tornado chases—and if you guys can make the tornado digitally, then we're going to make this film. Otherwise, we're not going to do it.' So everybody turned to me, because I happened to be the 'particle guy' going back to the work on *Jumanji* and *The Mask*. They said, 'Habib, we'll give you ten weeks, and we're going to do a test shot to prove that we can do this.' No pressure!"

Fortunately for Zargarpour, the test shot was so impressive that the film was green-lit. The shot was even cut into the trailer at the time of the film's release—an unusual degree of success, given that ILM's test shots are not typically seen by general audiences.

CHALLENGES, CHALLENGES, CHALLENGES

Stefen Fangmeier, visual effects supervisor:

"Creating tornadoes and the associated weather was a difficult task. This was due in part to the assumption that an audience knows what a tornado looks like. It was essential that the tornadoes in the film be absolutely believable. This challenge was further complicated by director de Bont's dynamic approach to cinematography. A lot of the shots were handheld, and sometimes de Bont would shoot as many as eight or nine cameras at once, so we had no idea which camera take he was going to use. It was almost impossible to accurately get all of the information we needed to incorporate our visual effects shots into the scenes."

Habib Zargarpour:

"You're going into the unknown on projects like this. Traditionally, we would shoot either locked-off or with an easy move, and then we could add a handheld shake later, as a post process. Our task was to convince de Bont that we could

PREVIOUS SPREAD

ILM's digital team customized its particle system software to create a variety of tornadoes depicted in the film. Each tornado was given a unique look and identity. Properties such as gravitational forces, along with wind speed and turbulence, were carefully animated to yield the desired effect.

ABOVE

Bill Harding (Bill Paxton) and Dr. Jo Harding (Helen Hunt) try to escape from a massive twister.

RIGHT

Visual effects supervisor Stefen
Fangmeier and director Jan de Bont

FAR RIGHT

A digital cow was added to a twister
sequence (no live-action cows were
harmed during filming).

do the high-frequency shaking ourselves after we've tracked the camera and done the visual effects. His response was, 'No, it won't look realistic; it's going to look fake.' We put a reel together that showed the camera shakes that we had done on *Jumanji* for the stampede shots of the animals. When de Bont saw the reel, he was satisfied and agreed to avoid the high-frequency shakes in his shooting so that we could actually track the camera."

Stefen Fangmeier:

"The typical techniques we used for creating CG creatures wouldn't suffice to produce something as amorphous as the larger tornadoes. Instead of dealing with well-defined surfaces that could be positioned by an animator, we needed a loose, large volume of particulate matter that would have inherent chaos, but could still be closely controlled."

Henry LaBounta:

"It wasn't sufficient to animate, light, and composite a surface model over the live-action background plate. The weather effects, including tornadoes, dust, rain, hail, and clouds, were often translucent volumes made up of anywhere from thousands to millions of independent elements reacting to complex natural forces. The flying debris required the unique animation of thousands of parts that would react to the tornado, each other, and their environment. The standard CG techniques of compositing these elements over the plate couldn't handle the volumes of dust they had to pass through."

Particle simulation software, called Dynamation, which had been used by Zargarpour on the 1994 releases *The Mask* and *Star Trek: Generations*, contributed both to the successful test result and to the impressive visual effects work in the final film.

As luck *wouldn't* have it, the production had to contend with one of the most *un*eventful tornado seasons in years. An actual tornado was never captured on film. The result was that all of the tornadoes featured in *Twister* were realized digitally.

Stefen Fangmeier:

"With a movie like this, you're completely tied to the weather and have no control over it. But with visual effects, we were able to *create* the atmosphere we needed in the film. So where there were blue skies, we would replace them with gray, and when they were just gray but not stormy enough, we would hang huge storm clouds in there and let the tornadoes come from that."

As a result of the uncooperative location conditions, the number of production aspects that had to be handled in post vastly increased, with the shot count for ILM doubling to more than 300, 135 of which included tornadoes.

LIGHTING, DUST, AND DENSITY

During principal photography, it became clear that the actors could not safely endure the amount of real dust and debris required to achieve the desired terrifying effect of a tornado. ILM therefore added approximately seventy-five dust and debris shots to the scenes. This made it

possible to include larger pieces of debris, which would fly close to the actors to heighten the sense of danger. The most challenging aspects of the assignment included the creation of CG clouds and dust.

Habib Zargarpour:

"The big breakthrough was drawing the particles to look like they're lit realistically, like the dust cloud that makes up a tornado. That was the breakthrough that no one had really achieved before in any way—to take a whole volume of particles and light it as though it's a mass of dust.

"It's not the same as shading a dinosaur. It had taken a few years to get different types of skin right, but we'd never done anything where you're actually lighting a cloud of particles to look like a clump of dust. What happens is there's no actual surface to light. It's this mass of dust but it still sort of behaves like a shape; the tornado looks like an upside-down cone, but the side that the light is coming from is brighter than the other side, so it has some notion of shading. But it's also a penetrable surface, so the light penetrates through many feet into the dust cloud giving it that volumetric look. This is what we were

able to create using a custom renderer that was written for the project, called P-Render, for 'particle render.' Along with the renderer, the simulation made it move realistically.

"To me, the most exciting things are always the first—the first time you do something. So here we had this particle renderer and the simulation, and we hit the button to render the first frame of this tornado. And the first image is starting to come down—it's kind of like getting images back from Mars. We're watching this image being created and what we see is completely *not* what we expected to see. We didn't see a tornado. We saw a tiny ball. It was like a little planet. But it looked perfectly photoreal, and it was lit correctly. And we're like, 'How come it's a sphere?'

"What happened was that the simulation software needs to give its position information to the renderer. It needs to say, 'Here's where all of the particles are. Here's my position.' And that information wasn't translated correctly to the renderer, so it had taken all of the particles and put them basically all in the same spot, at the origin. And because we had this technique to generate a lot of particles around that point, we ended up with this ball. But it was also a really lucky event, because the ball actually looked like a dust planet. It proved that the rendering was working, the lighting was working, but it also had this notion of shadowing itself, which gives you the dark side. So then we fixed the position and got the first tornado image."

BARN BREAKUP

To indicate the power of the tornadoes, objects had to be shown being picked up and tossed around by the high winds. The flying objects had to reflect the rotational force of the tornadoes and had to be integrated into the dust around and within the funnel. This meant that instead of using miniatures, more than one hundred CG models of flying objects were built: a cow, a drive-in theater screen, trees, a tanker truck—and even a large barn.

Henry LaBounta:

"The larger debris and props could be hand-animated and rendered using standard CG techniques. But the thousands of smaller pieces of debris required new procedural techniques to animate them so that each piece would have a unique chaotic motion, but the whole group could be choreographed to the director's wishes."

While CG animators were responsible for "tossing around" most of the objects, the barn that was broken up into three thousand pieces required a more procedural animation technique.

Stefen Fangmeier:

"Traditionally, you would do those kinds of shots with a miniature, but we did that all in CG, because the integration of the barn and the grain silo getting blown up had to move with the rotational force of the twister, and that's something that's fairly difficult to do if you work with miniatures."

Habib Zargarpour:

"I was actually turning the structures into cloth. That's because we had tons of reference footage of tornadoes from real tornado chases, and the one thing I kept noticing was that all

of these building parts keep behaving like cloth. When you see the tin pieces coming off the roof of barns, they always bend and twist in the wind like cloth. They don't come off like a solid tile. So that was the key, to make things bend and twist organically. Basically, we would take a roof piece, and we would convert it to a kind of semirigid cloth so the forces of the tornado could pick it up and twist it and bend it."

BANNED BLUE-SCREEN

To maintain the natural outdoors look of the principal photography, blue-screen and stage elements were avoided. Alternative techniques therefore had to be used to composite computer-generated tornadoes behind foreground objects such as trees, cars, and actors running toward camera.

Stefen Fangmeier:

"The advantage of avoiding blue-screen was that you could have the kind of staging that made it seem very real, because you're just running along with a camera. The director could pretty much do anything he wanted. But it didn't make our life any easier. For example, when they were shooting the sequence driving through the cornfields, one day when we showed up, the tips of the corn had suddenly sprouted little tassels. It was just a nightmare to get the edges right when we had to composite the element. The wraparound lighting on the tops of the corn plants and their leaves made these shots some of the most difficult composites in the film.

"It was also very difficult to create rotoscope mattes when you see Helen Hunt running in front of the tornado with her blonde hair blowing in the wind. For each element, we had to create sort of a cookie cutter on every frame to put our tornado behind that element. It was very difficult to do back then. And yet, because it had the action element and the drama and the stuff flying through the air, we sort of got away with it. It was also a film where pristine was not desired. We leaned on science for a foundation, but we often had to go a bit extreme to get the impact that the director wanted. The director wanted something that would shock people. We were creating an aesthetic art piece, not a scientific visualization."

DragonHeart

1996

Scott Squires, visual effects supervisor:

"The idea was, 'We're going to do this big project, and the main character is always talking and gesturing with his face—we've got to make sure that we can do that.' So our facial animation software, Caricature, was further developed for *DragonHeart*. Caricature became a big stepping stone at ILM; that technology and everything we learned from it has impacted all of our digital characters."

Director: Rob Cohen
Producer: Rafaella de Laurentiis

ILM Show Leadership:
Visual Effects Supervisor: Scott Squires
Visual Effects Producer: Judith Weaver
Animation Supervisor: James Straus
Visual Effects Art Director: Mark Moore

Academy Award® Nomination: Best Visual Effects
Scott Squires (ILM)
Phil Tippett
James Straus (ILM)
Kit West

ANOTHER ROAD TO ILM, OR "SO, HOW DID I GET HERE?"

Stefen Fangmeier, visual effects supervisor:

"When I was sixteen, I played guitar, I had long hair, it was 1976, and I wanted to be a rock star. But I didn't want to end up playing the top forty in local bars, so I came across computer science as something to study that would have a future; within computer science I found creating images with the computer to be the most creative and fascinating thing. This was the early eighties, the pioneering days.

"Then I worked at a company called Digital Productions, in their scientific division, which was funded by the National Science Foundation. They had researchers who would use the Cray supercomputer, because at that time, there weren't any powerful computers around that could handle the computational challenges of computer graphics like you could buy for a couple of thousand dollars today. What you have on your desktop now is probably ten times as powerful as that Cray supercomputer and is a fraction of the cost.

"Then, I moved on to University of Illinois, Champagne Urbana, and worked there with researchers taking their computational data from the supercomputer and turning it into little scientific movies. From there, I was hired by a German com-

pany called Mental Images, which is now one of the primary software providers.

"So when I moved to Berlin in 1989, I really wasn't that knowledgeable about visual effects at all. I wasn't a big *Star Wars* fan. My favorite movie from back then was *Blade Runner*. Then I got a phone call from Nancy St. John, who with her husband, Craig Upson, had worked with me at the supercomputer center in Illinois. They had moved back to California, and she was working at Industrial Light & Magic, crewing up their computer graphics department. She called me in Berlin and said, 'Why don't you come work for us on *Terminator II*?' ILM was just completing *The Abyss*, and they were increasing their computer-graphics department from twelve people to twenty-five.

"So I came to ILM in November of 1990 to work on *Terminator II*. It was an eye-opener to work at ILM. I remember seeing *Indiana Jones*, where this big ball is rolling after them. Back then, I never even thought about visual effects; I never thought, *How did they do that?* I just watched the movie and enjoyed it. As soon as I started working at ILM and I saw how these things were done with miniatures, suddenly my innocence in terms of looking and enjoying films was lost. After that, I was much more analytical. Anything I've learned about filmmaking, I've learned at ILM. It's not a career I ever chose. I studied computer science. I could be running a software company now. So it's not a goal I ever had, it's just something that gradually I moved into."

PREVIOUS SPREAD

Aside from the issue of animating Draco himself, *DragonHeart* brought new lighting and rendering challenges to the fray. In this scene, artists had to simulate accurately the light from the fire being blasted from Draco's nostril (the fire itself was a practical pyrotechnic gag orchestrated on set by Kit West).

ILM'S ACCOMPLISHMENTS in the creation of computer-generated dinosaurs in *Jurassic Park* (1993) inspired producer Raffaella de Laurentiis to move forward with a unique project: a film that required the creation of a CG dragon, Draco, who would walk, fly, talk, and express a full range of emotions. ILM, along with other effects companies, was asked to produce a computer-animated dragon test. ILM's test was deemed the most successful. Because the dragon was such a prominently featured character, nearly every shot in the film was a visual effects shot. As a result, ILM was engaged with the project for two years.

Scott Squires:

"We were faced with long scenes of dialogue between the dragon and real actors, where an audience could study and compare computer graphics to reality. Draco would be seen during the day, at night, in firelight, flying, splashing in water, holding an actor in his mouth and breathing fire. Most importantly, we needed to make him act and to try to ensure that the audience would develop an emotional bond with him."

Sculptor Mark Siegel works on an articulated hand puppet for Draco.

Model maker Erik Jensen (middle) and sculptor Bob Cooper in the Model Shop at ILM

Draco speaks to Kara (Dina Meyer)

Richard Miller (in apron) and Mark Siegel work on Draco's jaws.

Scott Squires:

"The main sequence where we used a full-size prop was when Bowen [Dennis Quaid] is in the dragon's mouth. The interior of the mouth, including tongue and teeth, was built in the ILM creature shop. This was mounted on a crane arm, and four puppeteers manipulated the numerous servos to lip-synch the mouth and tongue to the dialog with the actor inside. Markers were placed around the jaw and were later tracked, frame by frame, in the computer. We modified the CG Draco model slightly to wrap around the full-size jaw and then matched its motion exactly. This was a tricky matting process, since sections of the CG dragon had to be in front of the full-size jaw, while other areas had to be behind the jaw. We took full advantage of what both practical and CG effects had to offer."

James Straus, character animation supervisor:

"We created surface textures, the skeletal framework, and muscle relationships that would allow Draco to move about in a completely realistic manner. But the dragon needed a soul. We needed a method to allow Draco to express himself to the world (or rather, a method to allow the animators to act inside a CG dragon). We needed to create tools that would allow us to manipulate the dragon data in real-time—at a time when even our best computers could barely load-in the dragon model, let alone move it around. So we created what's called the Caricature system, and that changed everything."

CARICATURE

The facial-animation software Caricature was initially developed by Cary Phillips for *Casper* and was used first in *Jumanji*. But it was *DragonHeart* that drove key aspects of the software's development.

Cary Phillips, software research and development:

"Caricature ushered in a new way of dealing with facial animation and creature animation. Draco was the first time that a *main* character in a film was computer-generated. There were the dinosaurs in *Jurassic Park*, but they weren't the stars of the film, and they didn't talk. There was Casper, and he talked, but that wasn't photoreal. What you're seeing when you watch Draco is really the first believable character talking with a real voice and a personality. And it wasn't just a personality—it was Sean Connery. That was the dawn of the era of digital performances.

"There were several components of Caricature, and it evolved over time. What it did on *DragonHeart* was basically nothing but the face. Then, through a succession of other films, including *Mars Attacks!*, *Lost World* (see pages 63–67), and Episode I (see pages 120–131), more capabilities were added, and it evolved into a more full-featured system.

"Since its first application in around 1995, Caricature was basically used on every film that ILM worked on that had any kind of digital creature or character in it. It was the backbone

of the pipeline that supported our creature animation process until the emergence of the Zeno system in about 2005, when we stopped using Caricature."

But what was it about the inadequacy of *earlier* software tools that inspired the development of Caricature?

Rob Coleman, supervising character animator:

"Prior to *DragonHeart*, we were trying to come up with a better way to animate faces. There were different software packages out there that allowed you to move a character around, pose an arm, pose a head. But none of them had anything close to the tools that we needed to create facial performance and, therefore, believable digital performances on the screen. So James Straus and Cary Phillips and that team of very talented research and development people and animators got together and said, 'Okay, we *need* this tool. We cannot become the animation department we want to be, and we cannot create the characters that these directors want to bring to the screen without this new tool. We have talented animators, but we need the technology to come in and meet us part way.'"

Cary Phillips:

"What ILM has always strived to achieve and what set us apart, particularly in the early years, was the ability to deal with things at a much greater complexity than anybody else or anybody else's system. ILM has a reputation and a position in the industry that allows us to work on tremendously complicated and challenging projects. And the task of developing tools to support that wasn't so much about inventing techniques out of whole cloth. What we were doing was taking techniques that other packages and other systems had implemented and making them robust enough to stand up to the stresses and strains of the level of visual effects that we were trying to pull off. And most of that just comes down to complexity of images and the details of textures. We pushed those limits far further than anybody else, and our job, as software engineers, was to develop tools that didn't break down at those limits."

James Straus:

"From the beginning, we designed our Caricature software to give computer artists real-time animation feedback with a high-resolution shaded model. With this software, we could create the broad strokes of the acting very quickly, then fine-tune the performance to the very last detail.

ABOVE

Draco extends a wing over Bowen (Dennis Quaid) to shield him from the rain. Water cascading down the CG wing was simulated with shaders, which were employed in conjunction with practical water elements filmed on set.

"Ultimately, the animators would use Caricature to coordinate the complex muscle movements in the face that in concert created the lip-synched motion. With Caricature, we matched Mr. Connery's dialogue and did it with every bit of his irresistible charm. Special care was given to everything in the facial performance, from the subtle curves of the eyelids defining Draco's deeper emotions to the wet slimy tongue, which was perfectly timed to deliver speech."

SUPER MODELS

Draco was designed by Phil Tippett, who had worked at ILM on stop-motion animation for the original *Star Wars* trilogy, and who ultimately established his own company, Tippett Studio.

Phil Tippett, dragon designs:

"We showed the final maquette to the director, Rob Cohen, and he said, 'That's it!' He was very excited—but I could just see the faces of the ILM guys drop: *Oh, my God* ... I knew this design was going to be a pain in the ass for them when I was doing it, but it was what the director wanted. I kept their requirements in mind, but I didn't let the tail wag the dog. Engineering, whether it is computer-generated or practical, has to come second to design."

It took four people five months to build the computer model of the full Draco figure.

Re-creating Tippett's design in the computer involved a level of complexity ILM had never before achieved.

James Straus:

"The computer graphics team and I were building the largest, most complex, and realistic creature ever attempted by any of us. The resulting computer model was equivalent to four T. rexes from *Jurassic Park*. Staying true to Phil Tippett's design, we created exacting detail in the skin right down to the subtle nooks and crannies in the scales. We dubbed the dragon 'Phil's revenge' because there was seemingly no end to the lavish intricacies of horns, spikes, scales, and claws."

BEATING WINGS

Cary Phillips:

"When I came to ILM, I was determined that whatever I did, I was going to make darn sure that it was what the artist wanted. Early on, I gave a test version of Caricature to James Straus to play with. When I got in the next morning, there was a voice mail from James saying he played around with the software—and it crashed. Is there any way that he can get back the animation he was working on, because it was great, and now it's gone? So I remember thinking, *I swore I wasn't going to let this happen to artists*. An hour or so later the phone rang, and it was Judith Weaver, the visual effects producer on *DragonHeart*, and she said, 'Can you come down to the office?' And I thought, 'Oh my God, man, I am in *so* much trouble!'

"I walked down to the production office, and it was locked, so I looked in at the conference table, and all the heavyweights were there, Scott Squires and Alex Seiden. They were all huddled around the desk, and I thought, 'Oh my God, I'm going to get raked over the coals!' So I came in, everybody was quiet, and I think it was James who turned to me and said, 'We're trying to figure out how to animate these wings. Do you have any ideas how we can do this?'"

The challenge of creating Draco's wings was enormous. The design had to be both visually appropriate and structurally believable for a creature of Draco's size.

The team had to determine a wing structure that would allow for fluid extension and contraction. In addition, the wing membrane had to move with controllability and realism. For the flight scenes, computer animators had to vary the dragon's weight, depending on his actions and his interactions with people and the environment. Veins and other textures were painstakingly painted onto the translucent open wings by a digital artist.

James Straus:

"When Draco flies through the smoke of burning villages, watch for the computer-generated contrails curling off his wings. In front of the sun, notice how the light shines through his translucent wings, revealing a spider-work of veins. In addition to the many skin maps painted to create texture and dirt on Draco, these vein maps were added as a final touch."

THIS IS JUST THE BEGINNING

James Straus:

"There were an unprecedented variety of tricks for Draco to perform. This dragon had to fly through smoke and past sunsets, and walk through two-foot-tall grass—watch how the grass moves as he walks through it; it even ripples in the turbulence of his huge eighty-foot wingspan. Our dragon had to roll in the mud, swim underwater, pick people up, stand dripping wet in the rain, and talk, talk, talk. Some of the dragonfire breaths are carefully crafted from live elements, and some were conflagrations of synthetic computer geometry with fire-shaders. In the rain, Draco uses his computer-generated wing to shelter his human friend. Watch the CG water dance and spill off his skin, a perfect integration of mathematical water-shaders and real dripping water."

Overall, the challenges of creating Draco were a crucial test of the new technologies that were being developed by ILM at the time. And perhaps most importantly, the developments that came out of ILM's work on this film provided vital stepping-stones for the astounding accomplishments in CG imagery that were yet to come.

Mars Attacks!

1996

David Andrews, animation supervisor:

"We hope that in the creation of their characters, and execution of their behaviors, our efforts to bring these cute but malevolent Martians to life is worthy of the mantle of the great stop-motion animators, Willis O'Brien and Ray Harryhausen."

Director: Tim Burton
Producers: Tim Burton, Larry J. Franco

ILM Show Leadership:
Visual Effects Supervisor: James Mitchell
Visual Effects Producer: Mark S. Miller
Animation Supervisor: David Andrews
Visual Effects Art Director: Mark Moore

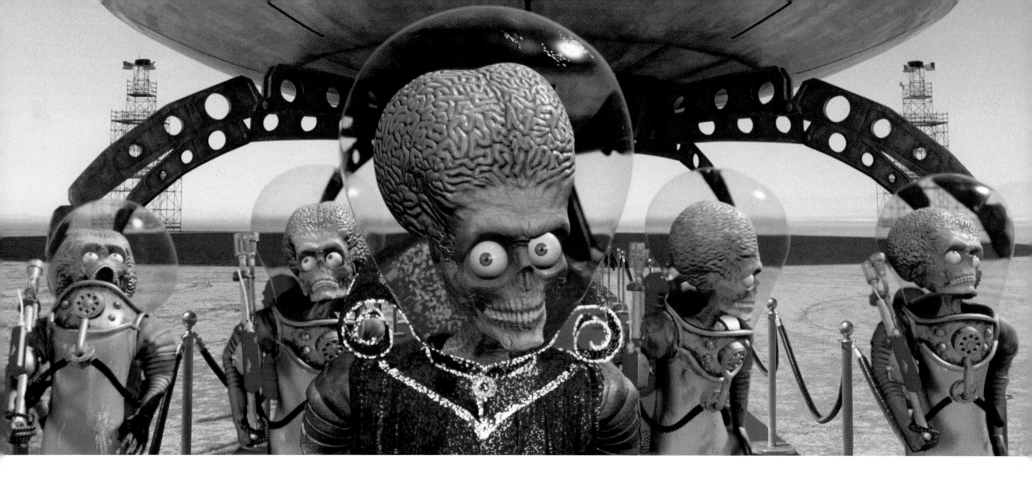

MARS ATTACKS! required ILM to assemble the biggest crew since the animation-heavy *Casper* (see pages 32–37). More than one hundred ILM team members were involved with *Mars Attacks!* at the height of production. Ninety separate computer models were built, including seven different Martian models. ILM also modeled Martian spaceship props, ray guns, and an enormous robot seen inside the mother ship.

Mars Attacks! was originally planned as a stop-motion project, much like director Tim Burton's earlier production *The Nightmare Before Christmas*, directed by Henry Selick. But this time, the animated characters needed to exist in the "real world" of the film with the actors, including Jack Nicholson, Sarah Jessica Parker, and Pierce Brosnan.

Jim Mitchell, visual effects supervisor:

"The plan was for ILM to composite the armatured Martian puppets over various live-action plates. But technical hurdles kept popping up for the stop-motion unit, so I pursued doing a test of Martians that would be completely built and animated inside a computer. The test was successful, and we showed Tim that computer animation, and the array of

digital tools we had to offer, would be the most effective way to blend his Martians into the live action. Most importantly, it presented computer animation as viable a method as any other for creating complex character animations. In a little over eight months, we created 304 visual effects shots, including 246 with 3-D Martian-character animation."

David Andrews:

"By blending the quirky vitality of stop-motion with the fluidity and technical malleability of computer animation, we created a hybrid style of animation. We began by revisiting the great stop-motion films like *King Kong*, *The Seventh Voyage of Sinbad*, and *The Nightmare Before Christmas*.

"Based on the preexisting stop-motion puppet, we created a model for computer animation. Beyond the necessary armatures, we added special controls in the Martian gills, face, and eyes. The fanning action of the gills expresses the Martian's inner state, as do the subtle brow animation and dilating pupils. In close-ups especially, these details add life to an otherwise doll-eyed skull. Our primary concern was with the quality of the performance."

PREVIOUS SPREAD

Two of director Tim Burton's maniac Martians attack.

ABOVE

Flanked by his minions, the ambassador Martian in a cape that represented a challenge to the CG cloth-simulation team.

Mars Attacks! featured breakthrough animation made possible using an updated version of ILM's Caricature able to handle upwards of twenty characters at a time. Previous incarnations of the software, like the one used on *DragonHeart* could only operate with a single character.

Jim Mitchell:

"The first Martian version was the 'nude' one clad only in red bikini briefs. This initial model was then clothed and modified to create other versions. For example, a sequined cape was draped around the neck and shoulders of the ambassador and leaders we see on the spaceship. The cape presented our first technical challenge because of the tricky nature of simulating cloth and the complex look of the material."

Animating and rendering the glittering capes was a challenge because, at the time, there was no such thing as surface detection in ILM's software. So, for example, if an elbow on a CG figure was moved, the CG fabric didn't automatically conform to that move; the elbow might wind up poking out of the cape. It was therefore necessary to animate each nuance of action as the cape moved and draped on the floor.

Jim Mitchell:

"For movement of the cape we favored a hands-on approach. Although time-consuming, it was in keeping with the way all the characters were animated. We wrote new software that added sculpting tools to our in-house facial- and shape-animation program, Caricature. This enabled the animator to clean up and contour detailed shapes on top of the keyframed positions. In addition, to give the characters their regal appearance, a special cape shader was written to make it sparkle and shimmer as it moved throughout the environment.

"Another set of Martian models were in green spacesuits. Shaders were designed to create the different parts of the suit made of rubber, hard plastic, burnished metal, and, of course, the glass helmets. Special care was taken to simulate the refractive quality one would expect from the helmet's curved transparent surface. To do this, we used rendering techniques to bend the background plate that the Martians were composited into. We also added details like scratches and smudges that interacted with the lighting, just like they would in real life. We even "dirtied up" the suits to take the clean CG look away."

UPDATING CARICATURE

ILM's facial-animation software, Caricature, had been refined during *DragonHeart*. *Mars Attacks!* inspired its further evolution. With earlier versions of the software, it was only possible to animate one character at a time in the same working file. For *Mars Attacks!*, the update of Caricature made it possible to animate several characters in the same scene, and render them immediately. This was a significant step in the evolution of ILM's tools for character animation. One of the most challenging sequences in the film is a fight scene in which fifty Martians appear in a single shot. Characters in both the foreground and background had to be individually animated. New software was written to help the animators work out the placement of multiple CG characters in the scene. The software, called Pawns, provided a

FAR LEFT
Nathalie Lake (Sarah Jessica Parker)
is imprisoned.

LEFT
Martian surgeons perform a vivisec-
tion on Nathalie and her chihuahua.

low-resolution geometry so that the figures could be easily moved around. In the years to come, the need to create CG crowd scenes would come up again and again. The work on *Mars Attacks!* laid the groundwork for efficiently and effectively handling the challenges of creating CG crowds in the future.

MARTIAN EXPERIMENTS

The Martian experiment sequences required the densest layering of elements of any shots ILM produced for the film.

Jim Mitchell:

"Here we, and the Martians, got to be a little like Dr. Frankenstein, cutting and sewing together body parts in the creation of some of the most bizarre images of the film. In most cases, we shot the plates of the quarter-scale operating room backgrounds before shooting the blue-screen elements of Pierce Brosnan and Sarah Jessica Parker. We then took the camera information, such as height, tilt, and lens, and figured out their relation to the full-scale blue-screen stage.

"For the sequence where Sarah Jessica's head is seen in a glass jar, we wanted to make her look like she was floating in some sort of liquid, so we over-cranked the camera at ninety-six frames per second. This gave her hair a more fluid action when played back at twenty-four frames per second. After extracting the blue-screen image, we stenciled away the neck and shoulders. These images were then texture-mapped to a patch that was parented inside the computer

model of the glass jar. To keep the image from skewing, due to the perspective change as the Martian walks away from the camera, we constrained the surface to always be parallel to the camera plane. The advantage was that Sarah Jessica's head inherited all the movements of the jar being carried by the Martian, and it always stayed oriented toward the camera. The set of bubbles you see surrounding the head were animated texture maps, while the bubbles coming from her mouth when she screams were actual 3-D spheres controlled by Dynamation."

YOU GOTTA MATCHMOVE

Mars Attacks! was the first film to benefit from an ILM motion control breakthrough that allowed digital artists to lock their animation into programmed camera moves.

Ben Snow, CG sequence supervisor:

"There was a sequence set inside the Martian ship, with a beautiful miniature that was created in the ILM Model Shop. Our director of miniature photography, Pat Sweeney, would shoot his motion control camera on stage with the model, and we would be able to take the data from that motion control camera and plug it back into our computer camera. That way, when we put the CG Martian into the scene, we didn't have to refigure everything that happened on the miniature set. The system made it a lot cheaper and quicker to match the camera and the computer."

Pat Sweeney, director of miniature photography:

"Typically in motion control, we're shooting miniature space-ships and assorted elements that are placed into a scene that has already been filmed or created in the computer. In the case of *Mars Attacks!*, it was essentially an all in-camera background. What I was doing was not only programming and lighting the background for the shots, but moving the camera in relation to what the CG characters would be doing. I used puppets for framing and timing. I could walk them through the shot, shoot a quick take on film or video, then adjust the camera move, if necessary, before doing the real take. It was as if I were shooting the Martians on the set—the only difference was that our set was miniature and our camera shot at a much slower speed than a live-action camera.

"For each shot, the animators could see how far away a Martian would be, the direction they would be looking in, and how they'd be interacting with any lighting on the set. All of that gave the CG artists a great starting point for determining a Martian's size and speed.

"This way, CG artists could use the exact data I'm using onstage, instead of spending three weeks trying to line up a move before they could add in their CG characters. About six months prior to *Mars Attacks!*, I had been working on our matchmoving tools to create software in which the motion control camera lens and the motion control crane axis would be the same as the virtual camera's. With this software—which we called 'mov2scn'—we now have an automatic interface between the motion control stage work and the CG computers."

The Star Wars Trilogy: Special Edition

1997

George Lucas:

"The first three *Star Wars* films fell short of what I wanted. Either we ran out of money, we ran out of time, or we didn't have the technology to do what we wanted. So I was frustrated that I couldn't actually bring together the vision that I had in mind, that I couldn't make the films I wanted. One of the reasons I wanted to do the Special Edition was to restore the films and rerelease them, but the other was to actually be able to fix some of the visual effects that, at the time, the technology just wasn't up to doing."

Director (*A New Hope*): George Lucas
Director (*The Empire Strikes Back*): Irvin Kirshner
Director (*Return of the Jedi*): Richard Marquand
Executive Producer: George Lucas
Producer: Rick McCallum

ILM Show Leadership:
A New Hope
Visual Effects Supervisors: Alex Seiden, John Knoll, Dave
    Carson, Dennis Muren, Joseph Letteri, Bruce Nicholson
Visual Effects Producers: Tom Kennedy, Ned Gorman
Animation Supervisor: Stephen Williams
Visual Effects Art Directors: Ty Ruben Ellingson, Mark Moore

The Empire Strikes Back
Visual Effects Supervisor: Dave Carson
Visual Effects Producer: Tom Kennedy
Visual Effects Art Director: George Hull
Assistant Visual Effects Art Director: Alex Laurant

Return of the Jedi
Visual Effects Supervisors: Dave Carson, John Knoll
Visual Effects Producer: Tom Kennedy
Visual Effects Art Director: George Hull

IN 1983, the year of the original theatrical release of *Return of the Jedi*, George Lucas and ILM had pushed the limits of what could be accomplished with the photo-chemically based visual effects techniques of the time. But the creation of imaginative characters and environments was limited by the processes used to realize these elements. These limitations were one reason for the lack of new *Star Wars* films following the completion of *Return of the Jedi*, the third film in the original trilogy. But a decade later, in 1993, ILM's groundbreaking work in digital visual effects made *Jurassic Park*'s CG dinosaurs possible. The new capabilities that ILM actualized in creating the creatures for *Jurassic Park* allowed George Lucas to consider not only a *Star Wars* "prequel" trilogy, but also to return to the original trilogy, to improve specific shots he had always felt were unsatisfactory.

In 1995, ILM began working on the *Star Wars* Trilogy: Special Editions.

Rick McCallum, producer:

"I think the most wonderful aspect of the Special Editions was that George's primary focus was on fixing things he couldn't do satisfactorily at the time. With digital technology, there's now a palette in which you can do whatever you want."

Instead of significantly reworking the visual effects elements of the original *Star Wars* trilogy, ILM implemented fixes and enhancements that were seamlessly interwoven into the three original films. Lucas was able to realize several shots in the ways he originally envisioned, but could not achieve twenty years earlier.

Rick McCallum:

"Since George foresaw the direction that filmmaking and digital technology were going with such clarity, he resolved that, given the chance, he would fulfill his original dream. So nearly

PREVIOUS SPREAD
The X-wing armada was enhanced for the Special Edition of *Star Wars* Episode IV.

ABOVE
Also enhanced and enlarged was Luke and friends' entry into Mos Eisley.

twenty years later, he was able to say, 'At the beginning, I didn't have the resources, the technology, or the support—but now I have those things.' To me, that is such an innocent and romantic notion—to go back and make the film in exactly the way he envisioned it, no more or less."

Lucasfilm's plan was to release the enhanced versions in theaters to celebrate the twentieth anniversary of the first *Star Wars* film. A 150-person team at ILM worked on Special Edition shots specified by Lucas. Digital tools were used to repair distracting elements in original optical effects and to integrate new CG creatures and cityscapes within existing footage. All three Special Editions were released in 1997.

For all of ILM's work on the Special Editions, it was important that the new footage match the original films, in terms of the look of the filters on the camera lenses and the amount of film grain. The film stock that was used at the time the original trilogy was produced is quite different from the stock that was used for the work on the Special Editions: The later-generation stock has richer blacks and smaller grain, which created a problem when new footage was shot and intercut with the old footage. In some cases, grain had to be added to the new elements to make it match the older material. The matching issue was complicated by the fact that the negatives for the original films had aged. Many of the problems of how to make the new shots intercut seamlessly with the old footage were worked out in the Special Edition of Episode IV *A New Hope*.

A NEW *NEW HOPE*

George Lucas:

"In *A New Hope* especially, and then *Empire* and *Return of the Jedi*, I couldn't get my whole vision on the screen. I fell short and people would ask me, 'How did it come out?' 'Well, it came out to be about maybe 50 percent of what I wanted.' And everybody would say, 'How can you say that about *Star Wars*? It's so great.' I'd say, 'Yeah, but I could see a better movie there.' And we got to a point where I said, 'Well, maybe if I went back and fixed up *Star Wars*, we could rerelease it and it could be the way I intended it to be originally.' It would also test all the technology for the new *Star Wars* films. We called

it an experiment in learning the new technology. So basically what I got to do was take this thorn out of my side."

Lucas's focus for the Special Edition of *A New Hope* was to transform the modest town of Mos Eisley into the busy spaceport city he had originally envisioned.

George Lucas:

"There were a lot of things about the original films I found frustrating, because to me the illusion was too thin. Mos Eisley, for example, was a half-block long. I made a town out of nothing—and to me it felt like nothing, even though other people bought it as a town. Now, in the Special Edition, I think it *looks* like a town. There are wide shots with lots of people and creatures and droids. Where before Mos Eisley was extremely simple, now it's kind of complex."

The challenge of integrating CG effects into footage that was not originally intended for visual effects processing was evident in the Mos Eisley street scene. The changes Lucas requested included the addition of CG dewbacks and a CG stormtrooper dismounting in the frame that shows R2-D2 and C-3PO watching stormtroopers interrogating a citizen. To integrate the new digital elements, it was necessary for ILM to use a virtual camera to duplicate the original camera moves. The challenge of matching included replicating the unique vibrations of the twenty-year-old camera that had been used to create the original scene.

Tom Kennedy, visual effects producer:

"We had to stay consistent throughout the trilogy and not try to 'wow' the audience with something obviously new. A new Special Edition element had to look like an extension of the original intent—so if someone other than an aficionado were to look at the film for the first time, an enhanced scene wouldn't stand out as a different type of scene."

The town of Mos Eisley was largely enhanced by ILM's digital matte department. One scene offers an angle of Luke, the droids, and Obi-Wan on a landspeeder entering the city. The shot shows a point of view ten feet above the vehicle as it travels down a street lined with pedestrians, a droid, and stucco-like buildings. The pedestrians were

blue-screened extras. The droid and the landspeeder with its passengers were computer generated. The surrounding environment was a digital matte painting, with the foundation for the Mos Eisley environment having been created by photographing physical miniatures in natural sunlight. The photographs were scanned, and then combined with other digital images using Photoshop. Paul Huston, who worked as a model maker on all three films in the original *Star Wars* trilogy, returned to the world of *Star Wars* as a digital matte artist for the Special Editions.

Paul Huston, digital matte artist:

"Rough building textures and outdoor lighting were still hard to do in CG, but easy to do in miniatures. When I first looked at the Mos Eisley shot, I realized that I could make some fairly crude models with simple texturing materials, paint them, then put them outside and photograph them. I shot them at the correct camera height to get the proper perspective; then, once in digital, I could fix edges and colors, take out things that didn't look right and add subtle details such as a crack along a wall. It was a lot easier than starting out in

the computer and having to add all the subtleties that make something look real. The lighting on the miniatures determined at what time and angle we would have to shoot the blue-screen plates. To perfectly emulate the lighting on the model, we had about a two-hour window of opportunity to film the live action."

The shot of Luke's landspeeder entering Mos Eisley is one of the most significant accomplishments of ILM's work on all of the Special Editions; it is a panoramic view that demonstrated a new level of accomplishment in digital matte painting techniques. Artist Yusei Uesugi created the establishing view with digital paint alone. Lucas was interested in creating a complex camera move for the scene, and Uesugi devised an innovative projection effect to realize Lucas's vision.

Yusei Uesugi, digital matte artist:

"George requested more and more camera moves, until I realized I couldn't do it with just a single painting. So I came up with the idea of setting up perspective points and selectively

ABOVE

Another view of the improved backwater town

BELOW

Concept art of Jabba the Hutt by Ty Ruben Ellingson

compositing painted textures. When I rendered the picture, I had a virtual camera set in a computer program with a specific focal length—just as you'd photograph something in the physical world. Then I projected the painting back from the same focal length onto the geometry, so each detail on the painting lined up on the original shape, giving me some freedom to move my CG camera around this environment. It was a big jump from a static matte painting—and I think the big camera move was a test to allow George to discover what was new in digital matte painting. He was thinking about the next *Star Wars* films, so he was testing a lot of areas, seeing what new things the ILM folks could do."

The projection technique created the illusion of perspective and dimensionality without the intensive processing time required for a CG model created in three-dimensional space.

Yusei Uesugi:

"We're usually given a very tight schedule to do our work, but the Special Edition was a rare opportunity where we were actually encouraged to make suggestions and just to say anything that we thought might work, even if we were not 100 percent sure. In this case, I said that I might be able to do some R & D and do something no one has ever done before, which is giving a perspective change to the matte painting."

Lucas was also interested in restoring a sequence in which Han Solo walks into a Mos Eisley hangar to check on his ship, the *Millennium Falcon*—and is confronted by the evil crime lord Jabba the Hutt. The incident was the beginning of a threat that ultimately ran through the entire original *Star Wars* trilogy. The confrontation with Jabba had originally been filmed with Harrison Ford on a hangar set with an actor playing Jabba, but the scene had never been completed—it simply wasn't possible to create the required Jabba creature effect using the technology available at the time. This was why, for the original release of the trilogy, Jabba was not actually seen until *Return of the Jedi*, when he was realized as a huge animatronic puppet.

George Lucas:

"The Jabba the Hutt scene was one of the key things that I wanted to put back. When I did *Star Wars*, the scene was superfluous, because if I never got the other films finished, Jabba didn't necessarily have to be there. And I didn't know technically how to do it. We were going to do it with stop-motion animation, but I was a little leery of that. Once I got the first three films done, however, I realized that the scene with Jabba the Hutt really should be back in there, because his problems with Han go through the other films."

For the Special Edition, Jabba was created as a CG creature. The CG Jabba "undulates" his way through the hangar and even interacts with

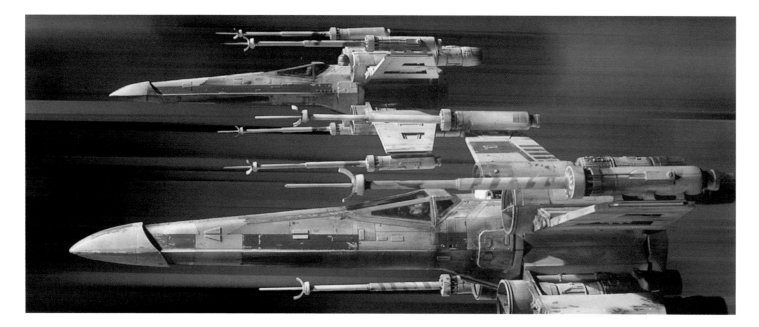

LEFT

An enhanced Special Edition frame
of an X-wing in the Death Star trench

the live-action actor, as Ford seems to step on Jabba's tail. Of course, the actual "interaction" of the characters was separated in execution by almost twenty years. To make the engagement convincing, Ford's eye line had to sync precisely with the position of Jabba's gaze. The animator responsible for Jabba, Steve Williams, had to work backward, animating the character to link with Ford's eye lines, instead of allowing the animation to guide the action.

Tom Kennedy:

> "We couldn't just digitally reanimate Harrison Ford's eye line, because eye lines are determined not just by the position of the eyeball, but by body posture as well. Other challenges involved integrating the new Jabba with the older film's grain structure and exposure variations, and dealing with various filters. Some of the original scenes had been filmed with a net in front of the camera, much like a nylon stocking, and we had to match the characteristics of its effect on the image."

THE REBEL UNIT

From 1993 to 1994, ILM's John Knoll experimented with the idea of using off-the-shelf software to create computer-generated final shots for the Special Edition of *A New Hope*. Knoll made an X-wing CG model,

along with a few TIE fighter models, and created a four-second-long dogfight. It was a technology test: Can work like this be done with off-the-shelf software?

At the time, Knoll had a new vision of how the ILM computer-graphics department might operate. The department had been built up around the idea of doing complex creature work. *Terminator 2: Judgment Day* (1991) and *Jurassic Park* (1993) had been the breakthrough films for which ILM was known. But the company didn't have a good way of doing some of the things that inexpensive commercial systems could do.

John Knoll, visual effects supervisor:

> "We weren't geared toward creating simpler hard-surface shots (vehicles, metal textures, etc.), since ILM didn't have trained hard-surface modelers. Everything went through the creature pipeline instead, which was great for doing these really complex things that nobody else could do, but we couldn't compete when creating simpler objects. Consequently, the numbers we bid for hard-surface CG shots were astronomical."

Several of the developments that came out of ILM's work on the Special Editions ultimately had a significant impact on how the company approached aspects of many future films; one of these was the establishment of what became known as ILM's Rebel Unit.

RIGHT
A view of Cloud City, with Princess Leia (Carrie Fisher) in a window, was modified for *Star Wars* Episode V.

John Knoll:

"The Rebel Unit was an alternate pipeline that let us do simple work with simple tools and allowed us to be very efficient. The artists that we pulled into the Rebel Unit would model, they would texture, and they would light and composite and do their own animations on the shots. (Later, we rolled that right into Episode I, so the majority of the space-battle shots were done in the Rebel Unit."

Including preproduction, the work on the Special Edition of *A New Hope* took two and a half years, the same length of time it took to produce the original version of the film. But by early 1996, the majority of the work had been completed. The success of this project inspired work to start on visual effects revisions for *The Empire Strikes Back* and *Return of the Jedi*.

THE EMPIRE STRIKES BACK—AGAIN!

For the Special Edition of *The Empire Strikes Back*, most of the work was focused on enhancing the Cloud City sequence and providing digital fixes, especially on shots that showed obvious matte lines and other elements that were telltale signs of optical processing.

The Battle of Hoth sequence takes place on a brightly lit snowfield battleground. In certain shots, matte lines were visible against the bright background. Removing the distracting matte lines was a priority. Another problem that had to be addressed was background elements seeping through into foreground elements, an issue known as transparency.

Dave Carson, visual effects supervisor:

"It's amazing that the optical department was able to get the quality of work that most of the original film has. All we could do back then was line the film up on an optical printer and try to play with different exposures of light. Now, in the digital realm, we have such tremendous control over compositing issues, with the ability to adjust color levels, the densities of black, and the size of the mattes that we use to composite."

The Cloud City finale required enhancements that Lucas had always wanted but were impossible to achieve at the time, given the limitation of shooting two-dimensional matte paintings with locked-off camera views. At the time of the Special Edition, three-dimensional computer graphics and digital matte paintings made it possible to construct photorealistic Cloud City buildings and flying craft, using flying virtual-camera views.

Rick McCallum:

"George was locked into a static camera on *A New Hope*, when he originally shot the movie. And he hated it. He felt so constricted by it. There were shots where he wanted to pan and move in, and kind of crane up and down with a ship, and he couldn't do it. Now, with the Special Edition, he could. And there were very specific shots that he actually wanted to do, that he had tried desperately to make happen when he was doing the original films but couldn't get there. So along comes this guy, John Knoll, and he just whips this stuff out week after week."

For the Special Edition, digital paint systems made it possible for artists to create photorealistic 3-D structures that incorporate perspective shifts and virtual camera moves to match the movements of live-action cameras. An impressive element of the digitally expanded Cloud City scene is a fully computer-generated *Millennium Falcon* flying through a computer-generated cityscape. The CG *Falcon* had been created for a scene in the *New Hope* Special Edition and was effectively put to use again for the view of Cloud City.

New Cloud City buildings were created with ILM's interactive Viewpaint texture-mapping software. The tool enabled digital artists to paint hundreds of textures onto 3-D wire-frame surfaces.

The *Empire* Special Edition also features a scene of Princess Leia gazing from the window of a Cloud City building. The structure was re-created digitally, which allowed ILM artists to produce a more successful composition, centering Leia in the window. This scene, set in the morning, presented the challenge of rendering CG buildings and passing cloud cars in bright, revealing sunlight.

Dave Carson:

"The huge amount of visual information we have to provide when something is in bright sunlight is really a strain, and the computer doesn't do it automatically. Someone has to make all the choices regarding the lighting, how rough the surface materials are and how they treat light, the color of the light, the bounce of light—all the things that determine the final rendered image. It's a very time-consuming, trial-and-error process, with no magical measuring device to let us know how far off we are from reality. We have to look at renders on the monitor, filming them out as we get closer to a final. Judging those shots on film is another step, in which we determine how the image is going to be modified as it goes from the digital to the film world."

RETURN OF THE JEDI RETURNS

The Special Edition work on *Return of the Jedi* included a much more impressive finale. Shots were added that provided views of celebrations across the galaxy, along with a wide view of the city of Coruscant. Lucas intended for Coruscant to be a prominent location in the planned new trilogy of *Star Wars* films.

John Knoll:

"When we were working on the space-battle shots, the lighting style, the motion style, everything had to fit as closely as we could to the original footage, But for Coruscant, nothing had been established yet. It was the first time that Coruscant was depicted in the films. We had designs that were coming from the art department that were meant for Episode I, but it was a chance actually to create some of that material and to start working out what the look of that planet was going to be for the Prequels."

The final Coruscant shot was a mixture of elements. Some of the buildings were miniatures, and matte paintings were also used.

John Knoll:

"The whole plaza had to be populated with extras, so we did a live-action shoot on the main stage. We had scaffolding built and put the heavy motion control dolly track on top of it, about twelve feet off the floor, which meant we had this three-thousand-pound camera just careening down the track—it was a scary thing to watch. By the time we got to the midpoint of the shot, the camera was probably going over fifteen miles per hour. But that was necessary, because it was a sixty-foot move that covered a lot of ground."

For the original version of *Jedi*, the idea of a Coruscant location had been considered. Concept artist Ralph McQuarrie had even created artwork of the city's wide plazas and pyramidal spires. In some ways, this final shot is actually the first shot of the second *Star Wars* trilogy.

Paul Huston:

"The rerelease of these movies was a kind of prelude to the new Prequels for the movie-going public, and the effects work was

The capital city-planet of Coruscant
was first seen in Episode VI as a
mostly digital creation.

a prelude for us, as we got ready to tackle the images George
wanted to see in the next trilogy. It was just the starting point,
and we ended up pushing the boundaries even further."

Rick McCallum:

"The Special Edition was the weirdest experiment you can imagine. I was just starting out in the film business when *Star Wars*
(1977) came out, and then suddenly to be working on films that
had been made eighteen years before was just so surreal.

"But we realized what we were doing and what we were
getting—it was just a beautiful two-and-a-half-year period.

And thank God for Twentieth Century Fox, because there
was a guy named Tom Sherrick who was the head of distribution. It was his idea to celebrate the twentieth anniversary
of *Star Wars*, which really gave us the freedom to say, 'Okay,
go spend some money, do whatever you guys want to, and
make them the way you wanted them to be, George.' And
that's what we did. George had a very specific idea, which
was 'Let's learn as much as we can about digital effects.
There are a couple of difficult sequences I want to do and
I want to see how much it costs us.' He was very specific
about what he wanted to achieve."

The Lost World: Jurassic Park

1997

Dennis Muren, visual effects supervisor:

"At the beginning, people would say to me, 'Why do you want to do this sequel? You've already done this—why would you want to do it again? How could you possibly do it any better?' Well, to me, figuring out how to do it better was exactly the point."

Director: Steven Spielberg
Producers: Gerald R. Molen, Colin Wilson

ILM Show Leadership:
Visual Effects Supervisor: Dennis Muren
Associate Visual Effects Supervisor: Rick Schulze
Visual Effects Producer: Ned Gorman
Digital Character Animator: Hal Hickel
Lead Digital Character Animators: Danny Gordon Taylor,
   Daniel Jeannette
Visual Effects Art Director: George Hull

Academy Award® Nomination: Best Visual Effects
Dennis Muren (ILM)
Stan Winston
Randy Dutra
Michael Lantieri

When ILM began work on the first *Jurassic Park* film, the feasibility of creating photorealistic animals using CG animation was uncertain. That exploration into new territory for CG resulted in a certain amount of conservatism in terms of visual effects shot design and camera movement. But after the phenomenal success of ILM's work in *Jurassic Park*, and further developments in CG capabilities during the ensuing four years, visual effects supervisor Dennis Muren and his team were eager to take on new challenges in the second *Jurassic Park* film, *The Lost World*. This time around, Muren already knew the team could create the photorealistic animals, so more energy went into shot design and character action. The goal was to design shots that had nuance and boldness. Muren wanted to treat the CG dinosaurs as if they were really being filmed in the wilderness. The project was a tremendous opportunity to explore the freedom and potential of CG.

DINOSAUR DOC

Dennis Muren:

"We wanted to maintain the sense of realism; we didn't want the audience to feel like these were trained animals. We wanted it to feel like you never knew what one of these dinosaurs was going to do two seconds from now—which is true of all nature. And it's hard to get that feeling into animation. We got it into the first film and we made sure that we kept that in the second film.

"I also wanted to be a lot more flexible with the camera, so that everything seemed more spontaneous and natural. For example, the *Stegosaurus* is walking through the shot and the sun is flaring the lens. You tilt up into these amazing

PREVIOUS SPREAD

Two T. rexes rip apart their victim in a scene that went back and forth between ILM and the ratings board until the level of blood and violence was deemed acceptable for the movie's PG-13 rating, and not an R rating. ILM's digital T. rexes augmented the work of Stan Winston Studio, whose practical dinos were used on set

ABOVE

The opening dinosaur shot featured much more complex CG creations than used in *Jurassic Park* (inset: wire frame of animation).

plates on his back. That was something that we found after we put the shot together and just treated it as though it was actually shot on a location. But of course it wasn't. We shot the empty plate and then we put the *Stegosaurus* in, and I thought, 'Wouldn't it be interesting if we tilt up and see these plates on his back?' And that tilt up gave the shot a documentary look. The documentary feel is the opposite of *Casper*, which is more theatrical. Even the first *Jurassic Park* had more theatrical staging. By the time we got to *The Lost World*, I was really pushing for that documentary look, because I felt we could successfully create more spontaneous camera movements and more spontaneous dinosaur behavior. I've always loved the idea of the shots looking like the camera is reacting to an event instead of cutting and seeing it. The camera pans all over the place to follow the action. You don't get a sense that there's an effects person saying, 'We can't pan the camera.'"

Dinosaur animation required not only technical expertise, but also the keen eye of animators who understood animal behavior and the nuances of performance.

Hal Hickel, digital character animator:

"The main thing we were trying to do, and we've tried to do on all of the *Jurassic Park* films, is to make the dinosaurs feel like animals rather than monsters. If you were out on safari and you were filming elephants and rhinos, you'd tend to think of that very differently from the way dinosaurs had been portrayed prior to the *Jurassic Park* films. They were presented more like Godzilla, something really outside of nature. In *The Lost World*, as had been done on the first *Jurassic Park* film, we were trying to continue the tradition of making the dinosaurs feel like they were animals that were part of our history, and they just didn't happen to overlap with humans—but if they *had*, this is what they would have looked like if you'd gone out and filmed them.

"Obviously, it's not that we had any real-world reference of dinosaurs to look at, but we have elephants and rhinos and other large animals with interesting physiques that in some way or other would help inform what we were doing. Dinosaur motion supervisor Randy Dutra had a laser eye to keep us on the mark in terms of making the dinosaurs really move the way animals move."

LEFT

A Compy dino on the shoulder of bad guy Dieter Stark (Peter Stormare). On set, the actor interacted with animatronic compys. The CG creatures were often hand-animated, with individual performances honed over a period of months.

ACUTE ANIMATION

In one sequence, two raptors are fighting over Laura Dern. They snap and bite and wrestle on the ground. The contact between the fighting raptors presented a particular challenge for the animators.

Hal Hickel:

"Because of all the contact between the CG characters, you have to work that out and try to make it feel violent and in the moment. One of the problems with computer animation is that it doesn't lend itself to improvisation very well. You have to conceive the shot in your mind and then carry it out in the animation, but it's a very time-consuming process. So you're laboring and laboring over a shot, and it can become very over-smooth and canned that way. A shot like that is always challenging because you want it to feel like it's just this raw action that you happened to capture on film.

"But what can an animator do to keep it fresh and energetic, to make the figures feel like they're really combating with each other? You have to look at reference—wildlife, lions fighting or something. You have to step away from it and come back to it. If you stare at it too much and just keep playing over the work you've done so far, you start to lose any real perception of it. The other thing is just inviting your coworkers to comment on it, dragging other animators in and saying, 'What do you think of this? What's wrong with it?' so you get fresh eyes on it."

Dennis Muren:

"There are many more dinosaurs, and they come into contact with people a lot more than they did in the first film, actually touching them, which makes the work a lot more difficult, but also a lot more successful. It's difficult because there's nothing touching the actor. For example, in the case of the little Compy, or *Compsognathus*, as he jumps on the guy's shoulder, it's got to stay on his shoulder, but it was never on his shoulder in actuality, so you need to be able to figure out in the computer where the actor's shoulder is, since you already shot the background and you have that image in the computer. Then you have to animate the character to move around the same way as the actor's body is moving, so it looks like it's attached to the body. And then the Compy has to create a shadow on the guy's body and has to animate as though it's holding on to the guy's moving body as he's thrashing around. At the time of *The Lost World*, this sort of work hadn't been done very much at all."

In some cases, live-action footage featuring puppet dinosaurs, created by Stan Winston Studio, was intercut with shots of CG dinosaurs. The sequence of the raptor chase, in which Sarah, Malcolm, Nick, and Kelly tumble down a hill, demonstrates how important quick and inventive intercutting between CG and puppet dinosaurs is, in order to create imperceptible transitions between the two depictions of the same type of dinosaur. The interaction between the CG raptors and the human performers was also a key element that enhanced the scene's believability.

Proprietary tools were incorporated into Caricature to provide subtle skin deformations for the dinosaurs. One such program, iSculpt, enabled modelers to build digital forms almost as if working in real clay. It also allowed animators to sculpt two muscle positions, flexed and unflexed, which resulted in a shifting movement when the computer interpolated between the two.

Ben Snow, CG sequence supervisor:

"We tried to get this sense of muscles for the dinosaurs, so when the animators moved a rig it felt like a muscle was moving under the skin. You could see the thigh become taught as the dinosaur flexed its leg. To do that we implemented a system called "joint-driven shapes." Joint-driven shapes meant that as the animators straightened the leg, it would automatically dial a flex shape on the leg of the character so you would get this sort of bulge in the leg. The software iSculpt allowed the artists to take a pose of the T. rex model they'd originally created, and more easily push and pull points on that to make a muscle-like shape. It was combined with Caricature to make it possible to say, 'Okay, as he runs along, I'll dial in these shapes.' Joint-driven shapes is another of the innovations that *The Lost World* allowed us to develop, and iSculpt was integral to that."

ANOTHER ROAD TO ILM, OR "SO, HOW DID I GET HERE?"

Hal Hickel, animation supervisor:

"By the time the first *Star Wars* came out when I was thirteen, I was already kind of interested in effects because I'd seen *King Kong*, so I'd started to get interested in stop-motion animation. But *Star Wars* really sealed the deal; that was when I really started to get interested in visual effects broadly. After *Star Wars*, I got interested in models and miniatures and motion control and matte paintings. So I always wanted to work at ILM.

"I was working at Will Vinton Studios as a clay animator, and I was starting to think that it wasn't going to happen because, after *Jurassic Park*, things were swinging toward computer animation, which at that time I really didn't know anything about. So it was very ironic for me a few years later to end up first at Pixar and then have the opportunity to bounce over to ILM, right when they were starting up the new *Star Wars* films, which was something I really never anticipated happening, and then a sequel to *Jurassic Park*. It was great timing. Ending up here and spending such a great long time here—it's been thirteen years now—it's just turned out better than I could have imagined.

"What I like about ILM is the history of the place. There are no other effects companies that are this old, that have been around this long, and that have principals in the company who were here from the beginning, like Dennis Muren or Paul Huston. I like that continuity and that history."

DISTANT LOCATION: THE PARKING LOT

Despite the sophisticated technological achievements in *The Lost World*, some of ILM's work involved a mixture of high- and low-tech.

Ben Snow:

"Dennis was very interested in looking at alternative image-capture approaches, so for the *Stegosaurus* knocking down trees, we actually went out with Hi8 cameras in the ILM parking lot, got some trees from a local nursery, and just tipped them over and shot it on video. Because the trees were going to be shrunk down so small in the shot, using consumer-grade video was completely acceptable. It was a low-tech, high-tech component. 'How do we do this easier or cheaper?' That was one of the things we were starting to realize: The effects were too expensive. We had to look for ways to make them cheaper and to use our heads to try and get better results."

PIPELINE PROGRESSION

Many of the effects shots were complicated by wild camera moves, high frame counts, and extremely tight close-ups. Several sequences included multiple interacting dinosaurs. This aspect of the work on *The Lost World* resulted in key developments in ILM's proprietary Caricature software.

Cary Phillips, software development:

"I remember feeling overwhelmed at the beginning of *The Lost World*. We had this emerging system in Caricature, which had started out simply being used for the face. And then, toward the end of *DragonHeart* and *Mars Attacks!*, it was extended to be used on the whole body, but it would still handle only one character at a time. But what just blew us away with *The Lost World* were the crowd shots; there were lots of sequences in the film with dozens of dinosaurs. Usually when we take on challenges, we've done a little bit of something before, but we'd never done anything on this scale. So in this case, we can animate one character, 'Okay,

so now do fifty. And do them all in the same shot.' So the level of complexity is really daunting.

"And this relates to the concept of our pipeline. You can compare it to an assembly line. We're a shop of specialists. Individual artists have their thing that they do, and they basically take some data from other people and use that data to generate some more data and then give it back to other people. There's this constant exchange. But when you get beyond just a few people and beyond just a little bit of data, the task of managing that, of making sure that everybody has the right version of the data and that it all fits together, becomes overwhelming. And the system that ILM had in place for coordinating all of this data, how it would be exchanged, how it would all be tied together and generate an image, was just hopelessly simplistic at the time.

"What we tackled on *The Lost World* was setting in place a system for managing that process. Euan MacDonald and I collaborated on a mechanism that we called Shot Files, which is a mechanism that still permeates ILM. A shot file is basically like a table of contents for everything that goes into the making of a shot. More goes into the making of an image than a computer can process at one time, so we have to produce the image in pieces. But somewhere there has to exist a definition of everything that goes into the shot, and ILM's mechanism for that is the shot file. It's the place that says, 'Here is all of the stuff that this image is going to consist of. And furthermore, here are subcomponents of that, which you might want to process independently.' So every individual dinosaur was made up of four or five different data files. There was one to describe the geometry, another the motion, the movement of the skin, and the appearance of the skin. The shot-file mechanism came to define what we refer to as the pipeline, as the way that all of the different artists make their contribution to the sum total of the image that appears on the screen. *The Lost World* was a large step forward in that regard."

RIGHT

An escaped T. rex runs amok; that is, a CG creature interacts seamlessly with practical elements on mechanical rigs filmed on location in Burbank (standing in for San Diego, California).

Men in Black

1997

Eric Brevig, visual effects supervisor:

"The constantly moving storyline demanded that no two sequences in the film share the same kind of effect. From crashing spaceships and exploding heads to alien life-forms, transforming vehicles, and giant cockroaches, the film required a surprising diversity of visual effects images."

Director: Barry Sonnenfeld
Producers: Laurie MacDonald, Walter F. Parkes

ILM Show Leadership:
Visual Effects Supervisors: Eric Brevig, Scott Farrar
Visual Effects Producers: Denise Ream, Jacqueline M. Lopez
Animation Supervisor: Rob Coleman
Visual Effects Art Director: David Nakabayashi

BAFTA Film Award Nomination: Best Special Effects
Eric Brevig (ILM)
Rick Baker
Rob Coleman (ILM)
Peter Chesney

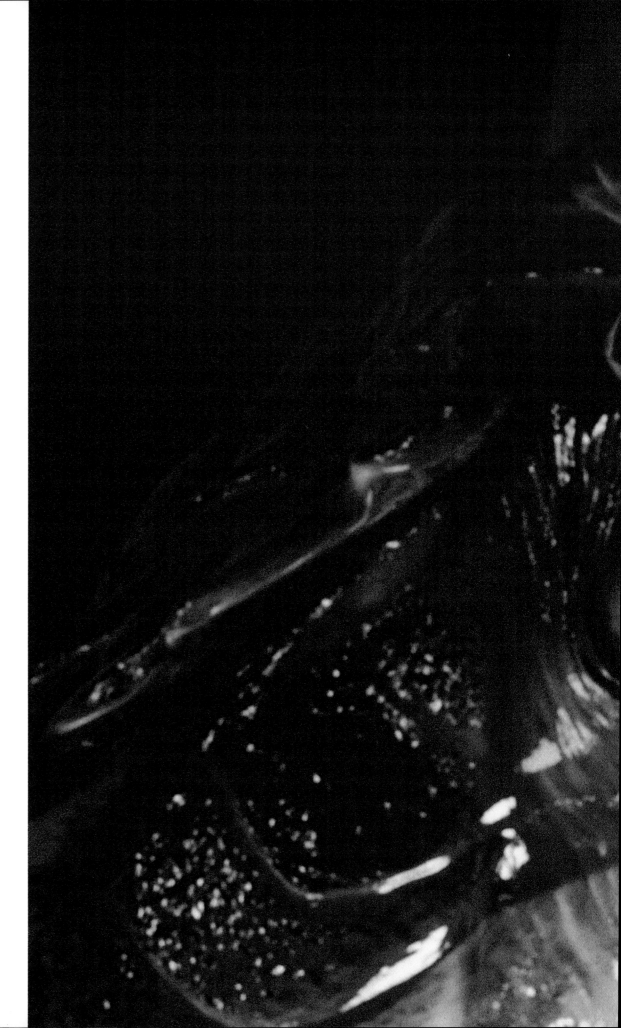

FOR *MEN IN BLACK*, ILM created more than 250 visual effects shots for thirty sequences. The work called upon every tool within ILM's repertoire of effects techniques.

A unique aspect of the CG work in *Men in Black* was that the computer-generated characters were called upon to deliver comedic performances with a precision as demanding as the technical aspects of their creation.

HEY, MIKEY!

Eric Brevig:

"Mikey, a seven-foot tall alien, is revealed as he feebly holds up an artificial head. While being interrogated, he angrily roars and attempts to escape, getting shot in the process—with explosive results. Throughout the sequence, the action moments of Mikey's initial reveal, angry roar, and suicidal escape attempt were accomplished by compositing a fully computer-

generated animated model of Mikey into live-action backgrounds shot on the set.

"The Mikey CG model was built using Alias software, then painted and textured using Viewpaint, ILM's proprietary 3-D texture painting program, to match a fully articulated Mikey suit built by Rick Baker. Because the CG shots were intercut with shots of the practical Mikey suit, the CG model of Mikey had to match its real-world counterpart exactly. Additional CG models of Mikey's 'roaring' mouth, teeth, and tongue were also built to allow for facial transformation. We added extensive controls to Mikey's muscles, skin, leg-flex, and belly wiggle to give the model the look of weight and mass while running."

David Nakabayashi, visual effects art director:

"With Mikey, we were doing work with socking and enveloping, which gave the skin the right viscosity and a sense of inner structure so it looked like there was muscle tone and architecture underneath, in effect giving it mass. Then the director

PREVIOUS SPREAD

The CG Edgar bug, which went through a very late design change when the script changed (introducing different actions, four legs to six, altering the eyes, and adding antennae, while preserving the the basic geometry of the original model).

ABOVE

Based on a creature design by Rick Baker, illegal alien Mikey was first shot with various physical props as held by an on-set grip (left); wire frame of animation (middle); final frame (right).

kept saying, 'Make it wetter,' so we had to do a lot of work with shaders to create a high-quality wet look for the slime. On stage, they take K-Y Jelly and rub it all over the rubber monster. At ILM, we had to create that through programming."

One sequence featuring Mikey involved the character running a considerable distance into the desert. This was a physical impossibility within the confines of the sound stage. The solution was to have the character transform from the onstage creature into an ILM CG image. As reference for the actions of the CG Mikey's muscle groups, the ILM team studied videotapes of world-class athletes and NFL slow-motion films.

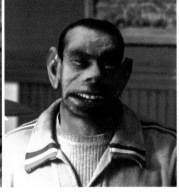

OFF WITH HIS HEAD

In a dramatic moment, Jack Jeebs's head is shot off and then quickly grows back. Creating the right look for the animation in this sequence was challenging because the audience would be intimately familiar with the look of an "authentic" human being. The successful creation of the Jack Jeebs head effect was the closest ILM had come, thus far, to simulating an actor on-screen.

Eric Brevig:

"The effect of Jeebs's head regeneration was accomplished by creating a fully animated CG close-up of actor Tony Shalhoub. This CG head was composited onto the image of his body, until the moment during the shot when the seamless substitution back to his real head is made. A live-action plate of Shalhoub raising his head and delivering his dialogue was filmed on the location set, and Shalhoub's head was digitally painted out of the sequence for the first several seconds of the shot.

"A series of seventy different 3-D CG models were sculpted, each representing a different stage in the regeneration process. These models, from embryonic to fully formed, were animated to grow, while lip-synching Jeebs's dialogue and following Shalhoub's moving torso.

"To simulate human flesh seen in close-up, custom computer graphics surface shaders were written, carefully matching the transparency and texture of Shalhoub's actual skin."

A HARD DAY'S SAUCER

The flying-saucer sequence was created by using a combination of CG and miniature techniques. A CG model of the saucer was used for the shot in which the saucer transforms in preparation for takeoff, and for the aerial shots of the saucer in flight.

A miniature Flushing Meadows set was fabricated, and model-makers created a one-sixth-scale miniature of the saucer. A one-sixth-scale Unisphere was also made to shoot the dramatic moment when the saucer crashes into this recognizable artifact from the 1964–65 New York World's Fair.

David Nakabayashi:

"The saucer crash was built as a miniature set, and it looked great. There we were, doing all of this breakthrough digital work—but the cool thing was we built and integrated something practical, which made for a really good-looking shot. Most people don't think about how dirt flies in front of the camera on impact, and it was very difficult to do that digitally at the time. Shooting it practically made it work."

Lorne Peterson, chief model-maker:

"One of the problems with doing that kind of thing is that people don't realize how incredibly dense the earth is. When a real airplane crashes into the earth, it might only make a groove that's three feet deep at the extreme. But emotionally, people think that big things happen. The only time that you get really big holes in the earth is if a giant meteor hits. But using real earth with miniatures just doesn't work because it's too dense; it isn't the right scale

TOP LEFT

Final frame of the alien ship (a miniature built at one-quarter-scale) about to crash land. The model was nine feet in diameter and, to withstand the crash, was built of fiberglass. The World's Fair Unisphere seen in the background is also a one-quarter scale model composited behind Agent J (Will Smith) and Agent K (Tommy Lee Jones) who were shot against blue-screen.

MIDDLE LEFT

The crash-landing of the alien ship was realized at ILM with a fantastic miniature set of Flushing Meadows Park, complete with electric lampposts, trees, and peat moss soil. For the crash sequence the craft was rigged to fly thirty-five feet at a speed of thirty miles per hour coming to an immediate and controlled stop at a precise mark or risk crashing through the stage wall.

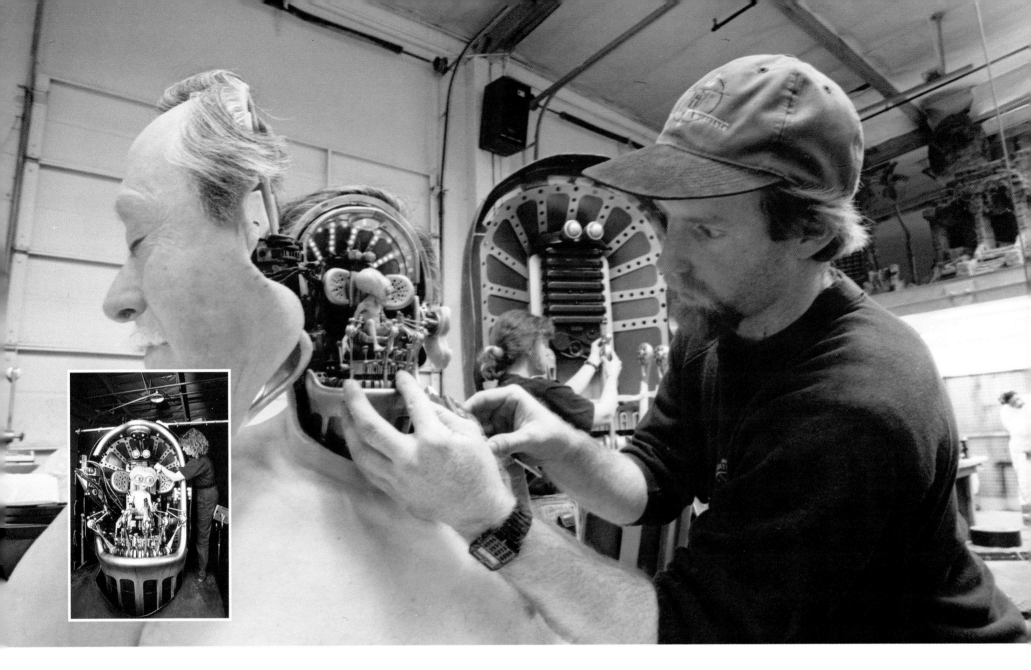

ABOVE

Model maker Danny Wagner working on Gentle Rosenburg, the Arquillian jeweler, guardian of Orion's belt. To accomplish the autopsy sequence, Cinovation built a replica of Rosenberg's head and shoulders and the alien within and ILM constructed the control booth interior.

ABOVE, INSET

ILM model makers fabricated a scaled-up control booth to house the oversize Cinovation articulated puppet that would allow for the nuanced performance.

and, of course, our ship doesn't weigh anything like what a real spaceship would.

"So I worked on different formulas to come up with a light-density dirt. I used vermiculite, which is a very puffy mineral, and peat moss, which I knew had the right color and the look of earth. I mixed the peat moss with the vermiculite so it would have a very low density and things could plow into it.

"At the same time, we're building, ten feet off the ground, the set that the 'earth' is going to be placed on. And the reason it's ten feet off the ground is that we have to create a railroad track underneath the set for the saucer.

The saucer has to be able to move very quickly: forty miles an hour. There's a rod that holds the spaceship, and in the center of the set, there's a groove so that whole set is split in half, and the rod can run down the center of it. The dirt moves like Moses parting the Red Sea.

"Right underneath the front of the ship, there seems to be a prow of a boat. To operate that thing, we had to have a little train car on tracks. A guy sits in there and he has a joystick. He controls the tilting of the ship so that it noses right into the ground, and he has a little video monitor so he can see what's happening up above. But we're having to do this all very fast because you have cameramen waiting.

So the guy gets in the little sled, and the ship is ready and the lights come on, and when they say go, the ship comes flying down through this trough—and as soon as the ship noses into the ground all of a sudden, it starts spewing up a tsunami of dirt.

"Once it comes to a stop at the other end, we have to do it again. You have to get all of the dirt that has fallen down through the gap and get that back up ten feet higher. So it's a lot of work, really fast, with a crew of people hoisting big containers of the peat moss and vermiculite. We take off the trees, the park benches, rake the dirt again, put the new dirt back in, roll it out, and put the green in again. We did it

eleven times in one day, between eight in the morning and eleven thirty at night. It was one of the hardest days I've ever worked."

David Nakabayashi:

"I think that's one of the things that makes ILM so successful, not just for *Men in Black*, but through the rest of the films, was that the effects were founded in this physical world of making models and building sets and making paintings to really understand what looks photorealistic, what looks believable—all of that influenced the digital work that was done for *Men in Black*. The digital part looked as good as the practical part, and vice versa."

ABOVE

Agent K (Tommy Lee Jones) inter-rogates an AWOL alien, whose wife is giving birth in their car—her CG tentacle grabs Agent J (Will Smith, filmed against blue-screen and composited into plates shot in NY). Ultimately, ILM created more than 250 shots for thirty sequences in *MIB*, contributing conceptually as well.

ABOVE

ILM's *Men in Black* Model Shop crew next to the one-quarter-scale model of the Midtown Tunnel. The crew put their names, abbreviated, onto the model-car license plates and placed cutout pictures of themselves inside the vehicles. The tunnel, complete with internal illumination and 50 one-eighth-scale vehicles, measured three feet wide, twenty inches tall and ninety-six feet in length.

RIGHT

Mounted to a rotating rig, Agent J (Will Smith) and Agent K (Tommy Lee Jones) drive their Ford LTD "Supercar" along the ceiling of the Midtown Tunnel, which was constructed as a one-eighth-scale miniature filmed separately and composited in.

Titanic

1997

Director: James Cameron
Producers: James Cameron, Jon Landau

ILM Show Leadership:
Visual Effects Supervisor: Dave Carson
Visual Effects Producer: Tom Kennedy
Associate Visual Effects Producer: Heather Smith

MOST OF THE VISUAL EFFECTS for *Titanic* were created by director James Cameron's own company, Digital Domain. ILM was called late in the game to pick up a total of twelve difficult shots.

Part of the work ILM was responsible for included four split-screens that reveal the entire ship, bow to stern, sinking. These shots combine elements of the full-size ship set that were never intended to be used together until Cameron came up with the idea in postproduction. During editing, Cameron realized that he didn't have a full panning shot of the *Titanic* as it lay foundering.

Cameron had a panning shot of the rear end of the full-size ship, and he had another panning shot—taken from a different angle at a different time—of the front end sinking. The two shots had to be aligned and blended. ILM exaggerated the rate of sinking in the final composites by adding water elements from other shots to create a new, higher waterline against the side of the ship.

Stars and a horizon line were added to the scene as well. Placing the stars presented a challenge, since the production footage included major crane and dolly moves. The solution for ILM was to employ a 3-D matchmove. This involved building a low-resolution CG model of the *Titanic* and lining the model up with the ship in the plate, which indicated what the camera was doing, making it possible to matchmove the shot.

RIGHT

The sinking *Titanic*

Deep Impact

1998

Scott Farrar, visual effects supervisor:

"*Deep Impact* was probably one of the most difficult
movies I've ever worked on. Nobody had ever done
water work to this extent: the large waves, the crashing buildings, the water damage…"

Director: Mimi Leder
Producers: David Brown, Richard D. Zanuck

ILM Show Leadership:
Visual Effects Supervisor: Scott Farrar
Co-Visual Effects Supervisor: Bill George
Visual Effects Producer: Denise Ream
Associate Visual Effects Producer: Jill Brooks
Visual Effects Art Director: Alex Jaeger

FOR *DEEP IMPACT*, ILM was responsible for effects shots in three categories: the comet itself, seen in space as well as in a series of shots as it approaches earth and makes impact in the Atlantic Ocean; miniatures for scenes of a spacecraft, the *Messiah*, entering the comet's tail and landing on its surface; and scenes of the massive tidal wave resulting from the comet's impact.

CALAMITOUS COMET

Bill George, co-visual effects supervisor:

"Often, directors are more shoppers than directors: They can't tell you exactly what it is that they want, but they know deep inside their head what they're looking for. Our job is to unlock those things. And often the best way to do that is to put a bunch of artwork out in front of the director and let them pick and say, 'Oh, I like this, I like that,' so you get clues as to which direction you're heading.

"My background is in the Model Shop, where I experienced the practical way of doing things back in the old days, when you didn't have computer graphics and you needed to figure out trick ways to do things. For *Deep Impact*, I sculpted a crude model of a comet. I poured sugar on top of it, which then cascaded off. I took photographs of it out in the parking lot and did long exposures to make it appear as though it was gas coming off of the comet. I then used those photographs as a basis for doing some concept art."

Scott Farrar:

"We live and die by very esoteric things like color and contrast. It's everything to us. We had a big symposium with NASA scientists who told us what they felt would be true about comets coming toward earth and what the impact might do. We then had to come up with the extremely difficult creation of layers of gasses streaming off the front of the comet as it flew through space."

Computer graphics were primarily used for the gas coming off the comet and the tail. Scenes on the surface of the comet involved a combination of elements shot on a live-action set on the Paramount lot with a miniature landscape built by ILM. After the miniature was photographed, layers of CG gas were added. ILM also shot practical elements of gas explosions that were composited over the other visuals.

Bill George:

"A lot of times people come to us to create things because you can't do it for real. But our goal was to be as scientifically accurate as possible. So that's where we started. At the same time, it's a little bit fanciful, because there was no real reference material; we were therefore able to steer it in the direction that we thought would be the most visually dynamic and exciting. However, we had the limitation of production having built a full-size set of the surface of the comet. We didn't want our design to be too drastically different, because it had to match the live action plates."

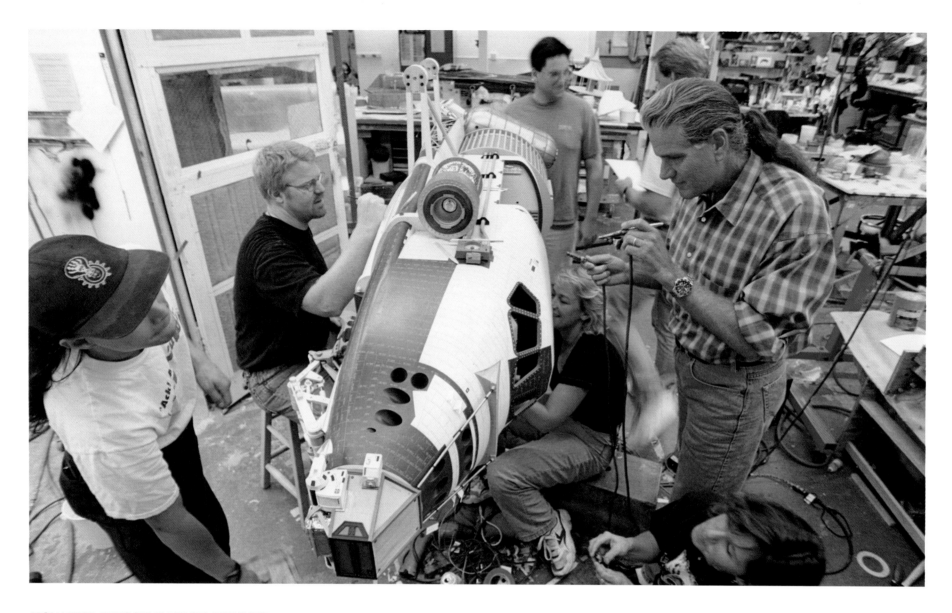

HOW THE *MESSIAH* FIRST ARRIVED

Scenes of the spacecraft *Messiah* entering the comet's tail and landing on its surface combined live-action elements filmed on an enormous stage with a variety of miniature and digital embellishments. The *Messiah* was designed entirely in a computer by the production art department team, and then built as a practical miniature by the ILM Model Shop. In addition to the ten-foot, one-forty-eighth-scale complete ship, model-makers constructed a six-foot, one-sixteenth-scale lander section, specifically for close-up views of the landing module approaching the comet's surface. The challenge in shooting the *Messiah* was that multiple passes were required, including a beauty pass, a matte pass, and a "comet interaction" light pass, to tie the spacecraft in with the turbulent activity surrounding it as it enters the comet's tail.

BIBLICAL DESTRUCTION

The massive tidal wave of *Deep Impact*, one of the most difficult aspects of ILM's work on the film, features prominently in thirty shots. The decision was made to use digital techniques exclusively to realize the wave.

Ben Snow, CG supervisor:

"I'd wanted to shoot a lot of practical water particles, but for budgetary reasons they asked us to do it all CG. So we had to rely on all-CG water particles and I have to say, no way would I ever do that again. We basically said, 'Okay, every water particle you see in this film is going to be CG,' so it was kind of crazy."

ABOVE

Water races through the asphalt
canyons of Manhattan, as CG cars
get tossed and flipped about like
toys. Realistic eddies and flow
patterns were created by a full fluid
dynamic simulation that produced
particles emulating water spray,
bouncing off buildings and into
one another.

Bill George:

"There's a horrible complexity to how water reflects and re-fracts light, and how it interacts with things it's hitting. And even though the average person can't paint or draw water, everybody knows how it operates; we're all experts, because subconsciously, we've spent our entire lives observing how it works.

"The great thing about ILM is that we always build on our past work. *Deep Impact* was one of the first big water films. The tools that we developed for *Deep Impact* would be used on *Perfect Storm* and were pushed even further. But the same issues always crop up with water simulation. One of those is that the computer has to calculate what the water is doing. You give the computer the parameters: 'The water is here, the force is coming this way, and this is what it's hitting.' The computer has to calculate how the water would move from one frame to the next. The computer has to calculate frame one before it can calculate frame two, and so basically you have to do it one frame at a time. It takes a tremendous amount of time and processing to do that."

A particularly difficult shot was an overhead view of New York City, as the wave fills streets and wraps around buildings. A full fluid dynamic simulation containing approximately ten thousand lines of code had to be written. Cars swept up by the rushing water were CG elements matched to autos in the live-action plates. Falling buildings were replaced with CG models, facilitated by obtaining plan views of city buildings, which established the relationship between structures.

Saving Private Ryan

1998

Roger Guyett, co–visual effects supervisor:

> "One of the reasons you haven't heard much about the visual effects in *Saving Private Ryan* is that Spielberg wanted you to feel that they photographed all of that action in camera."

Director: Steven Spielberg
Producers: Steven Spielberg, Ian Bryce, Mark Gordon, Gary Levinsohn

ILM Show Leadership:
Visual Effects Supervisor: Stefen Fangmeier
Co-Visual Effects Supervisor: Roger Guyett
Visual Effects Producer: Kim Bromley
Associate Visual Effects Producer: Heather Smith
Visual Effects Art Director: Alex Laurant

BAFTA Film Award: Best Special Effects
Stefen Fangmeier (ILM)
Roger Guyett (ILM)
Neil Corbould

FOR *SAVING PRIVATE RYAN*, ILM created effects that have been described as "invisible." The work included providing characters with unpleasant wounds and adding squib hits. In many cases, it was also safer for ILM to add explosions to a scene, rather than launching practical effects that needed to occur close to a character, which would have thereby put the actor at risk.

Roger Guyett:

"Spielberg's feeling was that if you started talking about visual effects, in some way you were diluting the visceral quality of it, as though the actors weren't having those experiences. I think one of his primary goals of that movie was to make it an immersive experience—to be involved in the D-Day landings and to have that very first-person experience of every aspect of it."

D-DAY DYNAMICS

Stefen Fangmeier, visual effects supervisor:

"The biggest visual effect in the film is a motion control shot. When the troops have arrived on shore, they get into a Jeep and drive away. The camera moves over, and we reveal the whole landing, the ships in the water and the troops on the beach. It's a big, epic shot that defines the whole scope of the invasion.

"We had eight hundred troops from the Irish army who were playing American soldiers coming up on the beach. We only had eight hundred, but the shot required that it look like there were thousands of them. That's why we had to do multiple passes. And in order to do multiple passes and combine them, we had to use motion control—so for each pass, you got the exact same camera movement. First we had the troops on top of the cliff, with our heroes driving by in a Jeep, clearing frame, and then the camera moving on to film an empty beach. Then, all of the people on top of the cliff move down, and we have them marching along the beach, and we did another pass of it. And we did this three times on the beach to get the feeling that eight hundred people were really thousands. That's often the case in crowd duplication. That's why you use motion control, which enables you to do several different passes of the same shot and then to combine them later on."

Roger Guyett:

"I still remember just how difficult it was to do the establishing shot of the beach and the ships and the ocean. We only really managed to finish that shot once, and fortunately it's the one that you see in the film. It sounds crazy, but it's a really long shot and required a tremendous amount of effort. That shot was about a thousand frames, and we were literally struggling to complete each frame, so we could only watch parts of it very occasionally. I was getting concerned that we were never going to see a completed version, and I think pretty much the only completed version is the one that's in the film."

OWNING UP

Stefen Fangmeier:

"I think visual effects really had more of a supporting role in *Saving Private Ryan*, because Steven was very specific about only using it when it is absolutely necessary and about really getting as much in reality as possible. It's a war film, and he didn't want to add any element of an artificial quality."

Much of ILM's work involved enhancing or solving problems that occurred in elements that were shot live-action. For example, the antique German machine guns that were used on set would frequently jam. To avoid slowing the live-action shoot down by stopping to repair the guns, production relied on ILM to keep the guns firing.

Roger Guyett:

"We contributed to the movie, but in no way would I want to take away what they achieved physically and viscerally in just watching that action play out. I think that *Saving Private Ryan* changed the way that modern war movies are made."

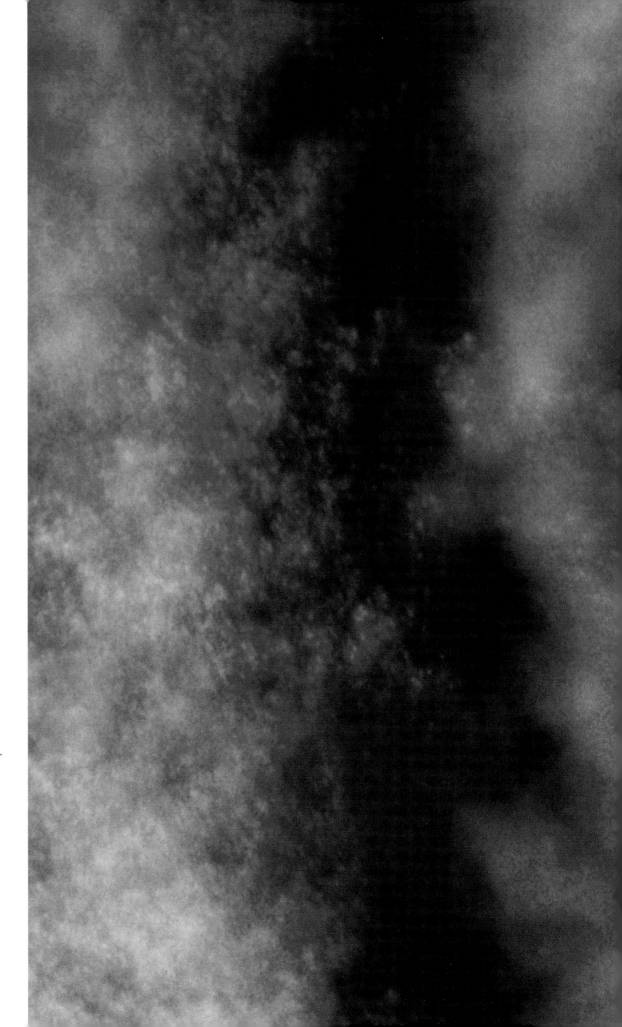

The Mummy

1999

Daniel Jeannette, animation supervisor:

"Rather than remake the title character from the
classic 1932 film, the mummy was completely re-
thought in concept and design. Bandages gave way
to a decayed body, complete with remains of skin,
muscle, sinew, and dangling bits of dried flesh. We
had to see into and through the body as it moved."

Director: Stephen Sommers
Producers: Sean Daniel, James Jacks

ILM Show Leadership:
Visual Effects Supervisors: John Andrew Berton Jr., Scott Farrar
Visual Effects Producer: Tom Kennedy
Associate Visual Effects Producer: Sandra Scott
Animation Supervisor: Daniel Jeannette
Visual Effects Art Director: Alex Laurant

BAFTA Film Award Nomination:
   Best Achievement in Special Visual Effects
John Andrew Berton Jr. (ILM)
Daniel Jeannette (ILM)
Ben Snow (ILM)
Chris Corbould

THE MUMMY PROVIDED an opportunity that ILM had been waiting for: to oversee the design and creation of a lead character. Typically, in preproduction, the studio will hire a creature designer. For *The Mummy*, the ILM team had a chance to show off their capabilities in creature design.

MERGING MOTION CAPTURE AND ANIMATION

Prior to *The Mummy*, ILM had used motion capture for the visual effects creation of background crowds and for digital stunt doubles (for 1997's *Spawn* and for animatics going back to 1999's *Star Wars*: Episode I *The Phantom Menace*), but motion capture had never been used to create a lead character in a feature film. During the course of the film, the mummy, Imhotep, evolves from a decayed skeleton, to a corpse brought back to

life, to a fully regenerated human, played by actor Arnold Vosloo. It was therefore important for the CG mummy to be animated in a way that would be consistent with the physical performance defined by Vosloo on camera. ILM developed new techniques to achieve this harmony, using motion capture to tie the CG creature to the real actor and his performance.

Daniel Jeannette:

"Because of the specific acting needs associated with a CG hero character, we designed a mechanism that incorporated motion capture data into our animation controls. It allowed our animators to work more effectively with the data when adjustments of timing or performance were necessary.

"Not only was Arnold Vosloo in the unique position of acting out all the various stages of the mummy on screen, but

director Stephen Sommers could also interactively direct the performance of the CG creatures. First, we filmed the scenes with all the actors (including Vosloo) going through their paces. This step was key to define a clear understanding of staging, acting, image composition, camera moves, and editorial continuity. Then, the final scenes were shot without Vosloo to generate clean background plates. Selected plates were matchmoved to be available in time for the motion capture shoot. In the last week of principal photography Vosloo reenacted his performance in motion capture attire. On set, each select take was immediately reconstructed into a CG skeleton figure and composited in the plates. Director Sommers could evaluate the validity of the performance in the context of the shots and we could recapture as necessary. In turn, Vosloo could effectively visualize his performance and adjust it more accurately. Ultimately, it gave us a way to ensure the complete success of the motion capture shoot and marked the first-ever performance-capture system with real-time feedback—a substantial breakthrough at the time."

ANOTHER ROAD TO ILM, OR "SO, HOW DID I GET HERE?"

**Scott Farrar,
visual effects supervisor:**

"I started making movies on a regular Super 8 camera when I was a kid, and I would beg my folks to let me shoot the vacation movies on a wind-up Brownie. I loved the excitement of shooting something, and I could hardly stand the wait between shooting it and getting it developed at the lab.

"This is pre-DVD, so if there was a famous movie out there, you may not ever see it, because all you could see was whatever they would present on TV or what was currently in commercial movie theaters; there weren't a lot of art or reperatory houses. I remember that I didn't see *Casablanca* until I was about twenty-two years old, because there was no way to do it. So I read about movies and about lighting. I went to UCLA film school. I didn't really have any relatives to get me in the business, so I was just sort of fumbling around with what I wanted to do.

"Then I visited a friend who was working on a science-fiction film. He said, 'You should check this out—we're working on this film, and we might get in the camera union.' I go over

and look, and they're shooting *Star Wars*. They didn't have the name yet. I meet Dennis Muren and a couple of other guys, and I see what a motion control track camera rig looks like. I say, 'Oh my God. You mean you lay down the move, and it's repeatable, and then you can get all of your various levels of exposure because you can run it slower and faster, because the lights on the ships require different exposures?! Oh my God. That's what I want to do.'

"It was literally like the heavens opened up. Then Dennis told me, 'There are a couple of movies starting, this one—meaning *Star Wars*—is all booked up, but *Star Trek: The Motion Picture* is starting and *1941* is starting,' and Dennis gave me a couple of people to call. I went with *Star Trek* because they were hiring first. And because of that film, I did get in the camera union. But *Star Wars* was the new birth of the era of visual effects that we're in today. It was palpable; there was something happening. Then I was working on *Galactica* when a friend of mine called about working on *The Empire Strikes Back*, but I'd already committed to *Galactica*, so I couldn't do that.

"But later on, ILM had moved up north, and I got a call from another friend who had moved up there to work on *Star Trek II: The Wrath of Khan*. My baby Katherine was one month old when I went up there and started working as a seven-month temporary hire. So here we are, twenty-eight years later."

Ben Snow, CG supervisor:

"The result on screen is a successful mix of Vosloo's performance, keyframe animation, and procedural animations. This was a significant advance toward the creation of a completely photorealistic CG human performer."

GUTS, BONES, AND CONTROLLABLE JELL-O

The CG Imhotep involved moving muscle mass and skin. This had been done before in a limited way as "cheats," but *The Mummy* required full anatomical detail, so that the character would hold up on-screen for long periods of time. A particular challenge for the ILM team was

being able to see through parts of the character, which required realistic rendering of successive layers of skin, organ remnants, bone, and muscle. ILM's R & D team therefore devised an entirely new skinning technology that provided sophisticated simulations for the movement of skin over muscle.

Ben Snow:

"We built up the hero CG character in layers, starting with a human skeleton model and adding guts, muscles, and skin over that. We created software to fill the space between the muscles and skin with a three-dimensional mesh simulation that provided 'virtual flesh.' This virtual flesh works like a controllable Jell-O: When animation is applied to the

ABOVE

A motion control arm extends over the Thebes City minature set on the ILM stage as a model maker adds a finishing touch. In addition to the miniature, ILM would incorporate matte paintings, blue-screen live action, and location photography to realize the shot.

ABOVE, INSET

Final frame

muscle controls, it's transmitted through this flesh material to anything suspended in it—veins or sinews—or on it—skin. We can control the properties of the flesh to make it more flexible—for guts and jiggly brains—or firm—for skin sliding over well-defined pectorals—in different parts of the model."

Cary Phillips, software research and development:

"*The Mummy* took the technology of cloth simulation and extended it to a three-dimensional volume that simulated the movements of the jiggly mass of shredded muscle and bits of skin that you could see through. The simulation techniques that we used in the past treated simulation and animation of the skin as just a shell, with nothing inside. The mummy was different in that it was a volumetric approach, the simulation of not just an outer shell but what's underneath the shell. We then got a better sense that the movement of the skin was motivated by what was happening beneath it."

The skinning technology developed for *The Mummy* represented an important breakthrough in the push for increasingly more sophisticated character animation. Ultimately, these processes and technologies would become standard to the build of all ILM-created creatures. The technology afforded the next level in creature realism.

PYRO, MATTE PAINTINGS, AND BLUE-SCREEN

Several miniature shots and matte paintings in the film required close work with various departments in the main crew and special effects units. The opening sequence is a *tour de force* visual effects shot, because it has a little bit of everything in it.

Ben Snow:

"The opening shot started with a plate featuring a wild camera crane of a chariot running along a wall. This was shot on a dressed location in Morocco. Match-animation was created for the plate, which was used for a computer-modeled previsualization of the final shot. This, in turn, was sent to the motion control stage to help create the move on a detailed miniature of the Sphinx and temple courtyard. The camera move was scaled up in motion control to provide blue-screen elements of people and soldiers in the courtyard and surrounds. These elements were all combined in the computer with a 3-D rendered matte painting of the distant pyramids and cityscape."

Scott Farrar, visual effects supervisor:

"Scale is always the issue. The best thing you can do is to add humans. The people running in the courtyard at Thebes sell it as real. We shot hundreds of people, and all of our 'extras' were ILMers. This is what we typically do. We put out a cattle call for crowd scenes, and ILM folks come in because they get to be in the movie. On *The Mummy*, one woman came in and said, 'Oh, I really apologize. I couldn't leave my dog at home.' I said, 'Wait a minute, that's great. Let's have the dog in, because there's this little magical thing that hasn't happened yet.' So we had her run across several times, left to right, right to left, and compositing that in suddenly brought the shot alive. It's like any painting or any sculpture or visual effects shot— you're looking for that *je ne sais quoi*. What is that little pizzazz, that little thing that you put in the shot that suddenly brings it alive? It's a little detail like the dog, so you never know what it's going to be."

ABOVE

The high priest Imhotep (Arnold Vosloo) surveys his empire, realized with a combination of miniatures, matte painting and a series of live-action elements composited together.

THE END BATTLE

Ben Snow:

"For the final destruction of Hamunaptra, computer-based previsualization was used to choreograph the action. Our pyrotechnic team created explosive smoke events to be combined with Chris Corbould's practical destruction effects. CG collapsing rocks and a miniature collapsing wall were built to match the practical plate."

In the climactic end sequence, Richard O'Connell (Brendan Fraser) battles a group of priest mummies and confronts a battalion of soldier mummies. Beside the sheer complexity of creating multiple performances within the same shot, these CG characters had to seamlessly intercut with shots of stunt performers wearing mummy suits designed by make up artist Nick Dudman. In some cases, CG and practical mummies existed within the same shot. This was further complicated by the large amount of direct physical interaction between mummies and O'Connell during the fight, as the same stunt performers acted out the motion capture. In order to maintain visual consistency in movement between live and CG Mummies, motion capture data was fitted into the CG models. Performance and timing adjustments were keyframed as necessary. In some cases, the data was used as a reference for the animators to keyframe all-new, custom performances.

The Mummy offered ILM great opportunities to push the envelope on character animation. The visual-effect facility's interest was in taking a humanoid figure and bringing him to the screen in a way that was more organic, realistic, and effective than anything that had been done before.

Galaxy Quest

1999

Bill George, visual effects supervisor, speaking on the Gelevator effect:

"I remember somebody taking an action figure and putting it in the refrigerator with some Jell-O. When we took it out, we shot some photographs of what the human figure would look like as seen through Jell-O, which is absolutely disgusting. I think it was blueberry flavored."

Director: Dean Parisot
Producers: Mark Johnson, Charles Newirth

ILM Show Leadership:
Visual Effects Supervisor: Bill George
Co-Visual Effects Supervisor: Ed Hirsh
Associate Visual Effects Supervisor: Ben Snow
Visual Effects Producer: Kim Bromley
Associate Visual Effects Producer: Janet Lewin
Animation Supervisor: Chris Armstrong
Visual Effects Art Director: Alex Jaeger

FOR THE SCIENCE-FICTION COMEDY *Galaxy Quest*, ILM was responsible for creating key fantasy elements, including space shots and CG creature effects.

SPACESHIP *PROTECTOR*

Bill George:

"One of the first things that we did was design the spaceship *Protector*, working with the production designer and the director to come up with its look. DreamWorks was concerned. They didn't want to be sued by Paramount because the *Protector* was too obviously like *Star Trek's Enterprise*. But we still wanted to evoke the design of the *Enterprise*. We kept getting instructions from the director: 'Do this, do that'; and then we'd get the lawyers calling saying, 'Wait a minute, it's too close.' So, as we were working on the ship and designing it, one of our production assistants had the idea that we should make the call letters for the ship: NTE, which stands for 'Not The *Enterprise*.'"

In *Galaxy Quest*, the *Protector* is featured in a half-dozen shots involving television clips from the series, as well as shots in the "real world" of the film. ILM's Model Shop created a highly detailed, eight-foot-long,

ABOVE

The *NTE-3120 Protector*—a miniature built by ILM—in action; "NTE" was an inside joke meaning, "Not the *Enterprise*"—that is, NOT the ship from the TV series *Star Trek*.

PREVIOUS SPREAD
Jason Nesmith (Tim Allen) runs from the Rock Monster.

Procedural animation was used extensively in creating the Rock Monster. The Monster was animated traditionally when it was walking, while rocks were independently simulated for other actions, such as the pieces coming together.

A software tool called Fred was developed by ILM for this work. The tool enabled the team to control how traditional animation and independent simulation were coordinated. As the Rock Monster moves, bits and pieces fall onto the ground. The new tool also made it possible to create automatic collision detection and debris generation.

TOP RIGHT

The model *Protector* composited into a CG environment in a final frame. Constructed at roughly $\frac{1}{144}$-scale, the model had multiple mounts for two-inch pipe and electrical connectors. The initial design was done by Erich Rigling, in the ILM art department; it was then turned over to model maker John Goodson, who added recognizable details and created the ship's paint scheme.

BOTTOM LEFT

In the Model Shop are supervisor Brian Gernand and chief model maker Grant Imahara working on a three-foot *Protector* model, which had internal lighting and multiple mounting points—like its big brother—but was much lower resolution, for scenes from the *Galaxy Quest* TV series.

BOTTOM RIGHT

Stage crew at ILM prep a large-scale shooting model of the NTE *Protector*.

one-two-hundredth-scale miniature of the *Protector* for the "real world" sequences. Computer-controlled laser-cutting equipment was used to make the model. A smaller, three-foot-long *Protector* model was also created. Because this model was used in clips from the "television" show, it was intentionally less detailed. This was the most used of the two spaceships, with the miniature photography session lasting six months. For those shots from the series, the effects had to look like they were created for television in the 1970s; conventional rules of model photography were broken in shooting the small model, as the *Protector* was lit flatly to make it look as "low budget" as possible.

Ben Snow, associate visual effects supervisor:

"We filmed the smaller-scale *Protector* model and took it into the composite. Then Marshall Krasser came up with a way of downgrading the image. He added scratches, missed out frames, and he even put in one frame upside down."

ROCK MONSTER

The creation of the Rock Monster was a challenge, in terms of modeling, animation, and compositing. The ILM team also had to devise unique ways to express the Monster's menacing character, given that the design did not allow for the usual cues derived from facial expressions.

Bill George:

"Reading the script, it's easy to say, 'Oh, there's this big Rock Monster that's attacking the captain.' But then it comes down to our responsibility—'what does the thing look like?' I'm a big fan of the architect Ludwig Mies van der Rohe, who subscribed to the idea that form follows function. You've got to figure out what it is, how it exists, and why it's a Rock Monster. So the idea we came up with is that it's a life force that has no form, but is able to grab physical objects to create a body for itself. It would be constantly changing and moving: What's an arm one moment will turn around and be its head the next. It's trying to put a body together. So the rocks itself aren't the creature. The creature is the energy that holds the rocks together. Our inspiration was *Forbidden Planet* and the 'Id' creature, which was basically a ghost."

Ben Snow:

"We had to have a pile of rocks form into this monster, walk along, and then fall apart back into rocks. That was a big challenge. Technical animation supervisor James Tooley and Jim Hourihan put a lot of work into this thing. We had to do directable simulation, which gave us the ability to say, 'Okay, we've animated something that looks like the Rock Monster shape, and now we have to go into simulation mode,' and control that. That was something that was new for us at the time."

Ultimately, the menacing character of the Rock Monster was suggested by the weight and mass of the creature and how it moved. There were subtle details that helped, too.

Bill George:

"When the Monster would step, it would hit the ground and cause fractures in its rocks. These simulations were incredibly complex, since all of those tiny pieces had to be driven by the animation of the rock creature lumbering through the frame."

"GOING UP?"

The ILM team called *Galaxy Quest*'s high-tech transport device the "Gelevator."

Bill George:

"The Gelevator was similar to the transporter in *Star Trek*, where, of course, they just stand on the pad and *poof*, off they go. The Gelevator was supposed to be an awful experience. And that was one of the nice things about this being a comedy. It took something like the transporter and allowed us to completely redesign it to make it a very different and unique visual effect. The idea was that Tim Allen goes out on this pad, and then this protective goo goes over him and encapsulates him."

To develop the look for the Gelevator, ILM used a unique visual reference: photographs of an action figure encased in Jell-O. The CG team then created a digital goo, which was animated to encase a computer model of actor Tim Allen. Computer generated light beams, reflections, smoke, bubbles, and a practical application of methocel were used to enhance the effect of the Gelevator.

ABOVE

Alien creatures courtesy of ILM

ABOVE
Blue Demons run amok, after being
created in part thanks to proprietary
software known as iSculpt.

DEMON BABIES

Some thirty-two shots feature digital representations of the Blue Demon. A maquette, built by Stan Winston Studio, incorporated ILM's design refinements. It was used as reference by digital model supervisor Geoff Campbell, who free-sculpted the digital version of the Blue Demon's head using ILM's proprietary software iSculpt. A library of face shapes to vary expressions was also built. Organic-looking skins were created, which built on technical advances in skin-layering techniques derived from work done on Jar Jar Binks in *The Phantom Menace* (see pages 120–131).

Lighting the CG Blue Demon Babies to accommodate the broad daylight conditions of the shots presented a challenge. This was the first production to use a new CG lighting tool ILM had been developing for some time, called I-Render. The tool made for a much faster workflow. The software was integrated into the pipeline for the first time on *Galaxy Quest*.

Ben Snow:

"In the past we could only light one frame at a time. I-Render allowed us to change the frame and update and light it. And it gave you a way to preview very quickly. It was a big step forward for us. Certainly it cost us money on *Galaxy Quest*, but to advance the technology like that, you just have to say, 'Okay, we're gonna do it now. And, yeah, it's not gonna be pretty and it's not gonna be cheap, but in the end, the whole company will benefit.' And you hope then, if the show ends up costing a little bit more, that ILM will say, 'But we got this great tool out of it.' So, it's one of the ways that we push technology forward: We talk about it for years, and then it finally takes a group of people to say, 'You know what? This is it. We're gonna do it now.'"

Star Wars: Episode I The Phantom Menace

1999

George Lucas, director:

"To me, Episode I was a huge development in the process of being able to make movies. Because suddenly I wasn't restricted by the size of the sets, I wasn't restricted by the epic quality of having 10,000 extras. I could imagine futuristic things, and the whole movie is immersed in a different world. That was a great milestone for me."

Director: George Lucas
Producer: Rick McCallum
Executive Producer: George Lucas

ILM Show Leadership:
Visual Effects Supervisors: Dennis Muren, John Knoll, Scott Squires
Visual Effects Producers: Jeff Olson, Ned Gorman, Heather Smith, Judith Weaver, Ginger Theisen
Animation Director: Rob Coleman
Visual Effects Art Director: David Nakabayashi

Academy Award® Nomination: Best Visual Effects
John Knoll
Dennis Muren
Scott Squires
Rob Coleman

BAFTA Film Award Nomination:
 Best Achievement in Special Visual Effects
John Knoll
Dennis Muren
Scott Squires
Rob Coleman

WHEN WORK BEGAN on *Star Wars*: Episode I *The Phantom Menace* it had been almost two decades since George Lucas produced the original *Star Wars* trilogy. The visionary director had to wait for the development of visual effects technologies that would allow him to realize the additional films in the series that he had imagined from the very beginning—and to create those films without compromise. The limitations of effects technology during the production of the original *Star Wars* trilogy had always been a challenge, even though the effects created for those films were nothing less than groundbreaking. And yet, Lucas was still waiting for the technology to catch up to his vision. While he was waiting to return to the *Star Wars* series, his effects facility, ILM, continued its pioneering work, moving the industry forward with each innovation it realized.

George Lucas:

"When ILM did *Jurassic Park*, you could see, finally, that a corner had been turned. And the work that had gone on, at least five years before that—which was very intense, with a lot of pain and suffering—was paying off. We were getting to a place that we would only hope to dream about. When I went to do Episode I, I was able to take all of the development, all of the talent, all of the things that had evolved at ILM over the years and use it for a movie that I wanted to make. When I did the first *Star Wars* films, it couldn't be done at all. It just was not possible. And now it was possible."

Much of ILM's work on Episode I involved breaking down limitations that were inherent in earlier eras of visual effects. For the Prequel films, Lucas was interested in the concept of working *within* the image—the idea that the image is no longer fixed on film.

PREVIOUS SPREAD

The Podrace was unlike anything attempted before. To realize Lucas's vision, visual effects supervisor John Knoll devised a program where computers rendered only what the virtual camera "saw," thus cutting down dramatically on rendering time and making the showstopping sequence possible.

ABOVE

Theed City on Naboo, as realized by ILM

George Lucas:

"In the course of working on Episode I, it became apparent that the ability to move things around, cut them out, and do a simple sort of Photoshop on the film, combined with the idea of doing digital previsualization, made it so that we could actually move anything we wanted, anywhere we wanted, at any time we wanted. That, then, made the idea of making a movie much more like doing a painting or something, where you can change your mind—something where you can look at it and make adjustments. In the process of making Episode I, we were able to develop a lot of techniques where we could actually have a great deal of latitude in what we did within the frame.

"It was really an evolution of the fact that we were able to do more and more blue-screen and just add sets in later. When we were doing blue screens, we were able to move the actors around and put them closer together, put them further apart, or have two different takes of the same scene with two people in it, and take one person from one take and one person from the other take, and if we were lucky, we were able to sync them up and get the best of both actors, which is something you couldn't do before. Those are the kind of things that really made a difference."

Of the 2,000-plus shots in *The Phantom Menace*, 1,900 were either entirely created or substantially enhanced using visual effects. In order to undertake this monumentally complex project, one half of the nearly 1,200 people who worked at ILM were dedicated to working on the film at one time or another. For more than three years, a significant percentage of the company's resources were occupied by the production. To oversee the work, three of ILM's most experienced visual effects supervisors were committed to the project: Dennis Muren, John Knoll, and Scott Squires.

Dennis Muren, visual effects supervisor:

"If you make a list of what's in that film—the Podrace, how many times has that been duplicated since in CG? And the battle scenes with two thousand droids fighting two thousand Gungans—you think back to *Spartacus* or the few times it had been done before, maybe eight hundred people and two different wardrobes, and that's about the most they could ever

RIGHT
Natalie Portman (Queen Amidala),
George Lucas, and John Knoll

do. In *The Phantom Menace*, we had fantasy characters by the thousands. So figuring out how to do it was a big deal at that time. There's software now that can make, fairly simply, those armies and people. But we had none of that, and we were doing it for the first time. We took a lot of motion capture of people fighting, and half of them we turned into droids and into Gungans. So that whole sequence has a lot of motion capture in it, which has also turned into another important tool. There were a lot of new applications in that film that I hadn't realized would become so important at the time."

Hal Hickel, lead animator:

"Up to that point, a really big visual effects project was in the three-hundred to five-hundred shot range. If you got above five-hundred shots, that was an enormous amount of work. And we leapfrogged from there to a project like *The Phantom Menace*, where we were up over a thousand shots. So just being able to wrangle a film of that size, to scale up, in terms of number of shots, number of characters, number of space ships, number of, you know, just everything, and keeping track of it all and moving it through the production pipeline smoothly and getting everything done on time? That was huge."

PREVISUALIZING THE VISION

Lucas used animatics to previsualize scenes before turning the concept over to ILM for execution. The challenge for ILM was to realize the imaginative conceptual material developed by Lucas, his art department, and his previsualization team.

George Lucas:

"I told the art department, just do the most stunning kinds of designs without worrying about how we were going to pull it off. So ILM was given a lot of visions that were basically not thought through in terms of how they were going to be accomplished. For the first three *Star Wars*, we very carefully designed the film *around* the technology of the visual effects.

"Now, on Episodes I, II, and III, I just said, 'We're gonna do whatever we want to do and we'll figure out a way of doing it.' And ILM did a *marvelous* job. They took things that seemed as if they were going to be completely impossible—and made them real.

"Previsualization made it somewhat easier for ILM. They didn't have to do a lot of experimentation. You say, 'This is the shot, this is how long it is, within three or four frames, this is where the ships go, this is what you want.' Then we can sit and talk through the parts that need to be changed or need to be improved. Literally, you can segregate out a dozen frames, and say, 'In this one, I want this ship moved over here a little bit, I want the wings to do this.' And no matter what you do with a videomatic, it's not real. It doesn't feel real. It doesn't look real. The gift that ILM has is they're able to take that and make it absolutely real, with enormous amounts of detail and subtlety that take it to a whole new realm."

THE *STAR WARS* LEGACY

Miles Perkins, director of marketing and communications:

"Having George come in was absolutely phenomenal. Everybody rallied around him because that's why the people had come to ILM, because of *Star Wars*, because of everything that had been done and because of the legacy—and here they are, working on the legacy."

Dennis Muren was the only one of the three visual effects supervisors on *The Phantom Menace* who had begun his feature-film career working on the original *Star Wars* trilogy. Twenty years later, he returned to that unique world.

Dennis Muren:

"To me, *The Phantom Menace* wasn't a *Star Wars* movie. It was something else. It had been so long, and the technology was so different. One of the things I appreciated as we were doing the Prequels was the size of George's imagination. What he was trying to get into *Phantom Menace*, however, was similar to what he was trying to get into *Star Wars* and *Empire* and *Jedi*: just sequence after sequence after sequence that you've never seen before, original idea after original idea after original idea."

Digital matte artist Paul Huston was another veteran of the original *Star Wars* trilogy who worked on the Prequels.

Paul Huston, digital matte artist:

"When you look at the original *Star Wars* and then you look at Episode I, a tremendous amount of time has passed. So many techniques and processes have gone through changes. It looks like a big change, but actually, from my point of view, it was like one day at a time from *Star Wars*. It's kind of a continuum because this is technology—things change almost daily, and it gets so that you kind of expect it. It's part of the job, and it's part of what makes things interesting. A lot of the thought processes, the problem solving that you go through, they're pretty much the same as they've always been. It's attempting to get an interesting-looking image just using whatever kind of methods that you have that make it happen in an efficient way. It's lighting, it's pacing, camera move, color, form, texture—the tools have changed incredibly, but it's still the same kind of people who are doing the work as have always done it: the artists."

DIGITAL AT FIVE HUNDRED MILES PER HOUR

Early on in devising an approach for the Podrace sequence, it became apparent that computer graphics would have to be a large part of

generating the terrains. Shooting live-action location plates was not an option, because of the exotic profiles of many of the background elements. The speed at which the racers travel also meant that there was no practical way of shooting plates.

John Knoll, visual effects supervisor:

"We're traveling a couple feet off the ground at five hundred miles an hour, and there's just no good way of shooting that stuff. If you shoot them with a helicopter, helicopters can't fly straight enough, and if you speed up the film, it starts to look jerky. So live action isn't going to work.

"We did do miniatures for some of the more closed-in environments. For example, the curved cave with stalactites sticking out of the top was done as a miniature. So we used miniatures where it was practical, and then everywhere else, the terrains were computer generated, one way or another. And while there are much better tools for dealing with it now, at the time, there really weren't any good tools for creating computer-generated terrain. Building organic shapes like rocks is hard to do realistically.

"On a few previous films, the matte department had started using a technique of projecting photographs onto simple geometry, so that we could do a camera move on them. Paul Huston and I got to talking about taking that technique and just pushing it to the ridiculous extreme on the Podrace sequence. So there are big sections of that sequence that are re-projected photographs: a good example of that is the arched canyon area, where we're passing through all these wickets. Paul had gone to the Model Shop and built a half a dozen arches as models out of foam and plaster and painted them. He then built a very low-res CG model of them. He took the arch models outdoors and photographed them in the parking lot in correct sunlight conditions.

"Next, we took those photographs and projected them onto the geometry. So when you're flying past them, they look completely real—because what you're looking at is a photograph of a real object. But by projecting it onto that geometry, we could then make as many copies as we wanted to, and we could fly past them as quickly as we wanted to."

OVERACHIEVING UNDERWATER EFFECTS

The ability to produce digital models also made it possible for ILM to create imagery for *The Phantom Menace* that simply wasn't possible for the original trilogy.

Dennis Muren:

"One of the reasons for going toward digital models was that we could build things with different types of camera moves and detail on them—the underwater Gungan city is an example of that. There are lots of views flying past those glowing domed buildings that would have been really problematic, or impossible, to do as physical models. It might have looked like they were models and not something as organic as what we ultimately created. What's limiting in the model world is there are only a few materials you can actually build things from—plastics and wood and steel and real materials—and they can be painted or sanded or textured or carved in a limited number of ways. Sometimes if you need a lot of tiny little details, there's no way you can get it into a model of a certain size. It's too small and the material just can't be carved any tinier.

"But in the CG world, the *real* physics of the construction materials is gone, because there's nothing in it; it's all mathematics. Whatever you can specify, a little sheen kind of halfway between an aluminum and a bronze or copper feel to

ABOVE

An underwater visual effects sequence features several homicidal fish attacking the heroes in their "bongo" (mini-submarine).

it, you can create. That's what CG has opened up: this amazing opportunity to really create, like a painting, something that didn't exist. It can be successful or it can be a failure. And when it's a failure, that's usually because you didn't specify it accurately enough—you didn't really imagine in your head what it should look like. And because of my history of doing this kind of work for so long and seeing real models, I've got a pretty clear idea of what things should look like. So I could specify to the guys building the CG models and lighting them what was right about them and what was wrong about them.

"Then I could take it to the next step beyond what we could ever do with a physical model. Once you specify it so

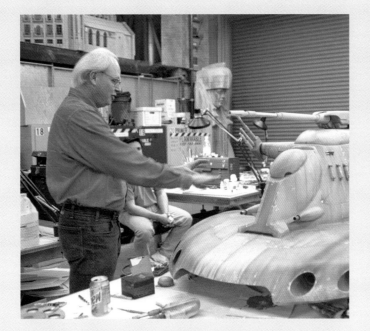

ANOTHER ROAD TO ILM, OR "SO, HOW DID I GET HERE?"

Dennis Muren:

"I saw *King Kong* in a movie theatre in the early fifties, and I saw *War of the Worlds* when it came out in 1953, and I thought about those images—I went home and with a little still camera, sort of tried to re-create them, to bring back the memories of seeing them in the theatre, because there were no VCRs or DVDs or photos at that time. And since that age, I just kept with it.

"But there didn't seem to be any future in that, because those movies were very seldom made. It's not like you could make a living doing effects. Now, with thousands of people doing the work, they don't understand that there was a time, I'm sure in the 1960s, when in the entire world, there were no more than fifty people at most that could do effects work.

"So, in the mid-1970s, I was about ready to get out of the business because there was so little work. At that time, occasionally there would be a commercial that you could do, and that was it. I was just on the verge of getting a job as an inhalation therapist, even though I had no idea what that was, but I saw an ad for it somewhere. Luckily, a friend of mine had heard that George Lucas was going to do a space movie. I really loved *American Graffiti* and *THX*, so I just started feeling around, 'Does anybody know anything about this?'

"Somewhere along the line I had heard that John Dykstra, whom I'd met once before for about fifteen seconds, had gotten the job to do this. I contacted John, and he said, 'Come on over, we may be hiring people.' I went over and met with him and Richard Edlund. This was in the beginning of 1976, and within three weeks or so, I got onto the film. It wasn't anything like a typical Hollywood movie. All of the things I feared about Hollywood didn't happen: There were no union restrictions, because I did all jobs myself, and that's the way I wanted to do it. I could light, I could do all of the camera work, design shots, everything. We'd follow storyboards, but there were no restrictions on anything.

"It was a different group of people than I'd ever worked with before. I had been involved in the old-fashioned school of visual effects, going back to the days of *King Kong* and *The Ten Commandments*, and this group essentially came indirectly out of *2001*, with modern technology. And I always thought *Star Wars* was a combination of Old Hollywood and New Hollywood. The Old Hollywood people being me and Ken Ralston, who could make corn on the cob look pretty with photography because we did that in commercials, and the New Hollywood, which was the technology that could make artificial corn on the cob that looked more tasty than real corn on the cob. And both of the groups together is what ILM was, and that's why the work was not all one or the other—it was something brand-new."

it looks real, then your imagination can kick in, and you can make it look like something the audience hasn't seen before. That's the whole purpose of it. I really wanted the underwater city to look more magical and inviting than we could have done with a model. Some of it was the glow around the lights, and some of it was the little tiny bubbles coming from the back of the submarine. We couldn't have really achieved tons of little things like that with physical models."

ANIMATING A GALAXY

The Phantom Menace contains eight hundred character animation shots. Close to one hundred creatures were digitally modeled for the show, but Jar Jar Binks was the most complex and expressive computer-generated character realized for the film. The animation of Jar Jar was based on the vocal and physical performance of actor Ahmed Best. During principal photography, the actor wore a Jar Jar suit and played the live-action counterpart of what would ultimately be a computer-generated character. Rather than having human co-

stars try to act with a nonexistent Jar Jar, scenes with other actors were filmed with Best on camera. This made it possible for actors to work out appropriate timings and reactions. Once the actors had successfully rehearsed the scene, production takes were filmed with Best out of frame to create a clean plate in which the CG character would be composited. In some cases, however, Lucas preferred the performances in the rehearsal takes that included Best. ILM's digital rotoscope department was then responsible for removing Best in those shots to produce a clean plate for the digital Jar Jar. Setting the challenge for ILM to create a CG character as prominent and complex as Jar Jar demonstrated Lucas's faith in ILM's animation and technical teams. The impressive results justified the risk.

A related challenge was the creation of digital clothing for the CG characters. In the past, ILM had primarily dealt with the computer animation of unclothed animals. *Phantom Menace* required that the company address the difficulties of animating fabric as it moved on a CG character's form. The creation of digital cloth that moved realistically was an issue that had challenged the CG world for years. While there were cloth simulations in off-the-shelf packages, these typically emulated lightweight fabrics like cotton. For *The Phantom Menace*, sev-

ABOVE

Gungans and Trade Federation battle droids engage in a gigantic land battle—the kind of conflict that studios used to wage with hundreds of low-paid extras in the early days of moviemaking. After costs skyrocketed, those sorts of shots became impractical for decades, until the advent of digital visual effects.

eral costumes were made of heavy burlap-like materials. In fact, Jar Jar's clothing had two layers. The bulky outer layer needed to emulate leather-like material, while the inner layer was made of lighter fabric. Previously, academics had attempted to create cloth simulations by cutting out patterns from flat pieces and joining them together. ILM's technique was to model the cloth in the form it would take when it was on a standing CG character. Textures were applied to give it the look of cloth. The cloth geometry was then modeled into the necessary costume, and driven by the animation of the CG character.

Innovations in motion capture were another milestone.

Hal Hickel:

"This show was when we really started to use motion capture more. We may have used it on some previous projects, but at that time, the animators were still very wary of motion capture. I think they saw it as a threat to their livelihood, and they weren't employing it very much. *The Phantom Menace* was the first show where we started to say, 'Look, this is a tool, and we're going to use it on some of the characters and not others.' So that's when motion capture really started to make its way into our animation tool set and to sit there more comfortably. Animators stopped seeing as a threat and started seeing it as something that was a good tool."

The complexity of the scenes and volume of effects for *The Phantom Menace* dictated that all aspects of ILM's production process had to be evaluated and, in many cases, streamlined and updated. For example, Caricature, ILM's proprietary character animation system, was used to create facial expressions and lip-synch positions for the film. It was necessary for the system to be completely overhauled for *The Phantom Menace*. *DragonHeart*, released three years earlier in 1996 (see pages 54–61), was their last film that had featured extensive facial animation. The animation requirements for *The Phantom Menace* were much more sophisticated. For example, Cary Phillips, the inventor of Caricature, revised the system's animation controls so that it was possible to handle several characters in conversation.

Cary Phillips, software development:

"Although on *Lost World* (see pages 78–85), we had the ability, with Caricature, to have multiple characters, the software still couldn't manage more than one talking character at once. So that was the major architectural retooling of Caricature that took place for Episode I—the ability to have two talking characters and two different facial shape libraries presented in the interface simultaneously. It really was the first major film that involved four primary characters that talked: Jar Jar, Boss Nass, Sebulba, and Watto, and each of those characters was intentionally designed in a way so that it really couldn't be a guy in a suit.

"If you compare a character like Jar Jar to Draco in *DragonHeart*, Jar Jar is much more complicated. He was more intricate around the mouth, wearing a vest and a little loin skirt. We could have gotten the face to move with the previous version of Caricature, but we had to be prepared to do lots and lots of that animation for dozens of characters for thousands of shots—and that was the thing that just blew us away. You add it up and ask 'How are we possibly going to get this done?' A tremendous amount of it came down to efficiency and just structuring things so that we could get work done and not kill each other in the process."

THE DIGITAL BACKLOT

To a greater extent than any previous film, *The Phantom Menace* used a "digital backlot" approach. Live-action plates were shot on set into which digital characters and sets would be composited. Actors were filmed on minimal sets or no set at all, in front of blue screens. Digital set extensions were added during postproduction. To make sure that the plates would work successfully with the digital elements that would be added, Knoll and other members of the ILM team took precise measurements during the shoot.

John Knoll:

"A very common problem in computer graphics, or at least it used to be, before good light-probe measurements, is that you would be looking at a render in dailies, and something wouldn't look right about it. It just wouldn't look real. And everybody in the room would have a different opinion about, 'Oh, well, the fill light's too bright,' or, 'The key isn't

ANOTHER ROAD TO ILM, OR "SO, HOW DID I GET HERE?"

Cary Phillips, ILM research and development, and inventor of ILM's Caricature software:

"I saw *Star Wars* seven times when I was fourteen years old, but I was never a true *Star Wars* fanboy.

"When I was a freshman in college at Johns Hopkins University in 1982, I went to a special lecture about computer graphics by a professor of chemical engineering. He showed a three-dimensional graph of a mathematical function drawn with a line plotter on huge sheets of paper. It was beautiful, and I was mesmerized. The next day, I went to his office and asked him if I could use his computer to write a program to draw pictures like that. He said that computer graphics was very hard, and that he didn't think I would be able to do it, and that he couldn't let just anyone use his computer. I found another professor, Joseph O'Rourke, who became my advisor and mentor. My first computer graphics image was a wire-frame drawing of two intersecting spheres.

"After graduate school, I worked at PDI, a company that primarily made TV commercials. I wanted to get into film and animation. PDI bid on *Casper* and lost the job to ILM. Then PDI bid on *DragonHeart* and lost it to ILM. At that point, a bunch of people left and scattered across the industry—to Pixar, Disney, Sony, and ILM. I mostly chose ILM because of its location; I didn't want to move. One of my PDI friends had already joined ILM, and I contacted her. I thought I would hate ILM, because it had the reputation, from the outside, of being a sweatshop, and for being arrogant. I think most of that was resentment toward its success. When I started, I was blown away by how smoothly things were working, at how much work was getting done without people completely freaking out."

bright enough,' or, 'No, it's just that it needs more reflection.' Everybody's got a different opinion, and it's hard to know what is correct.

"So we wanted to establish a ground truth. On films that led up to *The Phantom Menace*, I became more and more of the opinion that the more reference we had of something real, the better off we were. So we shot the grain chromospheres on every setup in Episode I; thus we always had references to key fill ratio, color, temperature, where the light was coming from, and the chrome side could actually be used to extract reflection environments for medium and non-specular surfaces.

"I was also concerned that our digital characters, like Watto and Jar Jar, look as real as we could make them. We actually had a full-size bust of Jar Jar made. It was a clay sculpture that had been cast in a sort of translucent silicone and painted all the right colors, so it really represented what we wanted Jar Jar to look like in the scene—and we brought him along. We dragged that thing in there and shot a reference of that head in the light for every shot we were doing with Jar Jar in it. We didn't always look at the reference, but any time we got into trouble, we could always look at that and say, 'Oh, well, here's the problem. He's getting a bounce from that wall that we don't have here.'"

On-set matchmovers used a laptop computer connected to an electronic transit surveying system to record and convert data into coordinates that were then fed into CG software. The evolutionary nature of ILM's work over the years is reflected by the fact that this setup was first developed by Scott Squires for *DragonHeart*. Scott Squires's responsibilities included supervising *The Phantom Menace*'s innovative digital backlot and set extension shots, all of which were executed at a level of sophistication never before attempted.

Scott Squires:

"We made real inroads blending CG environments with live-action sets. We'd built bits and pieces of virtual sets in the past, but never on this scale. Also, because of the number of effects shots, this film was the equivalent of doing ten movies—and that volume in itself was new territory."

RIGHT

Darth Maul (Ray Park) and Obi-Wan Kenobi (Ewan McGregor) stare each other down as a force field of energy separates them—another CG enhancement.

A NEW LEGACY

Cary Phillips:

"At the end of the film, George got the whole crew together for breakfast one day, just to thank us for the work that we did. I still have a very vivid recollection of what he said: 'When I made the original *Star Wars*, what I saw in my mind's eye was an oil painting, but all I had to draw with was a pencil. I created ILM to give me the oils to paint with.' I use that quote whenever I talk about ILM, because it sets out the challenges we face; in the films leading up to Episode I, what we were doing was setting these tools in place that would allow George to create the images that he had in his mind's eye."

Dennis Muren:

"*The Phantom Menace* spawned not only the massive battle scenes that you've seen since and the all-digital characters, which were a direct result of Jar Jar, but just having a movie of that scope had never been done before. It looked like it cost a billion dollars to make—if you could even do it for a billion dollars. Just look at the sets. If they had been physically built for the film, if the creatures had been physically built for it, the costs would have been unthinkable. It was an amazing thing that George said: 'We're ready to make this vast vision; for the first time, we have the tools to be able to do it, so go ahead and do it in a way that we can afford it.'"

George Lucas:

"When we did Episode I this way, everybody said, 'Well, this is great for science-fiction films, but it's not going to affect any other kinds of films.' But look how the industry has changed in just the time since then. At that time, the kinds of movies that you were allowed to make were very restricted. They were usually small and contemporary. The idea of doing an epic film had disappeared over the years, because nobody could afford the extras and the sets. So the industry was forced into a very limited kind of movie. If you wanted to do a historical piece, the studio would say, 'Well, the market isn't there for it'—which really meant that the market wasn't there for the price it was going to cost to make it.

"After Episode I, I said, 'You know, now you can do period pieces again. Many genres of filmmaking have been lost, but now they'll be back. You'll be able to see films from all periods of history, and you'll have epics and battles and all kinds of things that we've lost.' And that's what happened. This technology isn't really about science-fiction movies, anyway. We're just on the leading edge, pushing the envelope of the art form."

The Perfect Storm

2000

Stefen Fangmeier, visual effects supervisor:

"We knew that we were doing something very dramatic and something that had never been tried before. Most people actually thought that what we were trying to do was going to be impossible."

Director: Wolfgang Petersen
Producers: Wolfgang Peterson, Gail Katz, Paula Weinstein

ILM Show Leadership:
Visual Effects Supervisor: Stefen Fangmeier
Associate Visual Effects Supervisors: Doug Smythe,
    Habib Zargarpour, Tim Alexander
Senior Visual Effects Producer: Judith Weaver
Visual Effects Producers: Ginger Theisen
Associate Visual Effects Producer: Gretchen Libby
Animation Supervisor: Peter Daulton

Academy Award® Nomination: Best Visual Effects
Stefen Fangmeier (ILM)
Habib Zargarpour (ILM)
John Frazier
Walt Conti

BAFTA Film Award:
    Best Achievement in Special Visual Effects
Stefen Fangmeier (ILM)
Habib Zargarpour (ILM)
John Frazier
Walt Conti

DIRECTOR WOLFGANG PETERSEN'S VISION for *The Perfect Storm* was going to require a seamless integration of complex computer-generated simulations and imagery with blue-screen photography that utilized elaborate practical effects. Because the film's story is largely based on a real event, Peterson emphasized the importance of creating a highly realistic depiction of a severe storm at sea. The creation of a storm of this magnitude had never been attempted with computer-generated imagery. The difficulty of the assignment resulted in building up a crew of digital artists and technical directors that was almost as big as the team employed for *The Phantom Menace*—even though *that* film had more than five times the number of visual effects shots. *The Perfect Storm*, however, included more than 250 CG shots, a third of which involved placing a digital ocean behind the foreground stage element of a gimbaled boat. The remaining

two thirds of the shots relied on complex CG simulations that involved CG boats in CG water, often with CG characters on board.

Stefen Fangmeier:

"I remember that I didn't actually want to do the project. I heard that Wolfgang Petersen was coming to ILM to talk to a number of visual effects supervisors about *The Perfect Storm*. I only went to the meeting because I wanted to meet him. I said a few things and then, afterward, I walked out of the meeting and thought, 'God, I'm glad I don't have to do that film. It's just going to be too hard.'

"Then, after a couple of weeks, Wolfgang said, 'I want Stefen to do it.' It was mostly because of the approach I was

ABOVE

Up until *The Perfect Storm*, CG water on this large scale had not been possible to realize; the film was also the first to blend real water with virtual water. (Inset: the practical *Andrea Gail* was filmed against blue-screen with limited amounts of real waves released from five thousand-gallon dump tanks mounted above the set.)

ANOTHER ROAD TO ILM, OR "SO, HOW DID I GET HERE?"

Curt Miyashiro, director of production technology, ILM:

"I actually started out as an aerospace engineer working mission support for the Space Shuttles. In the early nineties, I was part of what is known as a data-engineering group at Rockwell International. At the time, the aerospace industry had hit its peak, and you could see the signs that it was moving into decline. So I knew that at some point, the group I was in would probably end up moving to Florida or Texas, so I started to examine what my career path would be, if I wanted to stay in L.A.

"Visual effects was something that, as a kid, actually from seeing *Star Wars*, I was always interested in, so I started taking film classes at UCLA. For one session, they invited a couple of people from ILM to come do a talk. At the end of talk, the teacher of the class, who was an exec at Paramount, said, 'If you're interested in getting into the business, why don't you come and talk to me and tell me what you're interested in.' So I went and told him I was really interested in the effects world. His office actually called ILM, and I ended up getting an interview.

"At the time, it was the beginning of *Jurassic Park*, late 1992, and they were looking for someone to work the graveyard shift for render support. When an artist launches a shot before they go home for the day, render support is the group that makes sure it runs and completes overnight and is ready to be seen by the key creatives and the artist in the morning. So I was interviewing and I said, 'I don't think I have enough skills to do this.' I was flabbergasted when they called me back and said, 'We want you to come up here and work on *Jurassic Park*.'

"So I quit my aerospace job, put everything I owned in the back of my Acura Integra, drove up here, got an apartment, and started working the graveyard shift on *Jurassic Park*. At that time, the job was only guaranteed till the end of the movie, so I figured, *If it doesn't work out, I will just probably go to Florida and work out of Kennedy Space Center.* But here I am, many years later; still at ILM."

taking: After reading the script, I had decided that everything couldn't be achieved by a full-scale water-tank setup, but should be designed by relying entirely on computer-generated visuals. While I wasn't sure that the work could be done in a timely and financially viable manner. I figured that an all-CG approach would give us the best shot at pulling off sequences that were to show a fishing boat plowing through eighty- and hundred-plus-foot waves.

"In the end, we produced about 340 visual effects shots for the project. Many of these turned out to be some of the most complex shots ever created, to date, at ILM. Creating photorealistic CG water is undoubtedly one of the more daunting tasks in visual effects, especially when it's to be seen in the context of a raging storm at sea. The complexity of the dynamics that occur in nature is quite mind-boggling, but it had to be considered in order to properly portray the forces that were at work."

ILM's previous experience creating CG water included the tidal wave sequence for *The Abyss*, which was eventually cut from the theatrical release, but was included on the director's cut DVD. *Deep Impact* also called for the creation of a CG tidal wave. However, the water effects for those films consisted of a single large wave, seen in only a handful of shots. In contrast, stormy seas are a prominent feature throughout *The Perfect Storm*.

OCEAN 11 FROM ILM

Curt Miyashiro, CG supervisor:

"It was the first really big water show at ILM where we were trying to replicate naturalistic phenomenon. For simulations, you can look at it and say, 'Well, that doesn't work.' But sometimes it's extremely difficult to describe or communicate exactly what's wrong with it—what's keeping it from looking

real. One of the biggest challenges was when everyone would say something doesn't look right, but then it was, 'Okay, *what* doesn't make it look right? Why aren't you buying this as real?'

"When we do a show at ILM, one of the things that's very important is to have a lot of reference. If we're trying to animate animals, we might go someplace like a zoo to look at the real-world equivalent. In the case of *The Perfect Storm*, we didn't have that. But what we did have is a lot of research that was done to create a large diagram of different ocean elements, defining all of the terms, the eddies, the waves, and the riplets, so when we talked about these shots in dailies, we were all talking the same language."

The R & D team, led by Habib Zargarpour, identified the essential visual details that needed to be represented and the techniques that had to be developed to achieve the required realism. Over a six-month period, new software was written for the water surface itself, as well as for the extremely complex particle simulations that would be used to model elements such as spray, crest mist, crest foam, and splashes.

Habib Zargarpour, associate visual effects supervisor:

"We wanted to find a way to allow the director to see, virtually, what it would be like to actually shoot on the open seas, giving him an idea of what kind of compositions we could create in these environments. John Anderson, a professor of fluid dynamics, developed a basic ocean-simulation software that we imported into a commercial 3-D package via proprietary plug-ins. We generated a tileable half-square mile of eighty basic ocean states with various wave sizes and wind conditions. I developed a hydrodynamic boat simulation system that could sense and react to the ocean surface. Using this system, an animator could select an ocean, position a specific boat within it, set certain parameters such as the wind conditions, boat weight, drag, buoyancy, and propulsion, and automatically get accurate boat motion. The boat dynamics were applied to ships of various sizes. Many camera and boat motions were keyframe edited by hand to fine-tune them for the individual shots."

LEFT
Bobby Shatford (Mark Wahlberg) clings to the side of his fishing boat, with CG water filling out the periphery of the shot.

WAITING FOR DAYS

Curt Miyashiro:

"It wasn't like a typical project at ILM with a lot of creatures where, in general, you could turn a shot around in about twenty-four hours. To simulate that naturalistic phenomenon took a huge amount of rendering power. For the water simulations, the turnaround on a typical shot was sometimes on the order of days. The problem was that when you made changes, you had to be pretty sure that you were getting somewhere, because you weren't going to see it until a couple of days later...."

Habib Zargarpour:

"It takes a lot of memory and computer power to simulate water, and we had to create a substantial chunk of the ocean to fit ships as big as nine-hundred-foot-long tankers. In order to make it even possible to do this back in 1999, we divided the ocean water into two layers: bottom and top water. The bottom water would be simulated on a larger scale by John Anderson's equations, which would take a week on a thirty-two-processor SGI tower. Then we used various techniques to re-create the top water surface with all the detail of small capillary waves and a half-dozen types of sea foam.

"The complexity of the rough seas makes it one of the most difficult things to re-create on the computer because of the movement and transitions of the water from liquid to mist. The movement was the key to how believable the effects would be, but we had to wait overnight for each iteration to see the results of the eighty-some parameters we were modifying to get it to look right."

OCEAN SPRAY

Habib Zargarpour:

"The crest mist was the spray and mist of water blown off the top of breaking waves by the powerful storm winds. The mist seemed simple at first, but when we started creating it, we ran into a big problem: These eighty-foot waves, from base to peak, would travel at extremely fast speeds and, as a result, would rise and drop anything near the surface at close to the speed of freefall. As the water surface dropped, it would leave a mist behind, forming a big gap. So we had to find a way to

ABOVE

George Clooney (Captain Billy Tyne) was filmed against blue-screen (inset), so that ILM could add the CG storm raging all around him in postproduction.

make the mist 'stick' to the ocean surface and stay with it as the waves dropped down from under it. Maki Oka, of *Heroes'* fame and who was a programmer at the time, brainstormed an idea that fixed the problem. It was a force that made the mist particulates stay with the water surface and account for the vacuum effect of the air above it."

Much of the finessing of shots was done during the compositing stage, where effects could be rendered more quickly in 2-D. Up to twenty-five compositors, more than on *The Phantom Menace*, were required to pull the ocean shots together.

One of the tweaks executed in the compositing stage was the addition of mist for shots that did not require any camera movement or change of perspective. Some of the 2-D mist elements were obtained the old-fashioned way, in an outdoor shoot at ILM where buckets of water were dumped in front of a giant fan and photographed. Shooting also took place on the set, using water cannons and dump tanks against blue screen.

The heavy use of practical on-set effects such as dump tanks, water cannons, wave-makers, and high-power fans was essential in generating a sense of interaction with the storm. However, this also made blue-screen extraction and the seamless extension of the tank water with CG water challenging in unique ways for each shot.

Stefen Fangmeier:

"The role of the visual effects work in *The Perfect Storm* was to create the setting of an evolving storm, really as a character within the film, against which all other action played. Rather than integrating a CG element into a photographic plate, we had to create the digital environment into which photographic elements would be placed. Wolfgang Petersen could not have brought this film to the screen without ILM's breakthrough work, which allowed him to show a storm at sea as it had never been seen before."

The Mummy Returns

2001

John Berton, visual effects supervisor:

"When Stephen Sommers first approached us with *The Mummy*, he had already written the script and was looking for ways to work in the effects. This time, he was looking for ideas even *before* he had a script. My advice was to go further than we had in the first movie, to top ourselves in every possible way. In terms of the visual effects, it had to be bigger, better, bolder—and all the creatures surrounding Imhotep had to be more amazing."

Director: Stephen Sommers
Producers: Sean Daniel, James Jacks

ILM Show Leadership:
Visual Effects Supervisor: John Andrew Berton, Jr.
Visual Effects Producer: Heather Macdonald
Animation Supervisor: Daniel Jeannette
Visual Effects Art Director: Alex Laurant

THE MUMMY RETURNS is an example of a truly collaborative effort; at this stage, ILM was no longer just a postproduction house. The company's work was integrated with production design *before* shooting began and, as a result, ILM had greater involvement with the creation of the film's environments and characters.

MOTION CAPTURE AT THE NEXT LEVEL

The Mummy Returns presented new challenges for character design: Even though this was a sequel, technological advances and the need for lingering shots of the mummy dictated a new approach to the lead character, Imhotep. ILM wanted to make use of the significant evolution of creature development that had taken place within the company in the two years that had passed since the first *Mummy* film. One of the most important advances had been an increased understanding of how motion capture can be used to create a great performance for a CG character. In *The Mummy Returns*, Imhotep interacts more effectively with the other characters, thanks to a revised technical approach to motion

capture. The new system allowed a motion capture performer to view, in real time, his own performance composited into background plates as a three-dimensional CG character.

Daniel Jeannette, animation supervisor:

"We wanted to retain more of Arnold Vosloo's performance than we were able to do in *The Mummy*. By allowing Arnold to perform his CG character to the pre-edited sequence, we enabled him to interact physically with characters that were in front of him in the scene, and we could guarantee that his performance would be integral to the plate. We could see his performance play in the context of the shot."

The kiss between the rejuvenated Imhotep and Meela (Patricia Velásquez) involved an interplay of motion capture and live-action, with keyframe detail allowing Imhotep's fingers to caress Meela's hair. The scene morphs to Vosloo, in human form, kissing Velásquez. A digital matte painting of the Egyptian palace balcony was generated and footage of the actors was inserted into a 3-D palace.

PREVIOUS SPREAD

An army of Anubus Warriors were among the new characters added to the film. Designed by the ILM department, the creatures stood nine feet tall and were essentially bipedal canines clad in Egyptian regalia.

ABOVE

On set for *The Mummy Returns*, ILM made use of the first real-time motion-capture technology; so when Arnold Vasloo (Imhotep) interacted with Patricia Velasquez (Meela Nais/ Anck Su Namun), the director and key crew could already see a gray shaded version of his mummified character walking around the live-action actress on a monitor; all of his undead details would be added later.

ABOVE

Stage and Model Shop crew prep a miniature for shooting at ILM.

ABOVE RIGHT

The completed Thebes city, with fire and smoke elements provided by the compositing team

RE-CREATING EGYPT

When logistics precluded an Egyptian location shoot, it was decided that ILM would re-create some of Egypt's ancient monuments. The model-making team constructed a one twenty-fourth-scale miniature of Thebes that covered a forty-foot square area. The model was given depth through the use of 3-D modeling software. An Epson printer was used to create less prominent panels, printing directly onto poplin fabric that was wrapped around the temple columns. A far-distance, layered digital matte painting was added to the miniature photography for this sequence.

VISTA OF THE OASIS

The vista of the oasis combined 2-D and 3-D elements. Digital matte artist Paul Huston used a variation on a technique he had used for the Podrace in *The Phantom Menace*. Rock pieces were sculpted, painted, and then photographed from a variety of angles. The sculptures were cyberscanned, creating 3-D digital versions. The photographs were then mapped onto the 3-D versions to provide a landscape. For the oasis vegetation, Huston sculpted a rough miniature of the terrain and detailed it with small trees and bushes. When the images were scanned into the computer, they provided a topographical model of the terrain. This was combined with 2-D photographic textures from Morocco and Huston's own 2-D

artwork. The effect of the growth of the oasis was realized digitally. A background-plate shot in Morocco was mapped with a growth algorithm that created ferns and grass and palm trees, animated to sprout on camera as the vegetation radiated toward the foreground of the shot.

GREAT BALLS OF FIRE

For the Scorpion King finale, stuntmen were put on stilts to walk at the correct height to indicate where the King would be. There were flamethrowers on the set in every shot. This created an interesting problem for the CG artists.

John Berton:

"A flamethrower makes a ball of fire, which travels across the room in a fairly unusual fashion. The light sources were not only moving, but they were moving in an uncontrolled way. That gave us quite a conundrum to match our CG character to the plates, but ultimately, because our character moved so dramatically, the lighting really added to the drama of the scene."

Pearl Harbor

2001

Ben Snow, associate visual effects supervisor:

"Unlike many of the fantasy-oriented projects we deal with, *Pearl Harbor* called for a seamless blend of visual effects with a familiar, albeit historical, reality. We needed to create complex scenes of destruction with myriad elements, simulate large smoke events, and make a virtual Pearl Harbor, Tokyo, and English Channel."

Director: Michael Bay
Producers: Michael Bay, Jerry Bruckheimer

ILM Show Leadership:
Visual Effects Supervisors: Eric Brevig
Co-Visual Effects Supervisor: Ed Hirsh
Associate Visual Effects Supervisor: Ben Snow
Visual Effects Producers: Ned Gorman, Janet Lewin
Visual Effects Art Director: Alex Jaeger

Academy Award®: Best Visual Effects
Eric Brevig (ILM)
John Frazier
Edward Hirsh (ILM)
Ben Snow (ILM)

FOR *PEARL HARBOR*, the focus of ILM's work was on the creation of panoramic battle scenes that tied together computer graphics, miniatures, and practical effects with first-unit footage. The resultant scenes contained thousands of elements.

One of ILM's great achievements on the film was creating a tremendous density of events in each shot. The complexity of any one shot was equal to the work that would typically go into ten isolated event shots. ILM created a modest 221 shots for *Pearl Harbor*, but the number of elements was equal to a 500-shot show.

Eric Brevig, visual effects supervisor:

"The elements were put into heroic, spectacle moments. What Michael Bay wanted, and what we rose to the challenge of creating, were shots where the camera flies down past twelve burning battleships or pushes right next to a ship that is literally turning over; and while that is happening, the tower of the ship breaks off and falls into the water, the sixteen-inch gun explodes, and people fall to their deaths. The subject matter lent itself to these kinds of sustained moments."

COMPUTER GENERATING HISTORY

Director Michael Bay's mandate was that shot designs be historically accurate in their depiction of the Pearl Harbor attack.

ABOVE AND INSETS
Computer-generated people were added to augment the live performers in wide shots of the action. Motion-capture data was used to produce a library of sixty-four performances from which animators could choose to animate the digital characters. A "sailor-management" tool was developed that allowed the motion-captured performances to be plugged in as they were or tweaked through hand-animation. With this interface, the animator had the ability to pick one of the motion-captured performances, select the uniform type and the accessory type, and then view it as a movie file.

PREVIOUS SPREAD

A CG bomb falls toward the USS *Arizona*; ILM created a completely synthetic world for this shot—even adding a camera shake and wobble to better mirror reality.

ABOVE LEFT

Working on a one-twentieth scale miniature of the USS *Oklahoma*, model maker Fon Davis (foreground) situates an articulated gun turret as Brian Dewe attends to deck details. The turrets and a variety of the other deck features of the model were interchangeable so the model could be redressed to stand in for a number of different ships.

ABOVE RIGHT

Lead model maker Brian Gernand working on the tower rigging of a one-twentieth scale USS *Arizona* model on ILM's backlot where it was photographed to provide lighting reference for the CG artists.

Ben Snow:

"There are shots in *Pearl Harbor* where I would defy anyone to pick which planes are real and which are CG. Now, Michael Bay is a man with a little bit of bravado, shall we say. He came to visit ILM, and Eric Brevig showed him a shot of an aircraft carrier, which we'd composited into a computer-generated sea. We'd refined some of the best water techniques that we had developed for *Deep Impact* (see pages 96–101) and *Perfect Storm* (see pages 132–139). And we had a bunch of bombers on the deck that were CG, alongside four real ones. Eric said to Michael, 'Okay, which bombers are real?' Michael says, 'Move aside. Let me point it out. That one.' 'No, that's CG.' 'That one.' 'No, that's CG.' So it was great, because, 'Argh!' Bay throws up his hands and had to admit that we'd nailed it."

BATTLESHIP MANDALA

Very few authentic ships were available to be shot by the first unit, so ILM had to create battleships, cruisers, and destroyers that would make up the Pacific Fleet moored in Pearl Harbor.

Ben Snow:

"I felt that, as much as possible, we should try to shoot motion control, so the Model Shop started building miniature battleships. But then it was looking like it would be extremely complicated to lock our motion control ships into our live-action plates. So each day another motion control shot would be cut out and changed into a CG shot. At the same time, we'd already built the miniature battleships and painted them. We were going over to the Model Shop every day and looking at this beautiful miniature ship they were making, the USS *Oklahoma*. They'd cut little bits of teak into tiny strips. And, you know, I'm the CG guy, but I had been pushing for more motion control elements.

"So it came down to Eric Brevig and Ed Hirsh, the two people who had a lot of experience with traditional techniques like motion control, saying, 'Ben, we're doing fourteen out of these fifteen shots as CG. We're looking at filming the one miniature outdoors, to get real sunlight, because that's the thing we feel can be improved over the miniature photography we did on *Titanic* (see pages 94–95). We're talking about filming outside in *January* in Marin County when it's always windy and rainy … for this *one* shot.

So don't you think this should be CG as well?' And I'm like, 'Oh no! I don't want to be there when you go to the Model Shop and tell Michael Lynch that we're not going to use the hero ship for its intended purpose.' So they tell Michael, and I've got to credit him. I mean, I would probably cry if I had to hear that my baby, which I'd been working on for months, is not going to get its hero role. We had photographed the miniature, so it was unquestionably the basis of the CG ship. But it wasn't going to be shot motion control, and I felt terrible, because I was one of the assassins there.

"So now we were wondering what we could do with the miniature ship. And we realized that it would have been hard for us to wrap real smoke around a CG battleship. We had come up with ways of doing CG smoke plumes, but

it looked like getting the CG smoke and CG battleship to interact would be very complex and expensive. So we came up with the idea of cutting holes in this beautiful miniature, piping smoke into it, and filming that. So I'm out on the backlot supervising the shoot, the wind comes up, and the smoke goes everywhere. We kept at it for a week, and we're like, 'Okay, you know what? This is no good at all. Still, we did actually get some usable elements; so, in a lot of the shots, the background ships are smoky miniatures."

But the saga of the miniature battleship wasn't over yet. Michael Bay decided he wanted a modern day view of the sunken, barnacle-encrusted USS *Arizona* sitting on the harbor floor, so the one-half-scale *Oklahoma* was transformed into an underwater *Arizona*.

ABOVE

To re-create the attack on Pearl Harbor, production detonated dynamite in the harbor and built a system of air valves under water to imitate strafing runs. For some shots, ILM added CG debris and airplanes—as well as huge black clouds of smoke with its new dynamic simulation technique.

RIGHT

Model maker Carol Bowman dresses the submerged battleship for a dry-for-wet shot.

Ben Snow:

"The final indignity done to this beautiful miniature was, and I'd like to think Michael Lynch did this himself, chopping it down the middle with a chainsaw and then dressing it to look like it's the USS *Arizona*, when it's been underwater for decades. That was how this gorgeous miniature ended up! And the great thing about ILM's Model Shop is that the artists there know that their work is going to be blown up or trashed, and yet it's still incredibly beautiful work. For *Pearl Harbor*, the model went from being this incredible showpiece that could be in a museum to being sawn in half, sprayed with green goo, and seen on the bottom of the ocean in only one shot. Damn good-looking shot, though."

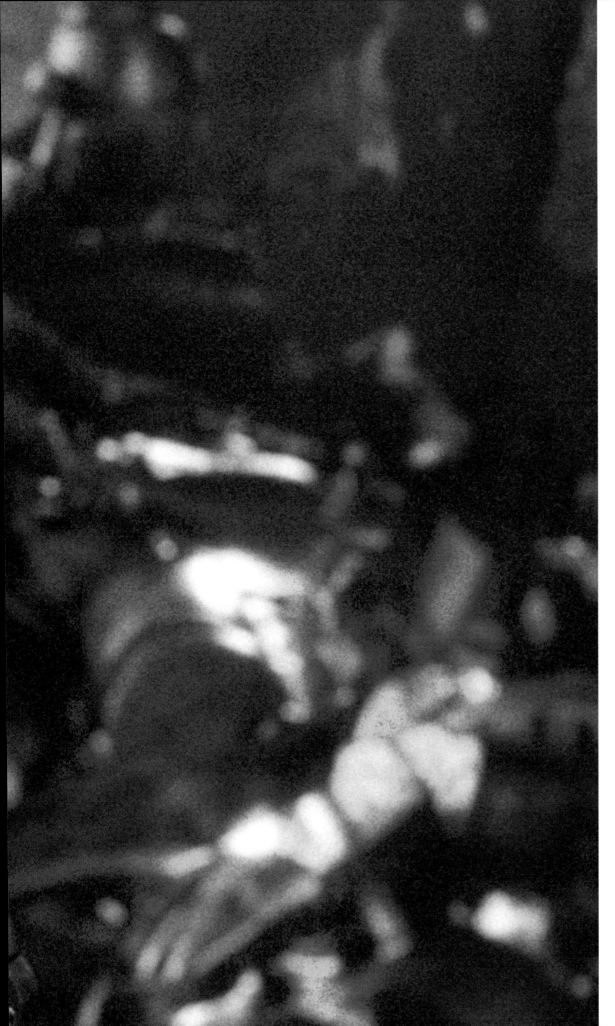

A.I. Artificial Intelligence

2001

Dennis Muren, visual effects supervisor:

"On Thanksgiving Day in 1993, I flew to England to spend the evening with Stanley Kubrick and discuss a science-fiction project he'd been developing titled *A.I.* A robot boy, his mechanical teddy bear, and Manhattan submerged by melted ice caps were some of the concerns we continued to talk about, by phone, over the next six years."

Director: Steven Spielberg
Producers: Steven Spielberg, Kathleen Kennedy,
** Bonnie Curtis**

ILM Show Leadership:
Visual Effects Supervisors: Dennis Muren, Scott Farrar
Associate Visual Effects Supervisor: Doug E. Smith
Visual Effects Producer: Ginger Thiesen
Associate Visual Effects Producer: Vicki Engel
Animation Supervisor: Hal Hickel
Visual Effects Art Director: David Nakabayashi

Academy Award® Nomination: Best Visual Effects
Dennis Muren (ILM)
Scott Farrar (ILM)
Stan Winston
Michael Lantieri

BAFTA Film Award Nomination:
** Best Achievement in Special Visual Effects**
Dennis Muren (ILM)
Scott Farrar (ILM)
Michael Lantieri

Dennis Muren:

"The unusual thing was that most of the thoughts we had over the years were never concluded. We'd submit ideas, but Stanley would always respond, 'We'll keep looking at this' or, 'That's not important anymore. Let's look at *this*.' Everything was changing all the time, and that made it very difficult to figure out how we were going to do it."

After Kubrick's death in 1999, Muren was surprised to learn of Steven Spielberg's interest in completing Kubrick's vision.

Dennis Muren:

"Around August of 1999, I read that Steven might be doing *A.I.* Two weeks later, I got a call and went to meet with Spielberg in L.A. That was when I saw all the artwork Stanley had generated in the period between when we had first met and when he passed away. I was shocked—I had no idea he'd done that much work. Stanley's longtime producer Jan Harlan sent over nearly 1,500 storyboards that no one outside of a chosen few had ever been shown. Stanley had done so much work on this film and had been talking to Steven about it for so many years."

For the lead character, David, Kubrick had considered building an actual robot boy and had also talked about making an all-CG boy. For Kubrick, using a real child seemed out of the question for many reasons, including British child-labor laws, skin textures, body movement, aging, and acting skills, etc. Ultimately it was Spielberg's decision to cast a real boy, Haley Joel Osment, which made the movie affordable.

TEDDY BOYS

For the character of Teddy, a combination of live puppetry and digital animation was used. Teddy was one of ILM's toughest assignments on the film, because the CG version of Teddy needed to match the look of Stan Winston's animatronic puppet.

Dennis Muren:

"Stan Winston's shop created the puppet for the close-up work. ILM created the walking, running, jumping CG Teddy. The

hair render was especially difficult, because each hair was wavy and there were patterns of wavy hair on the puppet that we had to copy. We ultimately got the CG Teddy looking good enough to be interchangeable with the puppet Teddy. There's one shot that starts on the puppet, pans off, then comes back to our CG bear, and the match is quite good. The lighting we created for the hairs on the CG figure was what really made the match work."

Scott Farrar, visual effects supervisor:

"What are you doing in trying to make a match? You're looking at photo references that you've scanned into the computer, side by side with your computer model. Do you have enough hair? Are the hairs curled the right way? There's one patch of hair that looks like it's the wrong pattern. And it's real easy to get wrong patterns when humans are trying to put something like fur onto a character. Wait a minute, the hairs don't quite have enough gold, there's not enough auburn, and you go back and forth on this stuff. It's excruciating trying to get matches to make sure it will hold up in the movie.

"The problem was that there were millions of hairs on this CG bear, so it took a colossal number of hours to render each frame. We ended up taking still views of the bear's body from all angles, so that we basically created a shell of the bear that allowed us to view Teddy from any angle. We rendered the bear from different views. Then we stuck those views onto an animated character and didn't have to render each hair every time. Once in a while, in a close-up, we would have to do a full-on render, but it really simplified the process."

PREVIOUS SPREAD
One of the abandoned Mechas in *A.I.*, half live-action, half digital wizardry

LEFT
ILM created an all-CG version of Teddy, which was intercut with the numerous articulated practical Teddys constructed by Stan Winston Studio. The CG version was used in a number of shots when the necessary action precluded the puppets from being used.

OPPOSITE
Rouge City as seen behind Gigolo Joe (Jude Law) and David (Haley Joel Osment) is actually a composite featuring live-action blue-screen elements, background miniatures, and digital set extensions. To aid in capturing the sequence, ILM created the first real-time on-set previsualization system, allowing director Steven Spielberg to see an approximation of the CG set in his viewfinder and videotape monitor.

OPPOSITE, INSET
Senior model-maker Grant Imahara works on a miniature.

FOLLOWING SPREAD
The surreal entrance to Rouge City

NAUGHTY ROUGE CITY

A digital team at ILM realized Chris Baker's concepts for the Rouge City entry. Shots inside Rouge City incorporated a blend of live-action miniatures and digital technologies, based on a Kubrick-Baker concept. The ILM art department worked with Baker to distill the many designs generated for Kubrick into a workable concept. A commercially available video-game engine was customized to allow interaction with the virtual set in real time. A copy of the Rouge City game engine was shipped to

Spielberg on a CD-ROM, enabling him to fly through the environment in real time, selecting camera angles and lenses, as a form of virtual location scouting to test the city layout, identifying the portion that would be used before investing in its final realization.

A foreground row of practical model buildings were constructed for Rouge City. Chris Baker worked with the model crew to supervise the sculpting of two key female figures. Model-makers populated the interiors with photo cutouts of ILM staffers and dressed miniature cocktail tables with dollhouse cutlery.

To create the half live-action actors/ half CG "Mecha" ILM made use of its proprietary "Motion and Structure Recovery System" dubbed, M.A.R.S. This system allowed for a highly automated camera tracking solution that enabled a CG camera to match its live-action camera counterpart and thus ensure acurate placement of CG elements in the scene.

ANOTHER ROAD TO ILM, OR "SO, HOW DID I GET HERE?"

**Lorne Peterson,
senior model-maker:**

"I wasn't interested in visual effects whatsoever to begin with. I was an art major in college, and the university that I went to had a very large industrial design and art department. I worked for a number of years in industrial design, and along with that, I was sculpting.

"McDonald's in the late 1970s used to have these parks with big hamburgers that have slides coming out of them, and I was the one that carved the originals of those things. I was on a Hollywood lot, because they had these big open spaces where we could carve these McDonald's pieces. Bob Shepherd, a guy who was in industrial design when I was in college, walked by and he said, 'Hey, Lorne, we're working on a science-fiction film, and we could really use some help from you as a model-maker and a sculptor. What do you think?' I said, 'Well, I've started a company with my partner, Jon Erland, but the work's kind of sporadic.' And he said, 'Here's the phone number, get in touch, because we've had a hard time finding model-makers.'

"My partner and I went over to see what they were doing. And here they were with machines cutting wood and doing plastic and starting to make the very first of the *Star Wars* spaceships. And we were in need of work, so we kept our clients; we would work for them at night, after nine until midnight, get up in the morning, and go to work on *Star Wars* again for ten hours.

"I'm not the best model-maker or sculptor in the world, but Jon and I had a lot of technical expertise; we knew a lot about materials and processes from working in industrial design for years. And maybe four days into working, I saw that they were using five-minute epoxy and gluing parts and putting tape on, and to me it was very laborious. So Jon and I introduced all kinds of materials, like Super Glue, so every time a new problem came up, people started coming to us to find out what the solution would be.

"Personally, I feel that I got to live in Florence during the Renaissance for visual effects. Everything was happening at ILM—it was the center of the universe, really."

MANHATTAN MINIATURE MYSTERY

The sequence featuring Manhattan submerged under ice caps incorporated real and CG water elements, miniatures, and 3-D geometry mapped with photographs of practical models. A water simulation similar to what had been used in *The Perfect Storm* was developed for this sequence. ILM's model department also created a miniature set with a nine-foot-wide Ferris wheel.

Lorne Peterson:

"The miniature set was pretty small, only about fifteen feet across, seven feet deep, and three feet high. Originally, they were going to shoot a live-action set, and then, as they closed in on it, they would have used our model in the distance showing the ice, with the Ferris wheel. Our model kept getting built in, with stalactites hanging down and snow and blocks of ice coming up from the bottom. One

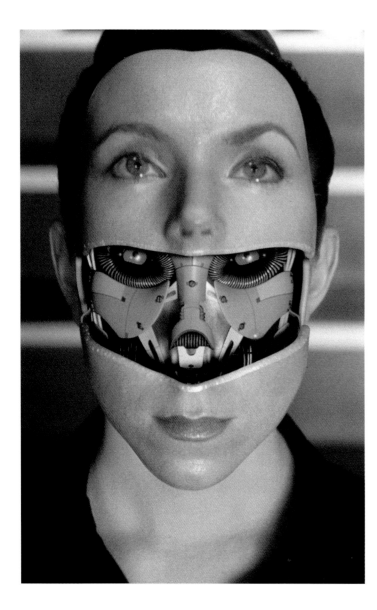

that sense of depth when the helicopter was only a foot long and the icicles were only a quarter of an inch long.

"Eventually, when Spielberg saw our miniature set, he liked it well enough that he used it full screen, which was really surprising because it wasn't intended to be seen full screen. You don't typically make something that's only fifteen feet wide if it's got to be on full screen."

Jim Morris, former president, ILM:

"The effects work in *A.I.* has a nuance and a poetry to it that you seldom find in visual effects. There's an understated quality to the work in *A.I.*, particularly in the scenes where the boy is underwater. As he falls into the water and floats down, the fish swirl around him and move him to different places. There's a cinematic element there that's really just poetic. It reminds you that visual effects don't have to just be about getting a story point across. It can also add to the ambience of the film and to the mood and the feeling of the film."

Dennis Muren:

"Many of the visual effects techniques I'd discussed with Stanley years before were used on the show, including realtime on-set visualization. At the time, Stanley wouldn't tell me what the environments would look like, but he was keen on being able to see a whole environment while shooting his actors on a blue-screen stage. I wish Stanley had lived to see our high-tech CG version of his Rouge City set, generated in real time, composited with real actors, and shot on film by a camera with six degrees of freedom. I know he would have been thrilled."

of the women model makers was helping me, since she was lighter and smaller than I am, because you match up the model maker with the size of the set. We eventually had her go in on a long board, on her belly, and work as if she were on a surfboard.

"You can't paint ice opaquely and make it seem real; it all has to be material that's translucent, so you actually see a bit into it. One of the things you do to make things seem translucent is to vacuum form. So we made a lot of the little icy parts by vacuum form. Then we would crinkle up some tissue paper and put it behind there. The crinkled white translucent tissue paper made it seem like you're looking more deeply into the block of ice. It was tough to achieve

ABOVE
The "opening" of the face of a human-like robot was a seamless blend from live-action to startling CG.

RIGHT
The problematic synthetic being of the future (audiences often thought it was an alien, not a robot) speaks with the ironic representative of the human race—their creators—as the film goes from the early model of robot at its outset to an almost god-like culmination of robotics at its close.

Star Wars: Episode II Attack of the Clones

2002

Rob Coleman, animation director:

"I was worried about that Yoda fight right up to the very last day. And the first time I got to see the movie with a non-ILM audience, I remember shrinking down in my seat before it happened, and then the cheer that came out from the audience just relieved all the stress in my life."

Director: George Lucas
Producer: Rick McCallum

ILM Show Leadership:
Visual Effects Supervisors: Dennis Muren, John Knoll, Pablo Helman, Ben Snow
Visual Effects Producers: Gretchen Libby, Jill Brooks, Heather Macdonald
Animation Director: Rob Coleman
Visual Effects Art Director: Alex Jaeger

Academy Award® Nomination: Best Visual Effects
Rob Coleman
Pablo Helman
John Knoll
Ben Snow

PREVIOUS SPREAD
An all–visual effects shot of a clone trooper and Yoda

FAR LEFT
Animation director Rob Coleman

LEFT
Wire frame for Yoda animation

AS WITH EPISODE I, the number of visual effects shots ILM produced for Episode II was phenomenal. Undertaking the creation of two thousand shots was the equivalent of producing work for three large-scale productions; thus, the ILM team was divided into three units. One was supervised by Knoll, one by Helman, and the third by Muren and Snow.

Much was learned in the course of visual effects production on Episode I that impacted ILM's work on Episode II.

Dennis Muren, visual effects supervisor:

"After Episode I, everybody became a lot more confident about the quantities of work that we could do and better at being able to detail the work. The creatures and the ships—everything looked better because we *could* make them better. And I think it opened up George's mind to go even *beyond* what he had for Episode I, feeling, 'Hey, I've done that. Now it's time to do something even *bigger*.' But we really felt we could deliver that, and everybody was getting very confident about the tools we were using and feeling that it almost didn't matter how broad George's palette was: Whether it's the color of the skies, or the distance of the landscapes, or the texture and the mouth of the talking creature, whatever shape it was, whatever quantity of shots it was, we could pretty much deliver it. So there was a real sense of being able to do it and, 'Let's go do it. And let's make it really great.' "

Rob Coleman was responsible for a team of more than sixty animators on Episode II. Seventy minutes of animation was created for the film, ten more minutes than for *The Phantom Menace*.

Rob Coleman:

"On Episode I, every Wednesday we would have the same meeting: 'Can we get the movie done? How are we going to get it done?!' We didn't even know how we could do the Gungan war for about six months of the production. I mean, we were living right on the bleeding edge. I didn't want to be there again. I wanted the tools to be in place so the animators could focus more on performance and acting. I wanted us to rethink how we did clothing and hair and skin, because a lot of our time was spent just trying to keep up with that on Episode I. I knew that Yoda was going to play a significant role in Episode II. He was going to wear the exact same clothing as Obi-Wan and Mace Windu, and I wanted the animators to be freed of that concern. I focused most of my attention with the animators on acting, on getting inside the head of the character."

YODA, READY FOR PRIME TIME

Except for a long-distance CG Yoda shot in Episode I, Yoda had always been achieved through puppetry or a small person in a Yoda costume, techniques that had the unavoidable result of physically limiting the character. The most astounding achievement of animation work for Episode II was the creation of a CG Yoda who appeared throughout the film.

George Lucas, director:

"We had decided that we would move to the next level on Episode I, which was to have digital actors that can actually do performances. We were able to do Jar Jar Binks, we were able to do Watto, we were able to do Sebulba, but we had a hard time doing Yoda. We worked on Yoda, and we kept working on it, but Yoda was never ready for prime time while we were doing Episode I.

"On Episode II, we were able to use the digital Yoda for the first time. And it really took about six years of development to get to the point where you could do a digital character who could actually have enough expression and movement and all of the facilities to have actually a good performance, especially one that we had to match to something that already existed. That was really the difficult part. In fact, we were trying very hard to get ILM to slow down a little bit because they said, 'Well, we can make him really good now.' I said, 'No, he has to match the old one. He has to match the puppet.' So they had to dumb it down quite a bit for it to be like the puppet rather than the way they could have done it, which was much more sophisticated."

John Knoll, visual effects supervisor:

"It wasn't that we weren't capable of creating a CG Yoda for Episode I. I think if you look at Jar Jar technically, the character is rendered very realistically, and there was really nothing about Yoda that couldn't have been done with the same technique. It was just that very early on, because of how much people loved Yoda from *Empire* and *Jedi*, doing him the same way as before seemed like the smart way to go. And we had enough on our plate with all the other characters we had

ABOVE

Gray shaded figures and vehicles in a virtual environment (inset) are then fully rendered for the final frame.

to do that we said, 'All right, Yoda's gonna be done as a puppet. Great. Should be fine. It worked great in the other films. It keeps our workload more manageable.'

"But there were story reasons why the puppet wasn't going to work for us on Episode II: in particular, the big fight at the end. Yoda was going to be so mobile that there was really no way of doing that with a puppet. So very early on, Rob Coleman started doing some tests, where we'd done a first pass at a sculpture on the digital Yoda, and he started doing direct duplications of the performances in some of the previous pictures. There were a couple of shots from *Empire Strikes Back* where they tried to do exactly the same performance, and did a split screen to see how well we were taking elements across. It was interesting that you couldn't match it exactly. I think people remember the puppet being better than it really was. If you look at the puppet, the mouth is not really articulating any of the shapes. It's just sort of opening and closing. And if you did that with the CG model, it just looked like you weren't trying very hard. So we found that we had to articulate the mouth shapes at least a little bit—not to do it like you would if you

were doing a character who didn't have this legacy, but where you really needed to form the phonemes a little bit better. We had to do something kind of halfway in between.

"The goal was to try to make Yoda look like you *remember* him looking in *Empire Strikes Back*, not what he *actually* looked like."

Rob Coleman:

"Before the May release of Episode II, I received a letter from Frank Oz. He had just returned from London, where he had recorded the final voice tracks for Yoda. He was generous and warm enough to write me a four-page letter about how moved he was by our work creating the digital Yoda. He had really studied our animation, which was on a big screen in front of him while he was doing the recording with George. And what he had noticed was that we had, in his words, copied his mistakes, that we had distilled Yoda down to the subtle movements in his ears when he turned and moved as a rubber puppet in *Empire Strikes Back*. And although Frank didn't want those in the original performance, that's just the nature of the material that the character was made of, and it became part of

who he was. I had always worried a little bit about what Frank would think, because I'd always wanted to ground myself in what Frank had done, but the fight took us to a whole different place; We were kind of making up a new Yoda, this new action-hero Yoda that he's now become. So to receive this handwritten letter was really a special moment for me."

Pablo Helman, visual effects supervisor:

"The Yoda fight was very difficult for lots of reasons. I think all of us had misgivings about how the audience was going to take that sequence and whether George had gone a little too far. And, obviously, we didn't want anybody to laugh at any of our work. It's just the sense that, logically, he couldn't possibly have done it because one, he's eight hundred years old, and if he's walking with a cane, how can he fight the most powerful Sith in the galaxy—in *any* galaxy for that matter? Who's going to believe this?

"The second thing was the movement. He was fighting and moving in a very odd way. I mean, why would somebody jump from one wall to the other when he's fighting, when the actual contender is just ten feet away from him? So that was a difficult thing to swallow. And then, the last thing for me was the fact that, physically, he is about two feet tall, and the opponent is six four. That, just from a framing point of view, is comical.

"Well, a lot of why it ultimately worked had to do with the way he looked. He looked very real—the animation and cloth simulation was very realistic. And so a lot of elements made that scene work. It was also the story. It was the fact that we really did want to see Yoda kick some ass."

NO NAKED ALIENS IN SPACE

Rob Coleman:

"We knew that we had to be able to take on the challenge of clothing. George kept saying, 'We're not doing naked aliens in space. We have to give these characters clothes, props, and weapons.' So we needed to be able to handle that on the technical side of animation. Clothing became one of our focuses for research and development. We have a very smart team of men and women who help write these new tools for us.

"The audience can look at Natalie Portman and her beautiful dress, and they can look at Yoda. If his clothing isn't moving and reacting in a very similar way to hers, subconsciously, or for some audience members consciously, they're pulled out of the scene, which means we failed in helping George create this world."

Another focus for the ILM team was the realistic creation of computer-generated hair and skin. Skin was a particularly complicated problem to solve, primarily because of its translucent nature.

Rob Coleman:

"If you look at your hand, you'll see it's not just one color—you get to see things subsurface. The way the light scatters around in there, we call that 'subsurface scattering.' As we move into creating these digital characters who are existing and coexisting with real people, and who are given more and more sustained close-ups, they need to have the same kind of realism in their skin and hair that you would see in Natalie Portman or Ewan McGregor. If they don't, they look, for lack of a better word, cartoony. There's a life force, there's something that comes out of us human beings, and as animators, we're trying to find out what that is."

THE HD CHALLENGE

Episode II was also a landmark production in that it was the first full-length, large-scale motion picture to be shot entirely on high-definition digital video, rather than on film.

ILM's use of the HD camera for visual effects photography resulted in some significant advantages. Of course, shooting on HD changed ILM's approach to creating the visual effects.

John Knoll:

"We had to build an internal infrastructure to deal with all the HD plates. We had to have digital projectors in the theatre for looking at all the dailies and footage digitally. And we had to have a way of shooting all our miniature work digitally as well, because we wanted to stay digital everywhere we could.

"One of the things I really like about working in HD is that you can see what you're doing at the time. So there's none of this guesswork about exposure levels and key-fill ratios.

You can just see it live. This allowed us to work more quickly and forge ahead with confidence.

"But there were a couple of downsides to shooting digitally. Generally, we had to light the models with a lot more light than we had to when we were shooting on film, which meant that you could only really have the lights on at full intensity when you were shooting, because the surfaces would get really hot and sometimes the models can warp. And sometimes, even with that much light, it was impossible to get enough depth of field. So we sometimes had to shoot the models multiple times with the focus planes in different distances and then split them together."

CREATING ENVIRONMENTS

The matte painting work was double that for Episode I, requiring a fourteen-member digimatte department led by Yusei Uesugi, Paul Huston, and Jonathan Harb.

A digi-matte painting of Coruscant

Paul Huston, digital matte sequence supervisor:

"Episode II had a great variety of imaginative locations, and by the time we worked on that film, we were doing entire sequences as digital environments. I was lucky enough to be able to create the pastoral images of the Naboo picnic sequence. The elements I created were combined with plates shot in Italy with Natalie Portman and Hayden Christensen in a pasture. George wanted waterfalls. So Pablo Helman asked me to photograph actual waterfalls, and I found two of waterfalls in Northern California: Burney Falls and McCloud Falls. I photographed them with different angles and lighting, because the waterfalls in the shot go from one side of the screen all the way over to the other side of the screen. So these small Northern California waterfalls were used to look like a waterfall similar in size to Niagara Falls.

"Aluminum foil was sculpted to look like cliffs and painted really quickly with some green HO railroad props thrown on it for foliage. I also used a section of synthetic fur for the foreground grass and blended it with the grass in the actual plates.

The model was photographed, and then the video waterfalls were composited into the image of the foil mountain ridges that made up the landforms. The skies for the environment were a composite of many different skies photographed in New Mexico."

The opening shot of Episode II features Coruscant, a city that was made up entirely of digital matte paintings.

Yusei Uesugi, digital matte sequence supervisor:

"I had worked on digital matte paintings of Coruscant on Episode I, and I worked on the same environment for Episode II. It's a capital city with skyscraper buildings and busy air traffic. We spent a lot of time designing and building and texturing new buildings for Coruscant, but we wanted to be efficient in making our resources, so we tried to design and build something recyclable; we designed a building formed by multiple components, and then we were able to reconfigure all of the components to make another version of the build-

ing. So we would build one building and then it was reconfigured to form three or four different kinds of shapes.

"On Episode I, the artists in the matte department had to learn how to share scene files; there were so many shots that needed to be done in one sequence, we started working in groups. This process carried over to all of the shows we worked on after that, and it was a very important way of working on Episode II. Everyone working on a sequence now shares information, tools, and resources. That's quite normal for the rest of the CG pipelines, but for matte painters it was a new concept back then."

DIGITAL DOPPELGANGERS

Pablo Helman:

"The Obi-Wan versus Jango Fett fight in the rain was a digital environment that was very difficult, because of the rainwa-

ter on the surfaces. It was also a very large and challenging environment, with lots of digital doubles, cloth simulation, and wet clothes.

"There's one shot of Obi-Wan being lassoed on the hands and then being pulled over, and that was one of our first digital-double shots. We were so excited, because it was looking so good. I remember the first time we showed George the digital double of Obi-Wan in the rain. He said, 'Hmm, that looks great. It looks like Richard Chamberlain.' We thought, 'Okay. I guess we need to work on it a little bit more.'"

Nigel Sumner, sequence supervisor and development lead:

"Obi-Wan and Jango Fett are out in the howling wind and the rain. But when it was shot, there was only a very small piece of set and the rest was green screen. Well, computer graphics are very good for clean shiny objects, but we really had to dirty everything up; we had to make them drip, we had to make

ABOVE LEFT
Jango Fett jets toward Obi-Wan Kenobi on Kamino, thanks to digital VFX.

ABOVE
The first battle of the Clone Wars made use of many entirely CG shots, with incredibly complex animation.

everything splash with water running off them. So we leveraged a lot of approaches that we'd done on previous movies like *Perfect Storm* to help us create all of that synthetic water in the computer."

Dennis Muren:

"It's very much like *Star Wars* was to The *Empire Strikes Back*. *Empire* was a so much bigger palette than *Star Wars*, and I think Episode II is way beyond Episode I. It looks like it was

by far the most expensive movie ever made because there are two thousand effects shots that not only could not be done any other way, but also look aesthetically great."

Pablo Helman:

"The sheer volume of work, organization, and management of having five hundred artists work on a film for two years—I had brown hair when I started on Episode II, and now I have gray hair."

Minority Report

2002

Scott Farrar, visual effects supervisor:

> "I like to tell people that I think the computer is still in the Stone Age. It's just a dumb thing waiting for input. Depending on who is doing the input, that's how brilliant the shot gets."

Director: Steven Spielberg
Producers: Jan De Bont, Bonnie Curtis, Gerald R. Molen, Walter F. Parkes

ILM Show Leadership:
Visual Effects Supervisor: Scott Farrar
Visual Effects Producer: Dana Friedman
Visual Effects Art Director: Alex Laurant

BAFTA Film Award Nomination:
Best Achievement in Special Visual Effects
Scott Farrar (ILM)
Michael Lantieri
Nathan McGuinness
Henry LaBounta

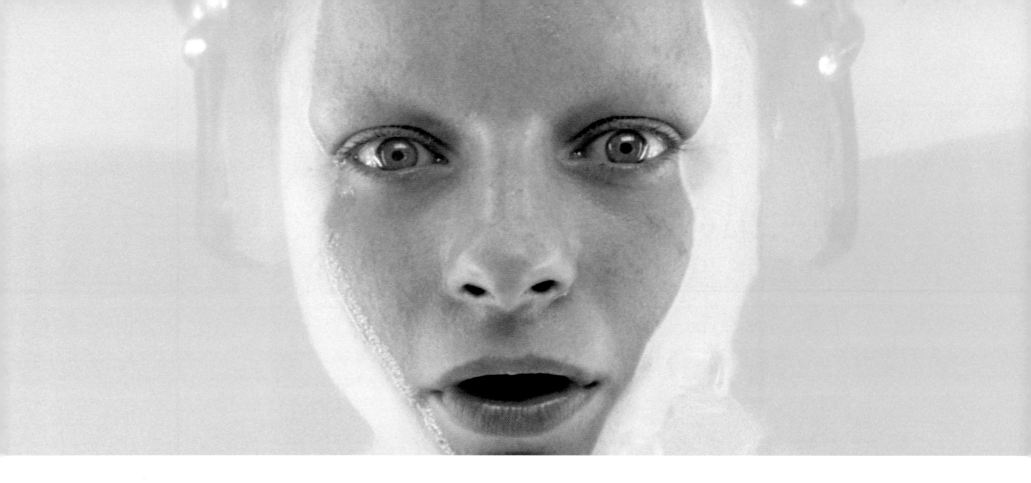

ONE OF THE MOST IMPORTANT ASPECTS of ILM's work on *Minority Report* was the development of new techniques for the creation of computer-generated models from photographic images. The photo-modeling technique had significant advantages over the creation of CG models by hand.

Steve Sullivan, software development:

"We tried to use photographs to come up with realistic-looking set pieces. The process was very new at the time and, ultimately, wound up being part of one of our Scientific and Technical Awards from the Academy. The award was given in 2006 for the design and development of the ILM Image-based Modeling System to Steve Sullivan, Colin Davidson, Max Chen, and Francesco Callari.

"We used the technique in the Hall of Containment sequence, where the camera is moving around hundreds of prisoners in tubes. The set was too ambitious to build and fill with extras. It's also a very difficult thing for modelers and artists to create by hand that many distinct humans who look very real, at different scales and in different positions.

"So we came up with a technique where a person would stand in this kind of containment chamber prop, and we would snap fifteen pictures simultaneously. Then the computer would help reconstruct their shape and their likeness in 3-D from those images. It was a very fast process—we just marched the extras right through. We could generate hundreds of prisoners that look totally photoreal, much less expensively than by either building a set and staffing it with people or using traditional techniques. And that was the start of a certain category of photo modeling for ILM.

"We had done things where somebody would take a bunch of pictures on the set, and they could reconstruct individual points. But actually to reconstruct a human being and make it look real was a step forward for us. We went from doing everything with tape measures and laser measuring devices on set to relying on lots of pictures and computer reconstructions in order to figure out what was on set and their dimensions or what a character looked like. It's called image-based modeling. 'Clone cam' is our internal term for it."

From 2002 to the present, ILM has gone from not doing photo modeling at all to using the technique extensively.

PREVIOUS SPREAD

Jetpack equipped precops surround John Anderton (Tom Cruise) in one of ILM's 261 shots created for *Minority Report*; the precogs were suspended from a hydraulic traveling rig built on the Warner Bros. backlot. ILM eliminated the wires and sweetened the sequence, supplying CG heat ripples and propane-burner flame elements captured on stage for the jetpacks (and tracked to match angles, etc.).

ABOVE

A precog—Agatha (Samantha Morton)—delivers a prophecy. Filmed on a full-sized set in a containment tank, ILM added prevision imagery and reflections into the precog's pupil.

ABOVE LEFT

ILM's first use of photo-mapping was used for the Department of Containment sequence. This technique allowed the effects facility to generate the 360 columns of prisoners seen in wide shots, with only a few pictures taken of the limited number of practical cylinders and nineteen containees; besides the cylinders, only the actors and the central tower existed on stage.

ABOVE RIGHT

Three-dimensional images of organ effects and medical readouts were supplied by Black Box Digital, which ILM tracked and composited onto the translucent cylinders.

FUTURE CITY

Director Steven Spielberg set an interesting challenge for the approach to creating exteriors for a futuristic Washington, D.C.

Scott Farrar:

"When we first had all the department heads together, Steven held up an artist's conception of a futuristic Washington, D.C., with all these fancy, shiny chrome high-rises, and he asked me, 'So, Scott, why is it that in so many science-fiction films the cities look so fake?' The answer was they looked fake because they looked so disconnected with what was there in the first place. All the new stuff that had been stuck in was obvious!

"We decided it should be like the freeway running by ILM. There was obviously a town here before, but when the 101 Freeway came through San Rafael, there was not a lot of room, so they built it up on legs. We applied that theory to Mag-Lev. It's obviously been added, but it's been added like a freeway. And in all cases, whenever we had buildings, we tried to prevent their looking too outlandish. We didn't want them to appear to have been made with materials that were not used today. I wanted people to see concrete, aluminum, plastic, glass; and then we aged everything to make it look integrated.

That was tough with Mag-Lev because the concept *was* outlandish; but wherever we could, we tried to make it real."

DEVELOPMENTS IN TRACKING

Matchmoving is the foundation of much of the work that ILM does. While an artist might match an element he or she creates quite closely to the rest of the objects in the frame, the viewer can still perceive a problem. If one element moves inconsistently against another even in the slightest way, it results in an unnatural "slipping" that audiences immediately pick up on. The complex 2-D work on *Minority Report* forced ILM to develop new methods for tracking matchmove data.

Scott Farrar:

"When Tom Cruise is playing back holograms of his wife and his son, he's there with a Rice Krispies cereal box, and the Rice Krispies characters come to life and start talking. On set, it was a blank box with a moving camera. The problem was that we had to track to the box, which was an object in the frame some distance away from the camera. So the layout people had to create that whole interior to accurately track the box. We had to know what lens was being used, the focus, where the table was,

LEFT

Several elements went into the holographic home movie of Anderton's kidnapped son, including a child (Spencer Treat Clark) filmed against green-screen (inset) with an array of synchronized video cameras; after further massaging, the 2-D image could be manipulated in 3-D space (ILM's tracking and matchmoving system, M.A.R.S., was transformed into "Zepo" at this juncture). The complete photo-modeling technique developed by ILM allowed Spielberg to focus on the actor's performance without being locked into a motion control situation.

the box, the wall, and where Tom was sitting. All of this data gets measured and recorded.

"But this one was tough because there was an increasing arc in terms of distance from the box, so we had a magnification change. Every one of these things added a new dimension of complexity, so we employed a new Zeno tracking tool to help with the process. Tracking and layout is the foundation of any shot; those are the unsung heroes. You can't do the explicit, beautiful lockdown work with moving cameras without exquisite layout tracking. And this was the breakthrough moment....

"What we do is we don't just look at that cereal box alone. We're looking at where it is in three-dimensional space. So if you were to see the Zeno scene, you'd see lines that intersect on the front edge of the table, as well as the box as well as the background wall. Just like when you have two-point perspective in a drawing. By doing that, you've got multiple points to track to, which help lock the box into its proper position in 3-D space. It is very similar to GPS tracking, but with images.

"We had a new artist at the time, Brian Cantwell, and he's the one that ended up solving this problem. Each one of our artists brings something in. He was pushing forward something as simple as tracking, but tracking is the life and death of us if it doesn't work."

The multiple track points made it possible to create a moving three-dimensional *shape* of a boy onto which an *image* of the boy could be projected. A virtual camera can then orbit around the character. This new technique was one of the key breakthroughs for ILM on *Minority Report*.

Scott Farrar:

"Now, we can walk around the character. What's there representing the character? Nothing. So, my new, patented, high-tech formula was to hang a washer from a couple of strings from the upper rafters of the set so the cameraman with the Steadicam could walk around, just photographing a washer, since the washer was a perfect eye line for Tom to look at. The cameraman can go all the way around and we will absolutely be able to lock to that washer and create this projected image."

COMPUTERS OF TOMORROW

Spielberg wanted transparent screens for all of the computer displays. The challenge was that the director also wanted to be able to see the image on the screen from both sides.

ABOVE

For the Mag-Lev chase sequence, CTEK created practical vehicles for live-action photography; ILM added more CG cars for wide shots, or all CG cars in shots where they are driving up and down vertical highways, in addition to the CG buildings and roadway (complete with weathering, reflections, and so on).

Scott Farrar:

"Nobody could figure out a way to do it live. We ended up shooting backgrounds for every shot containing transparent screen displays. ILM and Asylum Visual Effects composited them digitally. These composites were far more complicated than anybody watching the movie will ever realize. There were many times when the camera was on a crane arm moving three-dimensionally—with boom, tilt, roll, pan, tracking—starting close in, pulling back, revealing people—rack focus, and so on. I cannot overstate how difficult that was in the world of matchmove."

CHICKEN EYES

The creation of the eyeless gaze of the drug dealer, Lycon, involved a unique blending of physical and digital effects.

Scott Farrar:

"Alex Laurant was ILM's art director on *Minority Report*, and Mark Casey was the artist working on the sequence. We were trying to work out this shot, because there's a big reveal point, and Steven wanted it to be really creepy. The shot had a real actor, with real eyes, but we've got to get rid of them and make it look like he's got deep sockets with no eyeballs. We were struggling, but we had an idea of what it should look like, so I said, 'You gotta see stitches in there, you gotta see gristle, it's got to look gross.'

"Alex goes home that night and, fortunately for us, his wife was making chicken for dinner. He pulled the skin off the uncooked bird. Then he took some plastic modeling putty and modeled the eye socket interior. He got some thread and sutured the chicken skin into the clay and brought that in to ILM the next day. Now we have stitches and lumpy stuff and there's more like a Frankenstein's monster thing going on.

"Then Alex takes a bunch of photographs and in Photoshop, he plugs it all together. Yet you have only one moment for the audience to see what's going on there and it's got to read. So we also made sure that the lighting was such that we see that deep socket, with a lot of information there. I run it for Steven and tell him that we decided to go really gross with this. He says, 'Yeah, that's really good!'

"So the tool is a computer using a variety of programs—but it's not the computer, it's always the artistry behind it."

Terminator 3: Rise of the Machines

2002

Pablo Helman, visual effects supervisor:

"Photorealism was the main premise of this film. When I met with Jonathan Mostow, the first thing he said was, 'I want photorealistic stuff. Don't give me CG, because I won't approve it.' When I'm doing visual effects that are completely photorealistic, I want to be able to talk to the director in person and ask him, 'Is this what you want?' Being there gives me the opportunity to manipulate things on the set and to incorporate as many real-world references as possible."

Director: Jonathan Mostow
Producers: Hal Lieberman, Joel B. Michaels,
Andrew G. Vajna, Colin Wilson

ILM Show Leadership:
Visual Effects Supervisor: Pablo Helman
Associate Visual Effects Supervisor: Samir Hoon
Visual Effects Producer: Gretchen Libby
Animation Supervisor: Dan Taylor
Visual Effects Art Director: Peter Mitchell Rubin

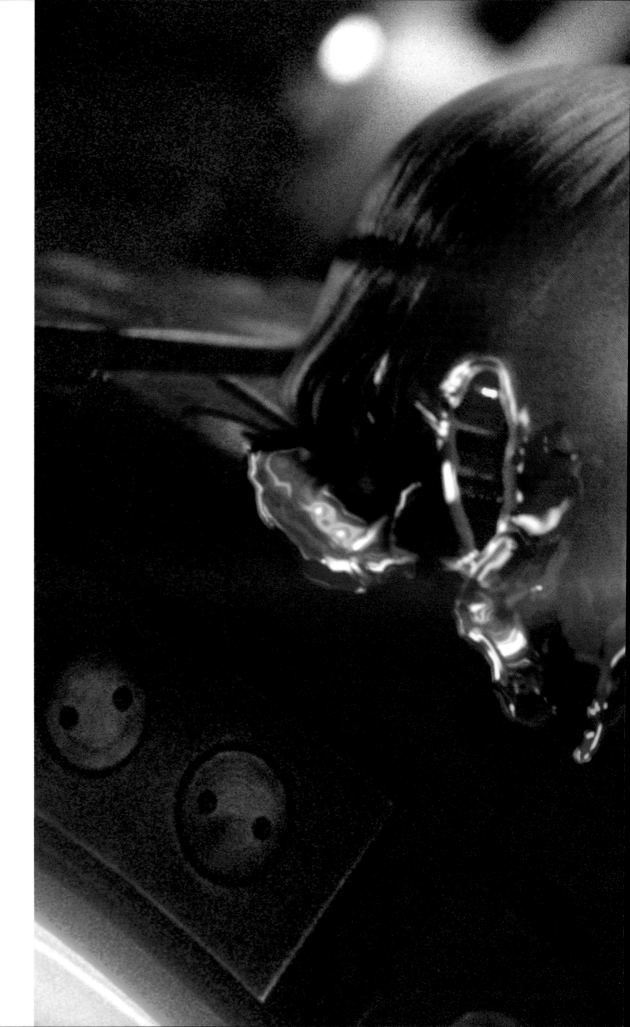

PHOTOREALISM WAS THE MAIN FOCUS of the visual effects work for *Terminator 3: Rise of the Machines*. The third film in the *Terminator* series adopted the effects philosophy used in the two previous films: Best results are not necessarily achieved by choosing digital over practical techniques. The most successful shots artfully combine the two—the art is in knowing how to use each approach to its best advantage. For example, for the dramatic sequence in which the Terminator's helicopter goes inside a tunnel, Pablo Helman evaluated the best approach to creating the required visual elements for the sequence.

Pablo Helman:

"I'll be the first to admit that I'm one of the people who thinks first, *How can we shoot this as part of principle photography? Can we do it practically?* If that's not possible, *then* I have to start think-ing about whether we do it as a miniature and then combine it with digital elements. When the Terminator's helicopter goes inside the tunnel, we had the tunnel in full scale, but we couldn't do all of the explosions and we definitely couldn't do a helicopter and all of the fire. So we decided we were going to do this as a miniature, combined with a Terminator digital double.

"Now, because the helicopter was going to go on explod-ing inside of the tunnel, clearly doing it CG was not an option, because we knew we would have to work out all sorts of things for months before everything would look like the real thing. But with a miniature, if you do your math right and you choose the right scale and detail the work, you get a lot of stuff for free. In CG, nothing comes for free."

PREVIOUS SPREAD

The liquid-metal-based T-X (Kristanna Loken) immobilized by the magnetic field generated by a particle accelerator. This 3-D liquefaction effect was the result of eight months of research and became the basis for the ILM Fluid Simulation System.

ABOVE

For the future war nightmare sequence, ILM created an army of CG Terminator T-800s composited into a background miniature.

RIGHT

On the ILM stage, concentric rings
of walnut dust were laid out so that,
when blasted outward by an air
cannon, they would simulate in miniature the shock wave of a nuclear
explosion. This element would later
be combined with a variety of CG
elements to create the final look for
the various explosions.

FAR RIGHT

Effects artist Willi Geiger works
on a CG simulation for the nuke
strike sequence.

RIGHT

Multiple nuclear detonations as
seen from eight miles above the
Earth. Using NASA imagery as reference, ILM matte painters created a
painting of the planet and layered
particle simulations representing
the cloud-like shock waves emanat-
ing from the nuclear detonations.

NUCLEAR EXPLOSIONS

The mushroom cloud for the nuclear explosion was a combination of 2-D simulation and 3-D particle animation. This and other simulations on *Terminator 3* involved input from Stanford professor Ron Fedkiw, a long-time associate of ILM. Fedkiw is a leading researcher in the field of computer graphics, specializing in topics relating to physically based simulations of natural phenomena. He pioneered a way to produce multiple iterations of a complex fluid simulation fairly quickly. To create the nuclear explosions, ILM artists ran numerous 2-D simulations of fluid to find an appropriate shape which, when rotated in 3-D space, would generate a mushroom-cloud shape. The final shape was used to create a virtual 3-D container, which was filled with a velocity field, and then particles were poured into the simulated currents. To complete the effect, ILM shot a series of practical elements to create the shock wave that traveled across the ground plane. The resulting effect was seen as one of the most realistic looking nuclear explosions ever created for a feature film.

Ron Fedkiw, Stanford University professor:

"Even though the smoke we had produced for *The Mummy* was successful, it was hard to make a large-scale smoke event like a nuclear explosion. So we had to come up with new ideas for how to actually build a nuclear explosion—and this particular explosion was a very big hero shot for the movie."

ILM's digital artists were concerned that it would take a long time to paint the changing shadows and lighting conditions in the environment for the nuclear explosion. To solve this problem, an appropriate location in San Jose was identified. ILM placed a photographer there from 5:00 a.m. to 6:00 p.m. Photographs were taken every five to ten minutes to capture the moving light and shadows. The sun was used as the source of light for the bombs. ILM digital matte artist Masahiko Tani then removed the sun and painted the middle-ground, while Sebastian Moreau composited the explosions into the area where the sun had been.

FLUID SIMULATION

Shots of the endoskeletons and the T-X in her liquid-metal form were digital creations. Most shots of the T-X endoskeleton were achieved using a digital model created by ILM. Stan Winston Studio designed and built several appliances to be worn by T-X performer Kristanna Loken. The appliances were fitted to custom prosthetics built from lifecasts of the actress's arms. ILM then created scans of the physical appliances to create digital versions. Next, the team worked out mechanical arm-to-weapon transformations. In the final battle between the Terminators, animation of the digital T-X was achieved by motion-capturing Kristanna Loken. This guaranteed that the T-X performance, even in its endoskeleton form, would be recognizably Loken's.

A particularly difficult shot required ILM to dedicate nearly eight months to research and development. The skin and clothing of the liquid-metal-based T-X begins to dissolve, exposing her endoskeleton. ILM created a three-dimensional liquefaction effect, filling geometry derived from Loken's CG model with a digital representation of liquid metal, distributing evenly spaced particles over the body and assigning attributes to them such as velocity and viscosity. Ultimately, the work on *Terminator 3* resulted in an important evolution of ILM's fluid simulation system.

Ron Fedkiw:

"The idea was to do liquid Terminators with a metal skeleton inside. In the earlier films, Terminators could change shape, but it didn't seem like a fluid. There was a technique that I had developed to simulate liquids. We could do harder liquids such as metal or molten steel, and softer, less viscous things such as water. So we needed somehow to get that into the ILM pipeline so we could use it for the liquid Terminators.

"We started building software tools that would allow more people to use it. And the work on *Terminator 3* was the beginning of the system we built for ILM that earned us the Scientific and Technical Academy Award from the Academy."

The award was given in 2007 for the ILM Fluid Simulation System. In development for years, the system ultimately contributed to many films, including *The Mummy*, *The Perfect Storm* (see pages 132–139), *Pirates of the Caribbean: Dead Man's Chest* and *Pirates of the Caribbean: At World's End* (see pages 266–271), *Transformers* (see pages 272–279), and *Evan Almighty*, among others. The award was given to Nick Rasmussen, Ron Fedkiw, and Frank Losasso Petterson.

ABOVE LEFT

ILM visual effects supervisor Pablo Helman holds a chrome and gray sphere as actor Arnold Schwarzenegger stands at the ready. After photography, the sphere images provide the CG artists all the clues necessary to match the on-set lighting in the computer.

RIGHT

To create the shape-shifting T-X's endoskeleton, liquefaction was achieved by filling geometry derived from actress Kristanna Loken's CG model with a digital representation of liquid metal, distributing evenly spaced particles over the body, and assigning to them attributes such as velocity and viscosity.

Pirates of the Caribbean: The Curse of the Black Pearl

2003

Hal Hickel, animation supervisor:

"Right away, they started talking about how we were going to have skeleton pirates and how they're going to be sword fighting. I said, 'Sword fighting. Wow, are you kidding me? I finally get to do a movie with sailors fighting skeletons—it's straight out of Ray Harryhausen!'"

Director: Gore Verbinski
Producer: Jerry Bruckheimer

ILM Show Leadership:
Visual Effects Supervisor: John Knoll
Visual Effects Producer: Jill Brooks
Animation Supervisor: Hal Hickel
Visual Effects Art Director: Aaron McBride

Academy Award® Nomination: Best Visual Effects
John Knoll (ILM)
Hal Hickel (ILM)
Charles Gibson
Terry D. Frazee

BAFTA Film Award Nomination:
  Best Achievement in Special Visual Effects
John Knoll (ILM)
Hal Hickel (ILM)
Terry D. Frazee
Charles Gibson

THE MEMORABLE SKELETON SWORDFIGHT sequence in *Pirates of the Caribbean: The Curse of the Black Pearl* was reminiscent of a film that many ILMers were inspired by in their youth: *Jason and the Argonauts*. The 1963 film featured the work of visual effects pioneer Ray Harryhausen.

Hal Hickel:

"I grew up on Ray Harryhausen. Just like Ray grew up on *King Kong* and he met Willis O'Brien when he was a young man, Dennis Muren grew up on Ray's films and he met Ray as a young man. And I grew up on all of their films, and I met Dennis as a young man. I feel like there's a history or a heritage that I'm proud to be part of.

"Harryhausen's films have a certain charming innocence about them and a wonder that I think Gore tried to

imbue his pirate films with. So it felt like there was a nice continuity. If Ray had made a pirate film, it might have been like this.

"Ray achieved a lot in *Jason and the Argonauts*, but then you kind of come to your version of it, and it's got to be something new and different. And certainly all of our technology is very different now from what Ray was using, but, as a point of inspiration, his films were the ultimate. We just had to take it from there and move into our own world."

John Knoll, visual effects supervisor:

"As soon as we read about sword-fighting skeletons in the script, everybody on the crew immediately thought of *Jason and the Argonauts*. But we had to do a much more complicated version of that, because we were working

PREVIOUS SPREAD

An undead pirate crew on the *Black Pearl*

ABOVE

The HMS *Interceptor*'s stand-in was a full scale replica of the real eighteenth-century sloop. Although the script called for the destruction of the *Interceptor*, the filmmakers knew they could not damage the rented ship in any way. The ILM model shop provided the solution with a one-eighth-scale model which they could blow to pieces without consequences.

ABOVE, INSET

The *Interceptor* model meets its fate during a run-in with the ILM pyrotechnics team.

with handheld cameras, smoky environments, and a much larger number of characters. When the whole pirate crew is fighting, there are scenes with thirty characters engaged in combat, all crossing over each other, with smoke blowing through the frame.

"If you look at the *Jason and the Argonauts* skeleton fight, the skeletons are all very clean, they have no clothes on them, and they're not grungy. In the design of our skeleton pirates, Gore wanted to make sure you could still tell who was who. So if they've all got just enough skin and enough of their costume, you immediately know, 'Oh, that's that guy.' So probably one of the biggest differences is the multiple layers of clothing and all the skin."

MATCHING THE MOVES

ILM made it possible for Verbinski to direct the skeleton performances in the same way he would direct a live actor. Each scene was shot twice: a reference take with Verbinski directing actors playing the skeletons, and a clean take into which ILM would place the CG skeletons. The shots of the actors provided a performance guideline for ILM to follow. Rotoscoping, keyframing, and motion capture were also used to create the skeleton performances.

Hal Hickel:

"We'd done a number of films where the director goes out and films something where an element is missing, where we're going to add, let's say, a rampaging dinosaur. The tricky thing on *Curse of the Black Pearl* is that we had a lot of scenes of

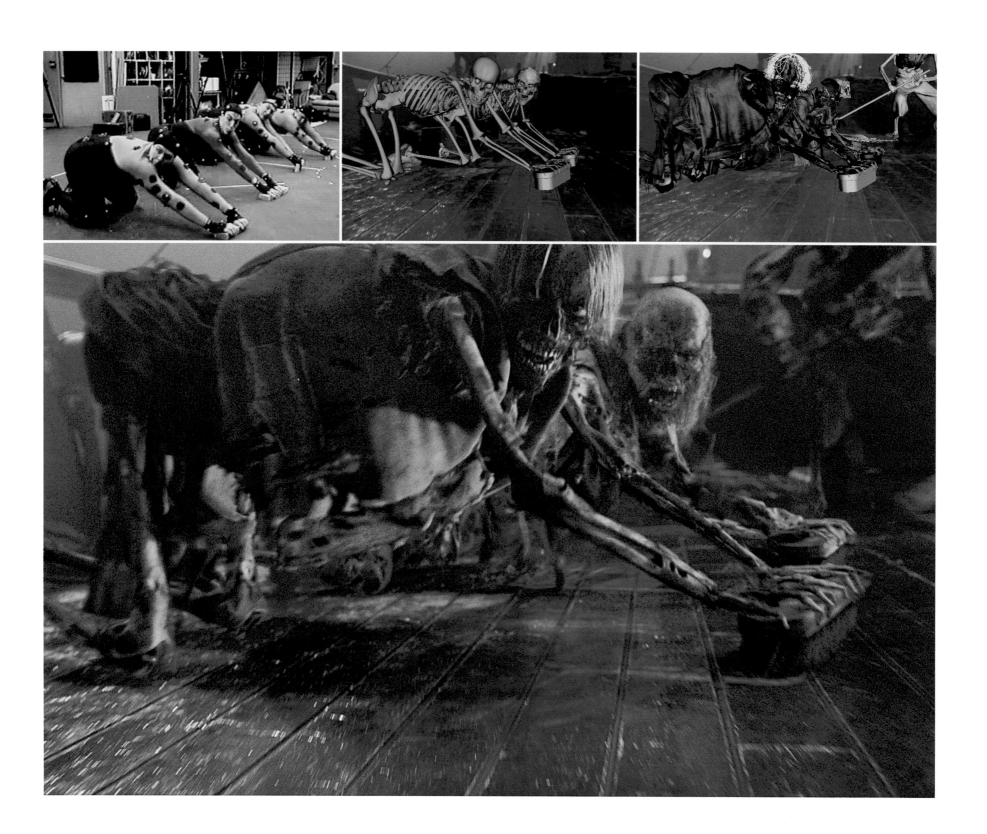

OPPOSITE

Actors were brought to ILM's motion capture stage (top left), and their performances then drove the digital animation of the specter-like pirates through the gray-shade stage (top middle) and cloth simulation stage (top right).

TOP RIGHT

A step in the transformation of live-action actor Geoffry Rush into an undead pirate: digital wire frame for match-move.

MIDDLE RIGHT

Another step included cloth and hair simulation.

BOTTOM RIGHT

The completed element of undead Captain Hector Barbossa.

essentially *humans* that were missing. They were going to be human-size skeletons, and they were often in close contact with the live actors in the scene, sword fighting with them. So the challenge was that we had to shoot the scene once with the actor sword fighting against a stunt man standing in for the skeleton. Then the stunt man steps out and they shoot the shot *again* with the actor going through the entire choreography, but against nothing. That's the 'hero' footage that goes into the movie, and we're going to add our skeleton to that. The previous take is reference for us.

"Then we go in and either animate the skeleton, or in most cases, because we wanted very naturalistic human action, we used motion capture. We'd have the stuntman on the motion capture stage watch the choreography from the original shoot and try to mimic it. Then their motion was captured and applied to the CG skeleton that's put into the footage. We had to do a lot of tweaking to get the two to match up, so when their swords clash, it really feels like there's an encounter.

"Now it wasn't a great process, because in the 'hero' footage, the actor ends up fighting against air, which doesn't look nearly as good as when he's fighting against an actual opponent, where their swords can hit against each other. There were also cases where the take with the actor fighting against air just didn't look as good as the first take with the actor and the stuntman fighting. If the director decided to use the other take, we would have to paint out the stunt man digitally and then insert our CG skeleton, which was extra work."

SUPER SIMULATION

Twenty-four skeletons have complex costumes that flap in the wind, which was a great challenge in cloth simulation. There were 139 shots of the pirates, which meant, at any given time, ILM had twenty-three people doing nothing but working on the simulation of different parts of the digital costumes. It was the biggest cloth-simulation team assembled to date. Fortunately, ILM's proprietary clothing-simulation software had been in development for several years. It had previously been used to great effect for the robes of the digital Yoda in *Star Wars*: Episode II *Attack of the Clones* combat.

John Knoll:

"We'd been doing cloth simulations in a, theoretically, physically correct manner since Episode I. Prior to that, we'd done *Mars Attacks!*, though it's not really showcased. *Curse of the Black Pearl* was probably the first film that really illustrated what our cloth-simulation tools were capable of. When we first bid the show, however, we were talking about skeletal pirates wearing some ragged clothing: 'All right, they'll be wearing some ratty pants and they'll probably

have a bandolier or something.' And we just thought it was
going to be a lot simpler. But when we started seeing the
actual wardrobe, a lot of us were shocked at how many layers there were. Some characters had as many as seven layers
that had to be simulated individually. And it was a little
alarming how complex that all was.

"The clothing the pirate characters are wearing is meant
to be torn and ratty, so all these strands are hanging down.
They're wearing a shirt and a vest and then a coat over the top
and a belt with all sorts of weapons hanging from it. So the
characters are very complex, and many of the elements that
are a part of that character really needed to be simulated—so
the film became a simulation showcase.

"But we just toughed it out and said 'Well, this guy needs
seven layers of simulation—we just gotta do it.' And I think
the process developed a lot of confidence at ILM that we
could do work like that in the future."

HANDHELD EFFECTS

ILM's approach to the visual effects work made it possible to shoot
live-action elements for battle scenes and swordfights with a handheld
camera—and still make extensive use of effects in those sequences.
In the past, it was difficult or impossible to interweave visual effects
with the free style of handheld camerawork. By the time of *Curse of the
Black Pearl*, matchmove tools had evolved to a point where it was no
longer necessary to restrict the camera movement for shots requiring
visual effects.

John Knoll:

"In the past, there were all sorts of constraints placed on
visual effects: Shots had to be locked down, you couldn't have
objects cross matte paintings—those sorts of things. And
all those constraints served to make a very artificial stylistic
barrier between the effects parts of the movie and the live-
action parts. Visual effects also had to be carefully planned in
advance. They were so carefully storyboarded, there was a sort
of deliberate, planned look to them.

LEFT
Early pirate concept art by ILM
artist Warren Fu.

"We'd been pushing to eliminate those differences, to
free up the filmmaker and treat the visual effects like they are
any other part of the movie, so you don't have to shoot with
special cameras, you don't have to lock 'em down. If you want
to do this handheld, just do it handheld—and so we went
completely free on *Curse of the Black Pearl*. For example, when
the skeletons are fighting, the sequence is meant to have a
spooky fog floating through the frame. The conventional
wisdom was that if you're going to have to put characters in
different depths through all this smoke, you'd be better off if
you just shot it clean, put the characters in, and then layered
smoke in later. But there were a lot of reasons why we didn't
want to do that. I wanted the best looking image that we
could get, and we'd figure out how to get the skeletons back
there. So we developed some pretty effective techniques for
matching smoke levels."

STEPPING INTO THE MOONLIGHT

ABOVE

This was a key shot in *Pirates*, because ILM had to "matchimate" (match-animate) its stop-motion computer to the live-action take in order to satisfy director Gore Verbinski. The time and effort it took to get this shot, of Jack Sparrow (Johnny Depp) looking at his hand, convinced ILM that for the next *Pirates* film, the facility would have to find a better way to translate live-action performances into digital animation.

Some of the most challenging shots in the film involved the pirate characters stepping into the moonlight to reveal their skeletal forms. It took a special effort to create a seamless transition from real actors to CG figures.

Hal Hickel:

"When Barbossa [Geoffrey Rush], is giving his monologue about the pirate's curse and he's walking toward Elizabeth, he steps into the moonlight and becomes a skeleton. We're in close-up, and we're starting on this awesome actor, and then we're ending on our 100 percent CG creation. And the CG creation has to still feel like Geoffrey Rush. So what we didn't want is to get to the end of the shot and have people in their mind saying, *Wow, look at that awesome CG skeleton.*

We wanted the reaction to be: *Good lord, look what they did to Geoffrey Rush!*

"The distinction there is that at the end of the shot, they should feel like, somehow or other, they're still looking at Geoffrey Rush—he's just been skeletonized. So we did a little trick on that shot. We knew that the audience would be looking right into Geoffrey's eyes as he's delivering those lines. So just after he passes into the moonlight and he becomes skeletal we preserved Geoffrey's real eyes from the footage combined with the skeleton, just for a beat; and then he does a little half-blink, and from that point on he's 100 percent CG. We just wanted to be sure that over that transition, the audience was still going to believe they were looking at Geoffrey. We just did it in that one shot, but I think it helped a lot."

The Day After Tomorrow

2004

Roland Emmerich, director:

"The wolves were the worst prima donnas I've ever worked with. It was like shooting with four Elizabeth Taylors on the set. Finally, we accepted that we'd made a mistake, and we went looking for an effects house that could do computer-generated wolves."

Director: Roland Emmerich
Producers: Roland Emmerich, Mark Gordon

ILM Show Leadership:
Visual Effects Supervisors: James Mitchell, Eric Brevig
Visual Effects Producer: Shari Hanson
Animation Supervisor: Dan Taylor
Associate Animation Supervisor: Scott Benza
Visual Effects Art Director: Alex Laurant

performances of the wolves. They were very well trained and would do just about anything we needed them to do on the motion capture stage. The dogs were able to hit marks and do several takes of the same action over and over again.

"You want those Lycra suits to sit as close to the skin as possible so that the fabric doesn't stretch while the actor is moving; otherwise, the data is somewhat flawed. German shepherds, however, have a very thick coat. But when you put these very tight suits on them, they look a fraction of their size. And since the suit doesn't entirely cover their heads, they've got this giant mane of hair coming out of the top, so they almost look like shaved poodles.

"It was also important that we have a couple of the motion capture markers attached to their heads, so we had a little bonnet made for each of the dogs."

Dynamic simulations were used to give the wolf fur lifelike movement. There were approximately seven million hairs on the wolves. This was considerably more than other hairy creatures ILM had created before. The result was a very fluffy dense look for the fur.

A newly developed blending tool was critical to achieving seamless animation: The tool allowed elements from different motion capture takes to be blended together into one smooth action to create the optimum performance.

Scott Benza:

"Having the resource of the dogs for motion capture gave us realistic results in less time than it would have taken to animate the wolves individually. Four-legged animals are very difficult to animate; it takes a bit of work to work out the order of the footsteps, how many legs are off the ground at once, and so on. When you're dealing with two legs, you just have to make sure the hips are balanced nicely above the legs to create solid animation. But when you have four legs, the hips can be in a number of different places, and it's more complicated to make the animal look convincingly real."

ILM was one of several visual effects facilities that worked on *The Day After Tomorrow*. The company's extensive experience in creating 3-D animated characters qualified ILM as the best facility to handle the wolf-creation work.

ILM executed approximately thirty character animation shots of wolves that stalk the lead characters through the hold of a wrecked ship. The all-CG approach made it possible to design wolves that looked exactly as director Emmerich envisioned them, rather than having to intercut CG wolves with live-action wolves.

Scott Benza, associate animation supervisor:

"It was one of the first times we used motion capture suits on animals. We used two trained ex–police dogs for the

ILM also generated interaction with the environment to make the illusion of the wolves' presence on set convincing. This included knocking CG items off tables, adding paw-skid marks on floors, and rattling cages.

PREVIOUS SPREAD

Once again, New York City takes a hit, this time frozen over by ILM for director Roland Emmerich. To create buildings and the Statue of Liberty encased in ice, the effects facility combined painted textures and 3-D procedural rendering techniques on 150 high-resolution LIDAR buildings. Early concepts of ice on the buildings was deemed too fantastical and distracting, with Emmerich preferring to keep things subdued.

LEFT

The movements of the dogs' ears and jaws were not included in the motion capture, and there was only one marker placed on each tail. The expressive movement of the wolf ears and tails was added by ILM animators using dynamic simulations. These simulations involved taking parts of a computer-generated character and assigning dynamic properties to individual pieces. For example, ILM artists "tell" the computer how much the individual bones inside the wolf tails weigh and how much tension there is between each of the bones. The software is then able to determine how fast the dog (wolf) is running and animates the tail, following the rules of physics. This is a starting point from which the ILM artists then adjust the animation to coordinate with the dramatic action in the scene.

In order to capture the right movement of authentic canines, an ILMer donned an attack suit used for training police dogs to record the motions of attack dogs. The information would then be used to animate the film's digital wolves.

RIGHT

In this completed shot of a partially submerged freighter, only the people are live-action elements.

Mike Conte, compositing supervisor:

"The plate we were given was just the camera dollying past an empty cage, but the director wanted the cage door to rattle and the camera to rack focus with the leaping wolf. To do that, we painted a still frame of the cage without the cage door, laid that still frame over re-created geometry of the cage, and animated the CG cage to bend and rattle as if the wolf were going crazy inside."

ILM's work on *The Day After Tomorrow* also included producing shots of Manhattan shrouded in ice. Baking soda and talcum powder were used to create wide expanses of snow-covered ground. Photographs of the setup were used either as reference or as texture maps applied to the CG terrain. Subsurface scattering techniques gave the icy cityscape a translucent, photoreal look.

Paul Huston, digital matte artist:

"They were having a hard time getting the buildings of New York to look photorealistic. So I took some building models and made a small miniature. I covered the buildings with baking soda and mounded it around the base of the buildings. Gravity makes the fine granules of baking soda settle around an object in the same way as snow. I photographed that and used it as a guide for digital matte painting and also as a photo element in a shot of New York City. It's so much easier using these common materials."

For scenes of ice-clad Manhattan, painted textures were combined with 3-D procedural rendering techniques on high-resolution buildings in the mid- and foregrounds, and on low-resolution structures in the backgrounds. Maintaining scale in the all-white buildings, which didn't have the typical scale-enhancing textures such as rust, watermarks, and stonework anomalies, was a challenge for ILM's ice-city shots.

ILM's proprietary crowd pipeline generated all of the survivors in the frozen city sequence at the end of the film. The composite consisted of more than three hundred layers, including simulated crowds, foreground high-resolution geometry, painted textures on background low-resolution geometry, dust elements shot on stage, and a real photographic sky.

Observations

AS A VISUAL EFFECTS SUPERVISOR, my ultimate goal is to maximize the reaction each shot gets from the audience. There are five broad elements that I consider:

1) **Purpose:** What does the Director see as the purpose of the shot in the context of the story and why?

2) **Timing:** How does the shot unfold and how does that fit into the sequence of surrounding shots?

3) **Composition:** Basic rules and theories of frame composition and how these affect the audience.

4) **Plussing:** Finding ways to give the shot even more than the audience expects.

5) **Reality:** Making sure that all of the elements in the shot look like they really belong in the frame and that the shot as a whole looks real.

In this essay I would like to focus on this last point. Creating the illusion of reality is much more complex than you might think. I learned a long time ago that if I recalled a visual image from memory, I would be wrong most of the time. Memories are simplifications of what really happened in life. If I had to model, texture, paint, and light an X-wing from memory, the result would probably not look very real. But they would probably be hard pressed to say what was wrong, just as I would be. Maybe I would have forgotten to add dirt and scrapes, or maybe the surface would be too shiny. Short of having a real X-wing in front

ABOVE

George Lucas (with bullhorn), director Richard Marquand, and visual effects supervisor Dennis Muren on the set of *Star Wars*: Episode VI *Return of the Jedi*.

of me, I really need a good reference to pull from. From this example you can begin to see how achieving a realistic-looking, complex shot of a 30-foot-tall ninja like Optimus Prime kicking some serious butt would be incredibly difficult.

The fact is that the visual effects we create with our tools—the Death Star, Davy Jones, the battle on Pandora—must follow specific rules of nature and physics. As effects practitioners, we need to seek out references—actual places and living creatures—that are similar to our fantasy scenes, and then incorporate the same principles seen in this reference into the shot. In my work I even like to take it a step further. Reference footage and photos are helpful, but you can learn even more by physically going to a similar space or actually touching a similar animal. By experiencing your references first hand you are better able to incorporate the true essence of that place or object.

The best way to understand reality is to become a perpetual student of nature. Nature is the master teacher. It is important to look deeply at the world around you and learn to develop an understanding of why things look and move the way they do. Be curious, take a walk, stop, look around and observe the details of your surroundings. You will soon begin to understand that there are certain universal truths that give our world its unique visual characteristics. Look for those commonalities, because they are the building blocks of our reality.

Sometimes one detail is all that's needed to turn a good shot into a great one. For example, in *Jurassic Park* there is a shot of the T. rex taking a step onto a muddy road outside the failed containment fence. As the foot hits the mud, we added a splash that really helps sell the shot. Because if this scene had played out in reality, the laws of physics would have dictated that the foot would displace mud on that rain-soaked ground. Without even seeing a mud puddle prior to the step the audience buys the splash and it really adds to the emotional impact of that shot.

Words like "hopeful," "intimidating," "suspenseful," "awkward," and "caring" are seldom used to describe a visual effects shot. Yet they represent descriptions of the feelings a shot needs to impart on an audience. To design a shot with impact you must learn to "feel" your work as if you were an audience member, yet maintain the ability to be a technician and critique the technical issues of your work.

Children observe their surroundings with curiosity and excitement, giving their fresh eyes the ability to always see something new, whereas adults tend to see only what they know and expect. Try to recover the ways you took in the world as a child. With this you'll find all the details needed to make your shots trigger the reactions you are looking for from the audience.

Dennis Muren, ASC

Harry Potter and the Prisoner of Azkaban

2004

Roger Guyett, visual effects supervisor:

> "The goal was to downplay the fantastical aspect of the story and, instead, make the visual effects and creatures as organic to their environment as possible. To achieve this, the film utilizes a look that is much darker and has more contrast than that of the previous *Potter* films."

Director: Alfonso Cuarón
Producers: Chris Columbus, David Heyman, Mark Radcliffe,
**   Lorne Orleans (IMAX version)**

ILM Show Leadership:
Visual Effects Supervisors: Roger Guyett, Bill George
Visual Effects Producer: Sandra Scott
Animation Supervisor: David Andrews

Academy Award® Nomination: Best Visual Effects
Tim Burke
Roger Guyett (ILM)
Bill George (ILM)
John Richardson

BAFTA Film Award Nomination:
**   Best Achievement in Special Visual Effects**
John Richardson
Roger Guyett (ILM)
Tim Burke
Bill George (ILM)
Karl Mooney

FOR *HARRY POTTER and the Prisoner of Azkaban*, the visual effects and animation work for almost a thousand shots was divided between eight different companies. ILM was responsible for 183 shots.

WILD BEASTS

The most complex CG characters ILM created for *Prisoner of Azkaban* were the Dementors. The Dementors are dark, decaying CG creatures made up of layers of rotting cloth, oozing debris, and decay. The main production unit in London created a practical one-third-scale puppet of a Dementor that was shot slow motion in a water tank. ILM subsequently processed the footage, reversing some of the elements, to give an elegant and ominous slow-motion feel to the horror.

Bill George, visual effects supervisor:

"Although production was very happy with the look of the footage, they realized that shooting blue-screen elements underwater that matched the live-action plates was very problematic. Our duty was to re-create the look of the graceful and organic underwater footage using computer graphics."

ILM's challenge was made greater by the fact that some shots included more than one hundred Dementors.

Bill George:

"One of our first challenges was how to telegraph to the audience the evil and dangerous character of the Dementors, even though they've got no faces for expression. The only

PREVIOUS SPREAD

Dementors, realized in computer graphics, fly toward Hogwarts School of Witchcraft and Wizardry.

ABOVE

Professor Remus Lupin (David Thewlis) the school's new Defense Against the Dark Arts teacher, protects the vulnerable Potter (Daniel Radcliffe) from a much-feared Dementor. Lupin agrees to teach Potter the Patronus Charm, enabling Potter to shield himself from the Dementors.

RIGHT
To create the motion for the Dementors, ILM's animators key-framed skeletons, which were then mapped with computer simulations providing the motion of the tattered, flowing cloth. To add a layer of complexity, dynamic forces such as wind and gravity were added in addition to hand-animated cloth tendrils. A CG approach was pursued by ILM when tests with a practical puppet—which production had created—produced motion that was too unwieldy to control. To guide the CG work, director Cuarón selected key moments from the puppetry tests that he felt conveyed the Dementor's essential character.

way to express their characters was through body posture— and fabric movement. It was therefore up to our cloth-simulation artists to convey the character of the Dementors. We have cloth-simulation software that calculates how the fabric behaves if there's wind and the creature is moving in a particular direction. But we had to take it to another level, because we wanted the cloth to do things that weren't realistic. For example, the cloth never came down and rested; it was always in a state of movement, which was counterintuitive. But because we were creating this in the computer, we could do wild and wacky things like change the direction of the wind."

For this film, the cloth had to perform. ILM used its cloth-simulation software in a particularly creative way, turning off gravity or running simulations backward. In a realistic approach, as the Dementor moved forward, all of the cloth would trail off the back of the figure. But now cloth tendrils led the way, almost as if they were searching. ILM called these cloth elements "tentacles," because they would do things like look around the corner. The cloth elements became characters.

NEW QUIDDITCH

Roger Guyett:

"The Quidditch game for *Prisoner of Azkaban* differs from the game in previous *Potter* films in that it takes place during a rainstorm. Other than the blue-screen elements of Harry on his broom and a few shots of the spectators in the stands, the entire sequence, including the stormy environment, was created within the computer. Shooting plates for these complex camera moves would have been impossible.

"Rather than generating 3-D environments using CG clouds, all of the backgrounds for the Quidditch game were created in 2-D by ILM's matte painting department. The paintings were projected onto CG cards, with 3-D camera moves plotted through the cards. Foreground elements were generated in 3-D."

Bill George:

"The way I looked at the Quidditch game was not: 'How would this be done realistically?' My attitude was, 'Let's say

ANOTHER ROAD TO ILM, OR "SO, HOW DID I GET HERE?"

**Bill George,
visual effects supervisor:**

"When I was a kid, I was very much into *Star Trek* and *Lost in Space*, and I built the models from the kits that were available. I kind of outgrew that by the time I was an early teen. Then, when I was nineteen, *Star Wars* came out—and it just totally blew me away, and it kind of brought back all of these passions that I had for science fiction.

"I'm the type of person that it's not enough for me just to love something, I have to manifest that love, and the way that I manifested my love for *Star Wars* was that I started making models again. Now as you know, merchandising came out much later, because they had no idea that it was going to be such a hit. So here I am, wanting to build the models, but there are no model kits available. So I had to start building things from scratch. Well, if you're going to build the things, you need to be able to know what they look like, so I started research-ing, getting magazines, and ultimately going to science-fiction conventions to get those magazines—and those magazines are how I discovered that the visual effects were done by this up-start company called Industrial Light & Magic, and that George had started the company for *Star Wars* because there wasn't an effects facility that could do what he wanted to do.

"I saw the photos behind the scenes, and it totally struck a chord with me. It was like, 'Oh my gosh, this is what I want to do.' I eventually started displaying my models at science-fiction conventions, and through that met a fellow who built models in Hollywood. He offered me a job in 1979, but of course my goal was to work at ILM. And a friend of mine, this girl that I met at one of the conventions, knew where ILM was, so when we would visit L.A. to go to the science fiction conventions, late at night we would drive out to Valjean Avenue where ILM was, and we'd go through the trash cans. I got some *amazing* stuff out of ILM trash cans. That's how it starts: You start in the trash can.

"In 1981, ILM called my boss, and they said, 'We're ex-panding, we're going to be working on three movies, and we need people—is there anyone you would recommend?' And my boss recommended me. Being a huge fan of the *Star Wars* films, when I got my job at ILM, I was so excited. I couldn't wait to go to work in the morning. If they'd set up a cot, I probably would have slept there.

"But I remember a couple of weeks after starting, they had, at the time, what they called model vaults in the building; they were basically just big closets where they kept the *Star Wars* models. I knew about them, but I was also a new em-ployee, and I didn't think that it was okay for me just to go in there. Well, I found out that Lorne Peterson, my supervisor, had the key to the model vault, and it came up in conversation. He said, 'If you ever need to go in there, the key's right here.' So that night, they're like, 'What's going on, Bill? Why aren't you going home?' I said, 'Oh, I have some stuff to do late tonight.' So I waited until everyone left, and I got the key, and I went into the model vault—and I must have spent an hour just star-ing at the X-wing and the big *Millennium Falcon*. They felt like holy relics to me. I was so in awe of these things. A total geek moment. There are a lot of *Star Wars* nerds at ILM, but at the company, we have a kind of 'don't ask, don't tell' policy. You kind of keep it to yourself that you're a total *Star Wars* geek."

kids could really fly on brooms, and we went and shot this.' You'd be shooting in the morning; you'd be shooting in the afternoon; some days would be cloudy; some days would be sunny. But the editor would put it all together and it would work. So it wouldn't be completely consistent. I see other projects where they make sure that the clouds always match and the lighting always matches; that's real reality. Then there's film reality. My idea for Quidditch was, 'Let's do it film reality.' And what was great was they shot the practical ele-ments of Daniel Radcliffe on the broom in exactly that way. It was over a number of weeks, so his hair would change slightly and the lighting would change slightly, so that helped us.

"When it came to the matte paintings, rather than having a cyclorama that was just a really big, beautiful matte painting that you could use for different camera angles, we used a different matte painting for every shot. And they were inconsistent. I purposely made sure that the lighting matched Daniel, but it was different from shot to shot.... And I think that made it look a lot more realistic for the film reality."

"For all the wide shots of Harry and other Quidditch players, we used digital doubles. Although the live-action elements had random cape movements, it didn't follow the action of the players. Our CG cloth-simulation capes moved and flapped based on the action of the animation and were much more dynamic and believable. One particularly difficult shot has Harry falling off his broom after he loses consciousness from the soul-suck effect. As the camera follows him, he tumbles, getting tangled and tied in his cape."

Lemony Snicket's
A Series of
Unfortunate Events

2004

Steve Sullivan, research and development:

"It was the first time we had created a close-up of a completely CG human in a feature film (well before *Benjamin Button* and other movies that used it more extensively). Most people didn't notice it. Only when you point it out to them later do they realize, 'Oh, that's a computer-generated baby doing these actions!'"

Director: Brad Silberling
Producers: Laura MacDonald, Walter F. Parkes, Jim Van Wyck

ILM Show Leadership:
Visual Effects Supervisor: Stefen Fangmeier
Visual Effects Producer: Jeff Olson
Animation Supervisor: Colin Brady
Visual Effects Art Director: Wilson Tang

SUNNY SIDE UP

THE GREATEST CHALLENGE in ILM's work on *Lemony Snicket's A Series of Unfortunate Events* was the creation of an entirely digital, photoreal, eighteen-month-old girl. The script required the baby to perform behaviors that no child actor could manage. For these scenes, the only option was to create the character as CG. The baby, Sunny, is featured throughout the film, and is seen at times in full-screen close-ups.

Moreover, ILM's digital baby required a precise correlation to reality, given that the CG shots would be directly intercut with scenes of a live-action baby filmed on set.

Steve Sullivan:

"The modeling techniques we had at the time weren't good enough to give us a matching baby. We had to invent a technique to capture the shape of the baby being used in the live-action parts, so the CG double would match. For a while in the industry, laser scanning was a common technique: You would put somebody in a chamber, the laser would revolve

PREVIOUS SPREAD

To create a believable digital version of the eighteen-month-old Sunny, ILM developed an image-based technology, CloneCam, to solve the problem of how to capture texture and generate corresponding geometry simultaneously.

ABOVE

A fairy tale–like house was constructed at ILM (inset: final frame).

that are connected together. I can attach that little soup of pyramids to the baby's animation and then, as she moves, those pyramids push on each other and squish each other. It's a great technology for simulating what happens when flesh gets squeezed or folds. It can give you a feel that there's actual flesh in a CG creature. At the heart, these things have a lot of math going on under the hood, and it's a constant battle to make them look organic."

The creation of Sunny also involved one of the most important early uses of a technique called subsurface scattering.

Steve Sullivan:

"Subsurface scattering was a technique that had come out of academia for modeling how light transmits through semi-opaque objects like skin. Light penetrates the skin and *then* it diffuses in different directions and changes color; that's what gives people their warm glow, makes them look alive. So we needed to use that rendering technique, or baby Sunny wouldn't look real. The role that our people played, especially Christophe, was to take that academic research and make it really *work*. That's what we always have to do: take the idea and figure out how to make it work in practice."

ILM first developed the production methodology for its use on the second *Harry Potter* film, where it was used on Dobby the mischievous house elf. (Hery would win a Scientific and Technical Award for his work from the Academy, along with Ken McGaugh and Joe Letteri, in 2003.)

around them, and it would give you a very dense 3-D mesh. We couldn't use this technique on *Lemony Snicket*, because babies don't stand still long enough for the laser to scan them, so we pushed forward our image-based techniques."

The needs of *Lemony Snicket* forced an important new development in image-based modeling technology at ILM. The technology, which became known as CloneCam, involves taking multiple, simultaneous photographs of an actor and using these images to construct a 3-D model, based on the computer matching up the images. (Developed for *Lemony Snicket*, CloneCam continued to evolve and later played a significant role in the creation of imagery for *Pirates of the Caribbean: Dead Man's Chest*. In 2006, ILM won a Scientific and Technical Academy Award for this image-based modeling technology.)

Jason Smith, creature development artist:

"We also did motion capture for the baby. Sunny wears a dress, so we had to set up her clothes for simulation. There's one scene where the CG Sunny hangs on the side of a table by her teeth. As she hangs there, swinging back and forth, all of the material for her dress is simulated.

"We also did flesh simulations. Because babies have such a soft cheek and neck area, as Sunny moved her head around, we were always looking for ways to get some of that really soft squish that you expect to see when a baby turns its head.

"We did the flesh simulation using the software Caricature. Caricature allowed us to select a portion of the model, like the neck and the cheeks, and generate a volume around the area that we filled in with tiny springy pyramids

ENVIRONMENTS

Two-dimensional and 3-D environments were the bulk of ILM's work on *Lemony Snicket*. More than twenty-six environments were a combination of computer-generated and mapped elements that included cliffs, oceans, cityscapes, rolling hills, cornfields, swamps, foggy beaches, raging storms—and unfortunate houses. Some of these were augmented with incredibly detailed miniatures.

For the home of Aunt Josephine, ILM extended the sets and painted backings for wide views, using miniatures as the basis for the

synthetic house and cliff. The library, which breaks away during a hurricane, was created entirely in CG. A miniature cliff-face set was used in the hurricane sequence. Long-time ILM veteran Lorne Peterson (known by ILMers as "the Machete King") carved the cliff face.

Lorne Peterson, model maker and miniature maker:

"We're talking about a big block of foam that's fifteen feet wide and ten feet tall and five feet deep, so I bring over the tools, the machetes, the knives, and I start carving this big block of foam. And Steve Gawley comes over and says, 'We've got to do this really fast, by Friday!' We would have worked on a rock that size for three weeks on *Attack of the Clones*. So I told Steve to send out an assistant to buy three chain saws. We were no longer going to make this thing with knives and machetes. Ultimately, it was just me and another guy who, in his youth, had been a logger in Northern California—so he was very familiar with chain saws."

The finished model was laser-scanned and duplicated in the computer to create 3-D models of surrounding cliffs on the lake. All of this al-

lowed director Silberling freedom in moving his camera through the environment. Still photographs of the model provided textures for the CG terrain.

ILM constructed a one-eighth-scale miniature for Count Olaf's house. Every feature of the replica was precisely scaled to the full-size set. The ILM team nicknamed the miniature the "Home Depot" house, because it had every building material imaginable in it—shingles, slate, copper, and brick, all beautifully weathered and covered with vines. Typical of the attention to detail ILM artists put into their work, there's even a scale bird's nest tucked into one of the eaves, complete with tiny bird's eggs.

Due to insufficient vertical space, the live-action set for Olaf's house could be built only up to a height of thirty-five feet. The uppermost forty-five feet of the house were created and tracked into the live action by ILM.

Views of the Baudelaire Mansion were realized with a combination of live-action footage shot on a full-size street set, location photography, and matte paintings derived from a miniature.

ABOVE

Count Olaf's dilapidated house as fabricated by the ILM Model Shop. The miniature measured roughly nine foot square and nine foot tall.

ABOVE, INSET

Model Shop Supervisor Steve Gawley applies final set dressing to the miniature prior to shooting. Constructed to match a partial set piece erected on a sound stage at Paramount, ILM's Model Shop built a highly detailed one-eighth-scale miniature of the fairy tale–like house out of redwood. Photos of the model were later mapped onto CG geometry for scenes where a digital version was preferable.

Paul Huston, digital matte artist:

"There was a set shot as live-action footage that had the front door of the destroyed house and the street with fire trucks in it. The production picked a mansion in Boston, and I went there and photographed it. Those photographs formed the basis for the main part of the background. I was just about finished putting all of the stills together when the director said that he wanted another fire truck. I searched on the Internet and found that for not very much, I think it was thirty dollars, I could get a high-quality die-cast model with a really nice paint job and lots of details. If you had to build a miniature like that, you're talking thousands of dollars. I built a little set for it to sit on, so I could get the street and texture, too, and photographed it and put it in front of the matte painting.

"I also designed a rough version of what the destroyed mansion would look like, and Steve Manchuk built a miniature. I took that miniature into the Model Shop and got a bunch of broken pieces of wood and sprues from model kits and various other pieces of trash and painted them gray-and-black and just tossed them all over the miniature, to make it look like a collapsed, burned interior. It was a lot easier and more effective than doing it in CG. I could very quickly come up with something that looked wrecked."

ILM created more than five hundred visual effects shots for *Lemony Snicket*. Overall, the film's dark and subtle tone was sustained in the effects, many of which were virtually invisible to the audience. While ILM's work on *Lemony Snicket* inspired a number of significant technological innovations, the project also recalls a more classic type of effects film, in which the effects don't call attention to themselves, but are there only to further the story.

ANOTHER ROAD TO ILM, OR "SO, HOW DID I GET HERE?"

Jason Smith, creature supervisor:

"When I was a little kid, life was all about *Star Wars*. I was watching not only *Star Wars*, but all of the Harryhausen creature movies. When other little kids were drawing stick figures, I was drawing Frankenstein and Dracula.

"As I got older, I found out about ILM and read everything I could get my hands on, including the two previous coffee-table books. I decided pretty early on that that was what I really wanted to do, but I ruled it out as kind of a pipe dream, so I was studying to be a doctor. At the same time, I was taking classes in sculpture and makeup, and I was making monsters. Then I would take computer-animation classes.

"Around that time I decided, *I'm going to try for this. But I better get my master's degree so I can really wow them.* But my wife convinced me just to apply. If they don't want you, they'll forget about you in two years by the time you come back with a master's degree. So I applied to be a tape IO assistant, which is somebody who comes in every day and backs up data and restores data and brings data online for productions and sends out film data over to the film printing companies. It's pretty low-level, but a great learning position. I applied, and I actually got the job.

"So I happily came down to ILM and spent a year on night shift, programming backup systems for the company. A year and a half later, I was a creature ATD, and started to do flesh simulations, so it was really kind of a dream come true for me to be working on creatures for movies. And at the time I was working on Mr. Hyde for *Van Helsing*, which was such a fun creature to work on, he had flesh simulations and beautiful facial animation. My very next show was *Star Wars*: Episode III. So the movie that got me started, the movie that really inspired me? I ended up working on that series, which was really fun for me."

Star Wars: Episode III
Revenge of the Sith

2005

George Lucas, director:

"Episode III has more technological breakthroughs, more major visual effects pioneering and accomplishment than any film had to date. Everything that's in *Avatar* was actually done in *Revenge of the Sith*. Be it sets, be it flying, be it realistic creatures, all of that technology, everything we did in Episode I and Episode II actually culminated in Episode III."

Director: George Lucas
Producer: Rick McCallum

ILM Show Leadership:
Visual Effects Supervisors: John Knoll, Roger Guyett, Pablo Helman
Visual Effects Producers: Janet Lewin, Jill Brooks
Animation Director: Rob Coleman
Visual Effects Art Directors: Aaron McBride, Alex Jaeger

As with Episode II, many live-action elements for Episode III were filmed in high definition against blue screen on minimal sets. ILM's major contribution to the film was nothing less that the creation 375 computer-generated models and hundreds of 3-D and 2-D environments. Forty-seven practical miniature setups were constructed and shot, several dozen major digital characters were created, and nearly 12,000,000 renders and composites were executed. Overall, ILM produced 2,151 effects shots and ninety minutes of animation for the film.

Because Lucas both established ILM and remained a major force in the development of the company over the decades, the director has always had a clear understanding of how to maximize the potential of ILM's capabilities.

Roger Guyett, visual effects supervisor:

"I think the three *Star Wars* Prequels achieved far more than people ever gave that series of films credit for. But from ILM's perspective, each one of those movies really achieved

PREVIOUS SPREAD
The opening battle over Coruscant

ABOVE
One of the Utapau miniatures is worked on by model maker Grant Imahara.

Next to ILM's C Theater was its big
stage, on which was constructed a
massive miniature for the volcano
planet Mustafar; the whole landscape was built at an angle so that
its "lava" (dyed methylcyl, usually
used as a thickening agent in milk
shakes) would flow downhill (below,
final frame).

some really big milestones. We were creating completely 3-D environments. To me, those movies really began to blur the line between just doing a 2-D matte painting, a flat image, and building entire 3-D environments. That's where digital environment work really came into its own.

"If you go back to the good old days, if you wanted to see a castle on a hill and you couldn't afford to do that, then you would shoot a shot of the hill, paint an image of the castle, and then superimpose one image over the other—then you'd have your castle on a hill. And it was down to the level of artistry on the matte painter's part. But because the image was painted on a flat surface, you couldn't move the camera, so most of those shots were locked off. Then, suddenly, in these *Star Wars* movies, there were tons of environments; you were seeing all of these fantastic places like Coruscant and Mustafar and really getting to move around them. These immensely complicated places were now being done digitally."

ANOTHER ROAD TO ILM, OR "SO, HOW DID I GET HERE?"

Richard Bluff, digital matte supervisor:

"When I was a child growing up in England, I was asked one Christmas what I wanted. I think I was about eight at the time—and all I wanted was the ILM book by Tom Smith, *The Art of Visual Effects.* I read that book from cover to cover, and I would memorize all the different pictures, hoping that I would work for ILM one day, never, ever imagining that I would get there or even knowing *how* I would get there.

"And I remember one of my favorite movies was *Return of the Jedi,* and I really liked the back of the book, because it would show the old posters and the old PR and marketing materials. But also it had the crew photo that was taken in Northern California, which doubled for Endor, where they were shooting the speeder bike sequence. And in there, well, of course I looked for George Lucas, and standing beside George Lucas was a gentleman that had a baby in his arms, which I thought was slightly odd. I didn't really give it much thought, but I still have the book today—it's actually still on my shelf right in front of me.

"Fast forward many years. I arrive at ILM, and one of the first projects I work on was *Star Wars* Episode III, so I felt like my life had come full circle at that point. I'd finally got to ILM to work on a *Star Wars* movie. One of the production assistants that I was working with was a girl called Katherine Farrar. Her father is Scott Farrar, who of course is a visual effects supervisor at ILM. And as I was talking to her, she told me who her dad was, that it's not exactly the first *Star Wars* movie she's worked on because, in effect, she was photographed for *Return of the Jedi,* she was the baby in the photograph . . . and she's now my wife. And she still works at ILM today."

For its work on Episode III, ILM revised its traditional pipeline by creating a Digital Environments Group, which merged the virtual set work that, in the past, had been divided between the company's CG and digital matte teams. The matte department became *part* of the CG department. This organizational shift was motivated by a promise Lucas had made, well before work officially began, that the project would require a much greater effort in terms of synthetic environments than the previous two *Star Wars* films. Lucas wanted to push what was possible with the creation of digital environments.

Paul Huston, digital matte artist:

"If you have an environment that's in a sequence, you can sort of amortize its cost across the number of shots in the sequence. But if you have multiple, really elaborate environments, using only one or two shots for each environment, it becomes a big undertaking—and that's what we did for Episode III.

"So that was really a turning point for the digital matte department. Up to that point, we had been a small group. We had idiosyncratic software, and we were on Macs, while everyone else was on SGI. Because we weren't working with industry-standard software or machines, it was really hard to find five more artists to hire so we could do more shots. So we switched over to Windows and to 3-D Studio Max software. There's a huge pool of really great artists who are available with those tools, so suddenly we could hire more people. We searched far and wide for really high-quality talent and doubled the size of the department."

The key to meeting the challenge of producing such extensive environments was a new module inside of ILM's Zeno software, called Zenviro, an enhanced version of a project technique ILM had been using for more than ten years. After Episode II, John Knoll spoke to ILM's R & D team about the development of a new projection tool for 3-D. The resultant Zenviro system used photographs of live-action sets, taken from many angles, to create 3-D environments. Zenviro's improvement over previous 3-D photomodeling was that it made dramatic camera movement possible using a layered texture approach. Textures could be derived from photographs of live-action sets as well as miniatures. The approach was extremely efficient and provided Lucas with great freedom in changing camera moves or shot composition as the project

ABOVE

A star cruiser is blown to pieces during the Battle of Coruscant.

evolved organically during editing. The desire had always been to have a virtual camera in a miniature set, and this is what Zenviro made possible.

John Knoll, visual effects supervisor:

"Back in the early nineties, we started transitioning matte paintings from flat and two-dimensional to three-dimensional. We did more and more of that, until that became how everything was done in the matte department. But we weren't doing a whole lot of that kind of camera-projection technique over in the computer graphics department—not because we didn't have the capability of doing it, but because it was a pain in the ass to do. I asserted that if we made it a lot easier for people to do camera projections in CG, we would do it a lot more. So we developed this very easy camera-projection technique called Zenviro, which was meant to support doing environmental projection work. And we made really extensive use of that on Episode III.

"I think three sections of the corridors in General Grievous's ship had been built full size for the live-action shoot, so that's a perfect case where what we see extended off in the distance really should be more copies of what had been built full scale."

STRIKING A BALANCE

As with all visual effects work in the digital age, decisions are constantly being made whether to shoot a particular element of a shot practically (that is, on a set or on location) or to create that element in the computer.

Roger Guyett:

"CG started years ago with the concept of doing very geometric, hard-surface solid objects. On the other end of the spectrum, you had all of these very complicated naturalistic and organic events, like liquids and tornadoes and dust, and all of these things have really complicated behaviors. Now, we're at the point where you could argue that a large number of those things are possible to re-create inside the computer. You use your own experience to adopt a technique that gives you creative flexibility, but to a certain extent, the decisions are driven by price. Generally, you don't have enough money. And that's nothing new. I've never worked on a movie where they turn around to you and say you need to spend some more money."

More than three hundred visual effects shots were created for the Mustafar sequences. A series of carved foam rock-formation sets were

ANOTHER ROAD TO ILM, OR "SO, HOW DID I GET HERE?"

Craig Hammack, visual effects supervisor:

"I come from a school that became well known for turning out technical directors and digital artists. But I went to that school to learn architecture. Then, as I got through the program, I didn't really want to spend eight years drafting or twelve years as an apprentice before I was able to do my own work.

"So I started looking for other avenues to explore. It just so happened that at our school, Texas A&M, there was a program called visualization sciences where they were doing computer animation, so I applied and was lucky enough to get accepted. At that time, there were probably seven other people in the program who were about to leave to go to major facilities like ILM, and that was the first wave of people out of that program to go off into the industry. The ones that got hired at ILM specifically became very well known and well respected.

"Then ILM started making recruiting trips back to the school, so I was lucky enough to talk someone into letting me have an interview slot. I applied for an internship with ILM, for what I assumed was working for free over the summer just to get experience and was promptly turned down for it. Then, a few months later, I received a call and was offered a job to come work full-time.

"So after a year in the program at Texas A&M, I left to come out to California. I didn't know what to expect, but when I got to ILM, it was their old facility, which wasn't the most impressive place in the world, visually. It was kind of hidden away in this canal district of San Rafael, in a complete kind of hodgepodge of buildings and trailers that were set up. But I was awestruck by the people and the work that was being done there.

"I started on *Speed 2* and went to a meeting where they said they had this water work to do, and no one wanted to volunteer to do it. I volunteered. And I thought, *Is this how it works? Are they going to trust someone right out of school to set up development on this major motion picture?* But that's how it worked, which was a bit of a shock. It was more casual than I expected. And somewhat trusting, because I was very much an unknown, green person and wouldn't have expected that kind of responsibility right out of the gate."

created. The riverbeds had translucent surfaces and were lit from below to create a fiery glow. The Mustafar miniature shoot took more than eight months—the longest miniature shoot in the history of ILM. Once the practical elements had been created, the ILM team developed substantial simulations to depict the "behavior" of the lava as it swirled around and poured over edges during the film's climactic duel between Anakin Skywalker and Obi-Wan Kenobi.

Roger Guyett:

"Mustafar was an incredibly complicated sequence. We were on that Mustafar set for more than a hundred days or something crazy like that, because there were so many shots that we needed to do. But it was at the point where to shoot something practical—for example, the lava, which is a very organic thing—it still made sense to create that as a practical effect, as opposed to creating it in a computer. In the end, 75 percent of Mustafar was a practical miniature, and 25 percent was digital."

As recounted in Lorne Peterson's *Sculpting a Galaxy*, production mandated that ILM devise an economically sound way to recycle the methocel (the thickening agent for the lava). An elaborate collection box, filtration, and pumping system filtered more than 15,000 gallons of methocel, pumping the goopy liquid back to the head of the flow. The lava footage was then intermixed with practical photography of lava explosions erupting from Mount Etna in Italy, which, in turn, was supplemented by footage of methocel blasts captured outdoors at ILM.

The main miniature built for Mustafar was the "river set," a confluence of three major molten lava flows that cut through the heat-blasted environment. The model environment was twenty feet wide by thirty-six feet long. The entire set was carved out of high-density urethane foam, hacked

away with sharp machetes and finer tools. Model-makers then sealed the foam, closing all the pores and leaving a tough skin over the entire model that enabled them to walk on the foam and maneuver around on the set.

The whole rear of the set was lifted with chain hoists to a grade of ten degrees, to enable gravity to pull the practical lava along the sculpted riverbeds.

Roger Guyett:

"It was an absolutely miserable set, because it was filled with smoke and atmosphere, and there were so many lights that it was boiling hot. Pat Sweeny was the visual effects DP, and every day he was sweating away in his shorts. It was kind of like being there on Mustafar."

BEST ACTOR: YODA

The Yoda in Episode III was even more lifelike than the character's CG incarnation in Episode II. Continuing evolution of the technology used for character animation made it possible to craft the character's physical performance more finely and to create added naturalism. Animators im-

proved Yoda's facial animation by creating eight new key expressions that could be accessed using ILM's proprietary animation software, Caricature.

Rob Coleman, animation director:

"Although I think we did pretty well on Episode II, on Episode III we really were able to delve into the acting part of it. On Episode III, I never had to worry about the clothing. It was more about Yoda connecting with the actors on a personal level. When we had scenes with Ewan and Yoda in the temple, I felt that there was a real connection between them, especially after they've realized what's gone horribly wrong with Anakin. That, to me, is some of the best acting that we've done with CG characters.

"The fundamentals of animation and how you set a scene up have been around since the golden days of Disney; there's nothing our animation team did that's different from what they pioneered on *Snow White*. We're trying to get into the characters' heads and make them move in a realistic and believable way.

"But what we're doing can be difficult, because we're blending it with real people."

GET GRIEVOUS!

General Grievous was a big bad guy for Episode III, and another fully digital, landmark character for ILM.

Rob Coleman:

"Grievous was a challenge in a number of different ways. One, he has no mouth, and he has no eyebrows—so we had none of the traditional building blocks that convey facial expressions and emotions to rely on. Grievous had to act with his body.

"The second challenge was that all of Grievous's coughing really only became part of the character in the last three months of our work. So, even though we had been developing Grievous for the previous *two years*, this aspect, which is a pretty significant part of his personality and also his physicality, because he's always hunched over and coughing, really came in pretty late in the game."

Grievous's newfound "ill health" meant that some of the already completed animation work had to be redone.

Rob Coleman:

"I remember George had this horrible cough. He was fighting a cold for the winter, and that's how Grievous ended up with the cough, because George said, 'Well, you should have this extra tick in his personality.' And the reason I remember this is that in the first shot of Grievous coming in through the door of the bridge, he originally didn't have a cough; we had rendered it, we'd finaled it, George was great with it, but then he came back and said, 'We've got new dialogue, and he's got a cough now.' I remember saying, 'Well, I want to reanimate it, because if he's got a cough, then he would move differently.' And he said 'No, no, it's fine, don't worry about it.' But the animators were so concerned that one of them stayed overnight and animated the shot over again with the cough in it. We showed it to George, and that's what you see in the movie."

John Knoll:

"General Grievous is a complicated character. I think we laid a little bit of the groundwork for being able to do *Transformers*

(see pages 272–279) with Grievous. He was probably the most mechanically complicated character that we'd done up to that point. He had very dense geometry, and all the pieces had to slide and move and work mechanically—and that was challenging just to build. It took longer than we expected, because we were redesigning pieces as we were building it."

EVOLUTION OF SIMULATION

ILM's simulation capabilities advanced significantly by Episode III. In character animation, simulations provide an extra level of realism to the work, and subsurface scattering was also improved.

Some of the biggest simulation challenges were shots with the Wookiees. For the scenes on Kashyyyk, performers in Wookiee suits were shot against blue screen. These figures were cloned to create the warriors in the first few rows. ILM then created CG background-Wookiees with realistic, simulated fur. One of the challenges in creating digital Wookiee fur was to match the familiar look of Chewbacca. The simulation of ambient occlusion for fur had been attempted for a long time, and ILM had created relatively successful approximations before. In this case, a new approach was used that resulted in a much more convincing look.

Rob Coleman:

"The Wookiees would have been impossible to do had we been asked to do them on Episode I, and would have been incredibly difficult to do for Episode II. The fur was still challenging, but certainly was less painful than what we would have had to go through in the past.

"We knew that they were creating eight Wookiee suits for the live-action shoot, and of course, we had Chewbacca coming back. We also knew there was going to be a battle on Kashyyyk. We didn't know how many Wookiees there were going to be, but we knew there were going to be a lot more than eight. So we were going to have to create digital Wookiees. I know from the technical side and from the compositing side, and certainly from the rendering side, that the first big shot of the mass of Wookiees would have pretty well ground any other facility in the business to a complete stop.

But ILM is big enough and powerful enough, and has the terabytes of space, that we could actually render something like that.

"In fact, we talk about people being 'middle-brained' at ILM. We have to have the artistic, performance side, but we wouldn't be anywhere without all the incredibly artistic *technical* people, like the technical directors and the compositors, who put the care into the rendering and the compositing and blending our digital characters into the real world, or the synthetic real world."

Craig Hammack:

"Everything was pushed further. Whereas in Episode II we had crowds that were robots, in this film, we had crowds that were Wookiees. So then you have to deal with a whole other set of things, like hair. Everything seemed to be pushed along a development line that was similar in scope to the previous movie but more difficult. You have a speeder flying through a city. Well, what if you have all of these vehicles on water? You have the addition of the interaction with the water and all the reflections of the battle going on. It also gives you opportunities of shooting explosions in real water and integrating that in, which was helpful because it brings some of the real world into this completely digital environment."

WELKOME TO KASHYYYK

To create the environment of the Wookiee planet, Kashyyyk, plates were photographed of a unique mountain range in China and incorporated into a digimatte cyclorama. Practical wake effects shot from a boat were blended with CG water to create the shots of digital tanks crossing the lake. A massive twelve-foot tall model of a Kashyyyk tree was also created.

ABOVE

An establishing shot of the Wookiee planet Kashyyyk, though entirely digital, made use of research plates photographed in China.

The scale of the tree model required enormous amounts of detail, according to Lorne Peterson. Forming the model out of urethane foam wrapped around a steel armature, the Model Shop sculpted alien-looking bark onto a brushed-on clay membrane. Pagoda-shaped wooden structures were then built onto the tree trunk by hand and finished with fine strips of teak planking. Architectural elements were created using a computer program called AutoCAD and produced with a laser cutter.

The Model Shop also built the Wookiee command center and the beachfront where the ground battle begins between Wookiee warriors and invading droids.

Craig Hammack:

"All of the action centers around a lake and the shoreline where the bad guys come and attack across the water. The Wookiees are in the trees so they're on the shore, but the integration of the CG water into the digital environment was our most significant challenge and accomplishment."

INCLUDING THE KITCHEN SINK

The opening space battle for Episode III runs almost eight minutes. ILM spent more than a year building all of the droids, starfighters, cruisers, and other CG assets the sequence required—for the most complicated space battle in any *Star Wars* film.

John Knoll:

"The battle isn't technically in space. The idea is that we're in the upper atmosphere of the planet, so we can see smoke, we can have fire, we can have other things that you can't really have in space. The addition of atmospherics was something that we hadn't had to deal with before.

"And then the actual opening shot of the movie is this very, very long shot: You follow the two fighters and get a really good look at pretty much everything that's happening in the space battle, all in that one shot. So that shot was quite a long time in the making because every effect that we had to represent was present. All of the high-resolution assets of the ships had to be looking good; we had to have

the missile trails, the atmospherics, the CG explosions that we had to fly through about halfway through the shot. The simulation and rendering on that all had to be worked out. It was full of everything. In fact, we were calling it the 'Kitchen Sink Shot' because it had everything but the kitchen sink—and so we thought it would be appropriate to put the kitchen sink in that shot. So in the big explosion that happens partway through the battle, there's a piece of debris that flies out of the explosion. The camera pans with it to get us onto one of the other fighters. That piece of debris is a kitchen sink."

FULL CIRCLE

As with most of the sequences in the film, the scene in which Anakin receives his black face mask and is transformed into Darth Vader was shot on a very limited set of a partial floor and operating table. Almost the entire environment of that scene was created in the computer.

Roger Guyett:

"I remember we needed a shot at the end of Darth Vader going crazy, breaking out of that operating table. George had realized he wanted a wider shot during editing. So one of the guys just put the Darth Vader costume on and he re-created that moment. We photographed it down on one of the stages. It was quite funny, one of our team actually playing Darth Vader there at the end, crashing around.

"And that is George's approach to filmmaking: put the thing together in stages, see where the holes are, and start filling them. Of course, a lot of our team working on the movie knew all about the reality of the different bits and pieces that had been used in *all* of the *Star Wars* movies, but you suddenly realize this sort of historic consequence and weight of some of the things that you're involved with. Suddenly, it was a great honor just to be part of that history."

FOLLOWING SPREAD
Darth Vader, in a mostly CG environment

War of the Worlds

2005

Dennis Muren, senior visual effects supervisor:

"We did practically the entire postproduction in only three months, which is really short. Everything got green-lit late, so we didn't have much time to prep. A lot of people still look at that film as an example of efficiency. But it only works if everyone is in sync with one another and is in their best form."

Director: Steven Spielberg
Producers: Kathleen Kennedy, Colin Wilson

ILM Show Leadership:
Senior Visual Effects Supervisor: Dennis Muren
Visual Effects Supervisor: Pablo Helman
Additional Visual Effects Supervisors: Ed Hirsh, Kim Libreri
Visual Effects Producer: Sandra Scott
Associate Visual Effects Producer: Lori Arnold
Animation Supervisor: Randy M. Dutra
Associate Animation Supervisors: Jenn Emberly,
   Tim Harrington
Digital Production Supervisor: Curt Miyashiro
Visual Effects Art Director: Christian Alzmann

Academy Award® Nomination:
   Best Achievement in Visual Effects
Dennis Muren (ILM)
Pablo Helman (ILM)
Randy Dutra (ILM)
Daniel Sudick

PREVIOUS SPREAD

An invading Martian looms over Rachel Ferrier (Dakota Fanning).

LEFT

Concept art by ILM's Christian Alzmann depicts a Martian death ray vaporizing a human.

ILM'S WORK ON *WAR OF THE WORLDS* involved the creation of a fairly modest number of visual effects shots. The work was complicated by the fact, however, that the 239 shots represented forty-five minutes of visual effects screen time and 123 character animation shots. The film has a documentary look, with some visual effects shots lasting for twenty seconds without a cut.

Dennis Muren:

"There's a scene at the beginning of the film where Tom Cruise is driving away in a minivan. In the background, you see an elevated highway being shot by a heat ray and blowing up. Then he turns down a street, and the houses on the left and on the right behind him are blowing up and crashing on the street. That whole shot is without an edit in it, and we used that approach throughout the film. We ran these shots as long as we could, and the camera didn't anticipate what was going to happen.

"That sort of spontaneous look is showing up in more shots now—sort of dashing around trying to see stuff. And once you start thinking that you can do that, then you start to design it into shots. The camera is going along the freeway and it goes down to the car, goes in and around the car, and then as they're talking, they're racing along, and the camera

pulls out, and there's no cut. People say, 'Oh my God, that's great!' Well, that style was then used in *Children of Men* (2006) and *Terminator Salvation* (2009) (see pages 297–301). But they're not doing the same thing. They're taking it to the next level. Which is a good thing. Let's go even further with it."

CLOTHES MAKE THE EFFECT

ILM artists created digital effects to represent the Martian heat-ray blast. CG particles were animated in perspective, and the beam was manipulated, blurred, and layered. Impacts were created digitally, incorporating blue-screen pyrotechnic elements and digital cloth simulations of the clothing that the vaporized figures left behind. Paint and rotoscope artists eliminated actors from the frame at the moment of impact.

Dennis Muren:

"I don't know where Steven got the idea, but I'd never seen anything quite like it—the way that people vaporize when they're hit by the heat ray, so that all that's left is their clothes flying around. In the old sci-fi days, people vaporized, and you'd see them on the ground as just dust with their clothes.

But the idea of them doing it when they were running was absolutely original. I didn't even know how we were going to do it, because it just hadn't been done before. But then I figured out how to shoot the backgrounds. The actors ducked out of the shot very quickly and we replaced them for a few frames. Then we shot some clothes against blue screen that we pulled out of the frame quickly and mixed it all together with the bright exposure and rays that were particle systems that we generated in the computer.

"In any event that's going to vaporize a body, and if you're looking at the person from six feet away, it's not going to be clear. There will be heat ripples and bright light when a body is vaporized, so I made sure we put a lot of those artifacts into the shot. That made it look like you were seeing an event that you didn't understand, but which was absolutely terrifying and that actually happened in front of you. I wanted you to believe it, going back to that documentary feel."

A NEW PIPELINE

Several years prior to *War of the Worlds*, ILM had begun developing a new technical initiative: upgrading the company's tool set and procedures so that artists could do more than one job. To accomplish this, the tools had to be both consolidated and easier to use. This new approach encouraged members of the ILM team to be generalists, rather than specialists. The new tool set was called Zeno and had been used successfully on *Revenge of the Sith*. On *War of the Worlds*, Zeno was invaluable in meeting what was a nearly impossible schedule.

Nigel Sumner, sequence supervisor:

"They gave us only about three months production time for the whole movie, which is extremely short; generally we get from six to eighteen months of production time. So it really was a testament to the hard work of the artists, to the well-thought-out technical issues and solutions that we needed.

ANOTHER ROAD TO ILM, OR "SO, HOW DID I GET HERE?"

Nigel Sumner, CG supervisor:

"As a kid, you play with computers, and when I was really small, the home computers that you could play with didn't let you do much with graphics—but it doesn't stop you trying.

"When I was at college, I was kind of in that middle ground of really being good at the science and the math side of things, but also really enjoying art and graphics. So I was studying physics, math, graphics, and art at the same time. Then I found this course at Bournemouth University; there were actually only one or two courses in Europe at the time offering a course in computer animation and visualization, and instantly I knew that's what I wanted to do.

"There was one movie that came out that year which solidified it: *Jurassic Park*. Seeing dinosaurs—living, breathing, sweating, spitting dinosaurs, on screen, running around eating things—once I saw that, I knew that anything was possible. If you can bring life to a virtual object, you can bring life to anything on the computer, and that pretty much made my mind up then and there that that's what I wanted to do.

"Once you start studying, you start to investigate companies, and you start to appreciate the work that they do, and ILM was and is the pinnacle; their back catalogue was endless, so naturally that's where everyone wanted to work. And how did I come to work here? Nepotism. I had a colleague whom I was studying with who ended up getting a job here. I came out to visit them one holiday, and inadvertently got an interview at ILM."

I think that changed future work schedules because it set a precedent. *War of the Worlds* was about the approach to a show, the volume of work, and how quickly we could do it, in addition to technical accomplishments."

Steve Sullivan, research and development:

"*War of the Worlds* is important because of when it happened, chronologically, for ILM. We went through a lot of soul searching in 2004 about what to do with our pipeline. Because the existing pipeline was getting old, it was more and more difficult to cram the high tech into that pipeline. It was just not built for that level of work. So in 2004, we decided to switch over our internal tool set to a new platform called Zeno.

"Zeno is kind of a software framework, almost like an operating system for ILM's tools. Somebody on a home computer might be running Microsoft Windows, and they'll run Microsoft Word to do word processing and Excel to do spreadsheets. All of these programs are compatible and running on top of the Windows foundation. The same thing is true with Zeno. Zeno gave us a foundation that we could then innovate and plug our tools into. Before there were many tools that were kind of built in isolation, so artists would go from one tool to another, and it would be a completely different paradigm. They'd have to relearn everything. The engineers might only know one piece of the software and couldn't help out on the others. It would kind of handcuff the facility in terms of both artist resources and engineering resources."

By creating a unified platform, ILM established a new home for all of its innovation, while making it easier for the ILM team to work collaboratively. For *War of the Worlds*, the implementation of the Zeno pipeline allowed a team of forty-five technical directors to handle matchmoves, animation, simulations, digital matte paintings, and lighting on a single platform.

Steve Sullivan:

"*War of the Worlds* was the first show to take the leap on the new pipeline. Dennis Muren made a major commitment to doing this. We knew it was going to hurt, but we were going to push forward and do it. And of course what we thought *War of the Worlds* was going to be about early on seemed very tractable with the new pipeline: rigid body simulations, rigid creatures—no big deal. But, of course, like every movie, once you get into it, and the director starts getting creative and

One day on location in New Jersey, director Steven Spielberg spontaneoulsy designed a shot involving the destruction of a bridge, creating a certain amount of anxiety in visual effects supervisor Pablo Helman, as Spielberg wanted the whole thing to take place in a single camera move. Starting from a live-action plate, ILM artists cleaned the bridge superstructure and supports from the shot and generated the collapsing bridge sections using rigid body dynamics. Approximately four hundred elements were layered by the compositing crew to yield the final shot. (Inset: the bridge before ILM's effects were added.)

everybody starts thinking of what you *could* do, it got much more complex. The scope of that show grew way beyond what we were comfortable setting out to achieve with the new pipeline, but we stuck to our guns and that really pushed ILM onto the new platform. So that tool set has grown since *War of the Worlds*, and it's what we use for all of our films now."

BRIDGE EXPLOSION

For the sequence in which a gas station explodes, Spielberg changed the shooting plan at the last minute. He added a bridge and houses blowing up, along with the crash of a tanker truck into a house. The ILM team collected additional matchmove information. Spielberg operated the camera himself to create additional elements for the visual effects shot. At least fourteen people worked on this one shot, using two hundred elements on the CG side and two hundred more in Inferno compositing.

Pablo Helman, visual effects supervisor:

"When the bridge falls, there're all of these cars. Let's say we started with twenty cars. Steven said, 'Twenty, do you think that's going to be enough?' Well, we ended up with hundreds of cars. I was just listening and agreeing with him—but all of the producers were behind me kind of throwing up in the corner, thinking *How the hell are we going to do this?* But Steven has that effect on people. He's super inspiring. He reminds you of why you wanted to get into this industry in the first place.

"When I was a kid in Argentina, I watched Spielberg films—all of the *Indiana Jones* films and *E.T.* and *Close Encounters*. And as a young person I wondered, *How do these people come up with these ideas?* And then, as a visual effects supervisor, being in the middle of *War of the Worlds* on location in New Jersey, I saw how they come up with these ideas. They get up in the morning and they say, 'How about if we

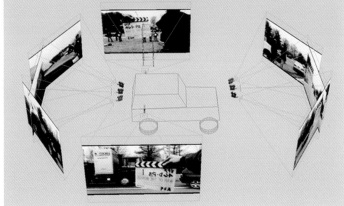

did that? Could you do that?' It was up to me to say, 'Yes, we can do it' or 'No, we can't.' And if we could do it, it was going to be one of those things that was going to inspire a young person somewhere else in the world to ask the same thing: *How do they come up with these ideas?*"

LEFT
A final frame from a scene that did not make the final cut of the film.

ABOVE
To realize a complex two-and-a-half-minute shot during which Ray Ferrier (Tom Cruise) and his family speed along a crowded road, a special camera rig was attached to a Jeep with an eight-camera array. ILM would be able to re-create a 360-degree view outside of the windows of the character's minivan by stitching together a virtual cyclorama from the camera footage. The footage was composited into shots of the principal actors in a minivan interior shot against blue-screen.

Jarhead

2005

Pablo Helman, visual effects supervisor:

"Director Sam Mendes had never really worked with visual effects, so he didn't know what visual effects could do. But when we got into post and he realized he could change things that weren't working for him, he got it right away. He found out what Steven Spielberg and George Lucas found out a long time ago: You can change the environment, you can change performances, and you basically have a lot of control."

Director: Sam Mendes
Producer: Lucy Fisher, Douglas Wick

ILM Show Leadership:
Visual Effects Supervisor: Pablo Helman
Visual Effects Producer: Jeanmarie King
Digital Production Supervisor: Grady Cofer
Visual Effects Art Director: Christian Alzmann

VISUAL EFFECTS WORK in *Jarhead* is very subtle. Because a large number of the shots called for emulations of reality, the four hundred shots ILM created are virtually invisible. In fact, every single shot in the third act of the film contains imperceptible visual effects.

Because the actual images of the fires of Kuwait were so memorable, director Mendes felt it was important to represent the burning oilfields accurately. Fires that rose four hundred feet into the air would have to be re-created. Initially, the ILM team had considered shooting numerous real fires on set, but the fires of Kuwait were so huge that ultimately only one fire element was shot on set; the rest of the fire was created by manipulating elements from a library of fire footage shot in Mexico.

Pablo Helman:

"We took a look at a lot of reference material from the Kuwait fires in the first Iraq war. There's no way that we could have done it other than using visual effects. But one of the most difficult aspects of creating the fires was due to one of the main problems with visual effects photography. It's hard to create a visual effect that really can't be shot in a particular scale. When you think about those fires, they were around four hundred feet tall."

It was important to Mendes that the scale of the fire was correct, so the ILM team never shot miniature elements.

Pablo Helman:

"We didn't use a fluid-simulation engine or anything like that. We shot the fires in Mexico and photographed them from different distances under different lighting and weather conditions. For one live-action fire, we were about 170 feet away, and the amount of heat that that thing created was incredible. My eyebrows are still growing back! We basically built a library of fire footage."

After Mendes embraced the fact that he could control many elements in postproduction, he realized that he wasn't tied to what had been shot.

PREVIOUS SPREAD

Added to the live-action plate of the actors and foreground was ILM's digital smoke and massive fires from the oil wells, as well as myriad details.

ABOVE

ILM's re-creation of fire went beyond generating imagery of the fire. To create the illusion that the soldiers were surrounded by flames, ILM painted fire reflections in the men's goggles, in the oil on their clothes, and on the ground.

More rotoscoping was done for *Jarhead* than any other ILM film to date, including *Revenge of the Sith*. "Part of the problem with not working in Kuwait was that the geography wasn't what we needed, so we had to replace the horizon for every one of those location shots," Helman says. "We had to do extensive rotoscoping."

a community during principal photography, things don't look right. So I was always working with Roger on lighting so that our post work would look great."

TWA ON A BUDGET

ILM also made it possible to transform a California location into a Saudi Arabian airport, a white commercial helicopter into a dark military helicopter, and even affect some magic on a 747.

Pablo Helman:

"There's a long shot tracking the soldiers coming out of the door of TWA 747 planes when they arrive in Kuwait. So we needed TWA planes, but of course there are no TWA planes anymore. So we went to a kind of plane cemetery or hangar, where they have all of these planes that are not used anymore. We asked if two 747s they had could be painted white, because TWA planes were white. They said, 'Sure, no problem.'

"But when we showed up at six in the morning on these huge tarmacs, the 747s said 'United Airlines.' And United Airlines planes are gray and blue, very dark, and they couldn't paint the planes white. So Sam Mendes turns to us and asks, 'Can you replace these planes?' I said I guess we could. Finally, we're shooting the scene and I'm just going, 'Jesus, how are we going to do that?' We didn't have the budget for it either, because it was a very low-budget film.

"So when I got back to ILM, we got on the web and found this guy that used to make model planes for the TWA company, two-foot planes that you put on a desk. So we asked him, 'Can you make two planes for us that have a little bit more detail in the paint?' We took those planes and we photographed them outside at ILM as a miniature, in different light conditions to match the scene. Then we rotoscoped the soldiers out of the plate and into our shot with the planes. If you actually look at the scene, those are miniature planes. So that was a great success story."

Pablo Helman

"He started using his eye, and he said, 'Maybe the top of that fire is too fast,' so we started splitting the fires into parts. The bottom of the fire might be used at the speed that we shot it, and then the top would be slowed down."

Helman was on the set nearly every day, both to track technical details and to absorb director of photography Roger Deakins's visual orientation. This close collaboration resulted in an aesthetic synchronicity between CG elements and the original photography.

Pablo Helman:

"We had a strong collaboration. For example, he put light sources on stage, close to the actors, as if the fire was illuminating them. Then we replaced those very small fires that he put in with huge fires that we had shot. Deakins and I talked a lot about the lighting. That's an important point about working in visual effects. Even though we do most of our work in postproduction when everybody else has stopped, if we don't work together as

The Chronicles of Narnia: The Lion, the Witch and the Wardrobe

2005

Scott Farrar, visual effects supervisor:

"The number one problem—and this was bad—is that they had photographed all the live-action actors in green tights against green grass. So extracting was a nightmare."

Director: Andrew Adamson
Producers: Mark Johnson, Philip Steuer

ILM Show Leadership:
Visual Effects Supervisor: Scott Farrar
Visual Effects Producer: Stephanie Hornish
Associate Visual Effects Supervisor: Lindy De Quattro
Animation Director: Jenn Emberly

Academy Award® Nomination:
   Best Achievement in Visual Effects
Dean Wright
Bill Westenhofer
Jim Berney
Scott Farrar (ILM)

BAFTA Film Award Nomination:
   Best Achievement in Special Visual Effects
Dean Wright
Bill Westenhofer
Jim Berney
Scott Farrar (ILM)

Three companies created visual effects for *The Chronicles of Narnia*. Initially, the plan had been to work with one company, but when the shot count grew from 800 to more than 1,400, it became necessary to split up the job. Sony Pictures Imageworks and Rhythm & Hues handled most of the shots, with ILM joining the project in postproduction. Its work involved the creation of CG leg and body replacements for half-human, half-creature characters. CG crowds were also added to live-action scenes. ILM's daunting task was to complete 211 complex shots in ten weeks.

Craig Hammack, computer graphics supervisor:

"The work on *Narnia* was frantic. As the supervisor, I had to give feedback on every shot each day, so we would come in at eight in the morning and go into our dark dailies screening room; we wouldn't come out again until lunch. We'd see daylight briefly, but the schedule would be so tight that we would bring in lunch so we could talk about the targets for the week. Then the afternoon was back-to-back meetings until we would go back in the screening room and be in nightlies for another hour."

Scott Farrar:

"Although ILM welcomed the opportunity to work on *Narnia*, it was a daunting task to not only complete 211 complex shots in ten weeks, but also to match the great look Andrew Adamson had achieved with shots from Rhythm & Hues and Sony Pictures Imageworks over the previous year. Because ILM was brought onto the *Narnia* team relatively

ABOVE

In order to finish their work on time, ILM created "Block Party," which enabled animators to use interchangeable digital parts to create fantastic creatures, such as centaurs, in a hurry; Block Party became the facility's premiere rigging tool for years afterward. (inset: live-action plate)

PREVIOUS SPREAD

ILM was responsible for embellish-
ing and augmenting a castle interior
for the coronation sequence. Sparse
live-action plates needed synthetic
environments, as well as CG characters. Production provided a green-
screen plate that included only a
short row of spectators, four thrones,
a background wall, and some pillars.
ILM then added several rows of
creatures and people, extended the
length of the front row of centaurs
and put in the palace and floor, as
well as the background and the sky.

RIGHT

The Ice Palace of Narnia is populated
by unlucky souls that have been
frozen solid.

late in the postproduction schedule, most of the CG creature assets came from Rhythm & Hues. The challenge then
was to add paint, texture, color, cloth, and hair simulations
as needed."

LOOK AT THOSE LEGS

ILM's main task involved replacing actors' green-legged tights with
animated lower torsos. The characters included satyrs and fauns
(both having the lower half of a goat), minotaurs (having furry animal
legs with hooves), and centaurs (having horse bodies). Locking the
animated hip to the very active actors was just one of the challenges
in this process.

Scott Farrar:

"Centaur horse bodies were often the most difficult to create,
with their layers of simulations, complex lightings, and the
delicate blends to the actors' waists. In addition, centaur actors performed on fourteen-inch green platforms to increase
their height. Our artists had to remove the green legs and
platform and then rebuild the missing background before
adding the horse body. Most shots needed a great deal of
reconstruction using digital painting and rotoscoping.

"The centaurs with actors wearing armor were easiest
to blend because of the solid leather waistbands they wore.
Next in difficulty were actors wearing draped cloth; for these
we built a CG waistcloth to join upper human and lower
horse. The most difficult were actors with only bare skin,

ABOVE

A very large crowd scene was first filmed on location with many extras in green tights (inset); however, in this case the green elements only complicated ILM's work.

which had to blend and transition into the horsehair body. Skillful compositing and delicate paint work got us through those shots."

The fact that none of the centaur performers were exactly the same height or size presented a further challenge, since ILM had one CG horse body of one specific size for all of the centaurs. If the horse body was scaled up to make it work with the taller performer, the horse would look taller, but he would also look fatter. If the horse body were scaled down, it would get shorter, but be too thin. The difficulty was ensuring that the waist of the human was the right size to join properly, while still maintaining a correctly proportioned animal underneath.

Lighting for the leg replacement was another major challenge, since most of the exterior plates included every possible variety of lighting: overcast skies, bright sun, left-lit and right-lit. The curly hair on the legs of the fauns was particularly difficult to light successfully. The horsehair on the centaurs was somewhat easier to create, as it was smooth and has a sheen to it.

Overall, ILM created sequences containing more than forty types of furred creatures that were replicated to produce hundreds of figures for crowd shots. Often, there were only two actors in the frame before ILM added the creatures around them.

BLOCK PARTY

Because the ILM team had only a few months to complete the assigned shots, the creature setup schedule was tight. Other facilities had had

more than a year to set up and animate their creatures, while ILM had only a few weeks to accomplish its work on thirty creatures. Luckily, a new technical development helped make the tight schedule manageable.

Jason Smith, lead technical animator:

"Jeff White and I had been working on a new way to set up creatures that allowed you to take different animals and put them together to make a new animal. It was an idea we were developing without any project in mind. But when *Narnia* came up and thirty creatures had to be rigged in a very short amount of time, we were able to use this system that we had developed and called Block Party.

"In the past, when we rigged a creature, we'd have to place each bone, by hand, and set up all the math for how the bones work together and how the animators could pull the puppet around. The new Block Party system enabled us to create these sort of Mr. Potato Head components, like a human

arm, a human head, or a horse leg, things like that. And then from these components you could kind of mix and match to make creatures. In *Narnia*, there's a werewolf, so we took a human body, took off the human legs and popped on two cat hind legs for him and a cat tail. You've got all of these rigging components available, so you can pop some things off and pop other things on."

Jeff White, creature development supervisor:

"With Block Party, the new idea was, 'What if you took all of that information, like where the shoulder joint is, and encoded it in a geometric mesh?' We were able to use that software to take all of the rigging and all of the musculature and encode it in that geometric volume. You could then start mixing and matching between characters. We were able to create a centaur in a couple of days, whereas it would have taken several weeks of custom rigging."

Letterman Digital Arts Center (2005)

Jim Morris, former president of Lucas Digital Ltd., 1994–2004:

"ILM's move to the Letterman Digital Arts Center was a profound event in the life of the company. It's a fantastic facility—in such a spectacular setting, you can't help but be inspired when you go there."

WHEN ILM WAS FIRST ESTABLISHED in 1975, the company was based in a warehouse in Van Nuys, north of Los Angeles. In 1978, the company moved to a facility on Kerner Boulevard in San Rafael, fifteen minutes north of San Francisco. The Kerner Facility

was home to ILM for twenty-three years. But in 2005, the company moved once again, this time to Lucasfilm's state-of-the-art Letterman Digital Arts Center (LDAC) in the heart of San Francisco's Presidio National Park.

Congress had mandated a unique funding model for the Presidio: economic self-sufficiency by 2013 or liquidation. The Presidio Trust was established and charged with maintaining and enhancing the cultural, historical, and recreational resources of the park, while achieving long-term financial stability. The Trust selected the twenty-three-acre site of the vacated Letterman Army Medical Center to be redeveloped and

ABOVE

The Letterman Digital Arts Center, or LDAC, home to several Lucasfilm companies—including ILM (the Golden Gate Bridge can be seen in the background).

leased. Following a design competition in 1997, a team led by Lucasfilm Ltd. was selected to replace the hospital with the Letterman Digital Arts Center, a new home for the company.

The Letterman Digital Arts Center integrates motion-picture, visual effects, and gaming technologies in one world-class digital-arts facility. The twenty-three-acre campus brings together ILM, LucasArts, and Lucasfilm's corporate activities for the first time in Lucasfilm Ltd.'s thirty-year history.

SIDE-BY-SIDE

Early on in the development of the Lucas companies, George Lucas saw the potential for a symbiotic relationship between film and games production. The physical proximity between LucasArts and ILM at the Letterman Digital Arts Center works to encourage this relationship to develop even further.

George Lucas, chairman of Lucasfilm Ltd.:

"At the Letterman Digital Arts Center, LucasArts and ILM are right next door to each other. We're encouraging the work concepts to drift between the two companies, much more than we ever did before. The game company has expertise in some things, and ILM has expertise in other things; I think letting them share their ideas and technology changes and improves the way they both work and advances the methodologies that they're both using."

The Letterman Digital Arts Center houses the engine for a "virtual studio" in which graphic artists, game developers, and motion-picture directors can collaborate on visual effects and digital creations in real-time, connecting them to anywhere in the world.

At the time of this writing, it is home to one of the largest computer networks in the entertainment industry, a high-performance system designed to deliver large volumes of data and high-resolution images to artists' desktops, encouraging interactive collaboration on the creation of synthetic scenes and characters.

BUILDINGS

George Lucas was the primary conceptual designer for the Letterman Digital Arts Center.

Jim Morris:

"The Letterman Digital Arts Center is in a beautiful, historic setting. George, in his traditional fashion, has created buildings of great beauty and function. He's really an architect deep down inside."

George Lucas:

"When we were awarded the privilege of building in the Presidio, we knew we had to create something to honor this special place. We wanted to create a campus that would speak to the history of the Presidio, fit into the environment, and make it look and feel like a natural part of the larger park."

The design of LDAC incorporates the same palette of red brick, white stucco, and terra cotta roofs that is seen throughout the Presidio, bringing the facility into harmony with its neighboring buildings, some of which are nearly a century old.

THE MOVE

ILM's move took place in four stages between August and October 2005. The change in facilities has been likened to changing the tires on a Formula One racecar while the race is still in progress. ILM had at least one major motion picture in production during the relocation: *Pirates of the Caribbean: The Curse of the Black Pearl.*

During the move, the Kerner and LDAC facilities were run as if they were one unit. ILM team members on both sides of the Golden Gate Bridge accessed the same data. A fiber-optic cable was leased that ran from San Rafael to Berkeley and then across the Bay Bridge to San Francisco to link the servers in San Rafael to those in San Francisco. The data showed up as one virtual disk. Running the two facilities simultaneously made it possible for ILM to move people from one location to the other in waves—so it was never necessary for anyone to stop working. Without this system, ILM would have had to completely shut down its facility—an action that would have cost millions.

Chrissie England, president, ILM, 2004–2010

"Moving to the Presidio was a daunting challenge. ILM had been located in an industrial park for thirty years. We had started as half a warehouse and ended up in twenty different buildings on the same street. We worked on our own. We didn't work in a corporate environment. We were perceived by corporate as being the rebels. And I'm sure we were proud of that. The move was done very smoothly, but there were certainly some difficult moments in the beginning, not only in people getting used to a more corporate environment, but also corporate getting used to us. And you know, I could equate Lucasfilm to the bank and ILM to the circus. And the two of those identities now had to coexist in the same space."

Miles Perkins, director of marketing and communications:

"Moving to the Presidio was a major cultural shift for ILM. We left a place where we had an overhead paging system, which was going on constantly. You'd hear them yell, 'Fire on the slab!' and then you'd feel the impact. You'd go outside, and there were mechanics and people wheeling filmmaking equipment from here to there. You really felt like you were a part of the filmmaking community. Moving to the Presidio, we were in a brand-new building, just the way George wanted it for everybody; he created something beautifully idyllic, so people could be as creative as they can be. But initially, that wasn't necessarily the feeling that the artists had. They felt, 'Oh, my goodness, I'm in this beautiful place, I don't wanna mess anything up. How can I express myself?' So it was a little bumpy coming in. But we were able to rally around the accolades that we were getting in the press. The pipeline started getting ironed out, and the artists realized they were able to accomplish this Davy Jones character, which no one else could do. It made people feel a little more comfortable about being in this new facility."

The campus was designed and wired for integrated, real-time work-flow among digital artists. Everything at the Letterman Digital Arts Center—the campus itself, the digital tools, the network—had been created to make possible real-time collaboration and facilitate creative decision-making.

The computer network at LDAC delivered a capability similar to working on a live movie set, only "virtually." Distance boundaries were eliminated, and digital artists could collaborate internally throughout the campus, as well as with creators of entertainment anywhere in the world.

What's more, some of the artists at ILM feel there are important ways in which things *hadn't* changed much.

Scott Benza, animation director:

"There's a different breed of artist at ILM, and almost all of them are here because they are hugely passionate about the work they do and are fulfilling childhood dreams. Everybody I talk to here saw either *Jurassic Park* or *Terminator II* or some of the very early work that ILM had done and knew that they wanted to work for this company. Everything they did in their career path was ultimately leading them to work for ILM. So I don't think it matters where the company resides or what the physical space is where we do our work—it's the projects, the people, and the legacy of ILM that keeps everyone happy, and which keeps everybody at this company. I can't really think of how my work has changed since moving to the Presidio, because the people haven't changed."

OPPOSITE

Another view of the LDAC campus, situated in San Francisco's Presidio Park, founded in 1776.

Mission: Impossible III

2006

Roger Guyett, visual effects supervisor:

"*Mission: Impossible III* involved the invisible-effects approach to making movies. You weren't doing things that people were supposed to be aware of. We were able to take advantage of this concept of creating digital environments for filmmakers, which was an important landmark around that time."

Director: J. J. Abrams
Producers: Tom Cruise, Paula Wagner

ILM Show Leadership:
Visual Effects Supervisor: Roger Guyett
Visual Effects Associate Supervisor: Russell Earl
Visual Effects Producer: Shari Hanson
Animation Supervisor: Paul Kavanagh
Digital Production Supervisor: Patrick Tubach
Visual Effects Art Director: Alex Jaeger

THE CHALLENGING WORK ILM UNDERTOOK for *Mission: Impossible III* involved creating 530 visual effects shots generated in less than four months. The core crew of approximately 100 nearly doubled at its maximum of 185.

Like *Jarhead* (see pages 233–235), *Mission: Impossible III* is an example of a film in which the visual effects are "invisible." And also like Jarhead, as well as *War of the Worlds* (see pages 225–231), *Mission: Impossible III* is an example of visual effects providing the director with complete flexibility.

While production did a location shoot in Shanghai, it was necessary for ILM to do blue-screen work in cases where shooting angles were difficult or getting the shot was impractical. The infamous Shanghai pollution also made shooting conditions unpredictable, so the ILM team created a library of photographs and moving plates in

Shanghai. Three hero buildings on a virtual set were built to a high level of detail, and the rest of the set had all of the dimensionality of 3-D without using real architecture. The stills that were pasted onto models of the buildings made it possible to "fly around" the structures inside of the computer. This relatively new technique had been developed in-house at ILM.

Roger Guyett:

"ILM had developed the ability to project images onto simple pieces of geometry. By *Mission: Impossible III*, we'd realized that you can photograph a skyscraper from specific angles and then re-create it from the photographs you've taken, giving you the flexibility to design your camera moves in post. By taking the still images and projecting them onto very simple

PREVIOUS SPREAD

Ethan Hunt (Tom Cruise) charges off a skyscraper into the Shanghai cityscape created digitally by ILM.

ABOVE

Because shooting in Shanghai presented too many obstacles (lights turned off too early, uncooperative military helicopter pilots and smog), director J. J. Abrams allowed ILM to build a more modernized, cooler version of the Shanghai cityscape, which also allowed him to "direct" the skyline (inset: an intermediate stage). The live-action plate was recorded at Universal Studios, where Tom Cruise leaped off a parking lot roof three stories high, doing the stunt himself.

ABOVE

Because it was logistically impossible to shut down the bridge over Chesapeake Bay, production moved to a field in California and constructed its own bridge (inset)— whose surroundings ILM greatly enhanced in postproduction.

pieces of geometry, you are able to move your virtual camera around them. All of the detail comes from the real image. Using this technique, we were able to build up an incredibly realistic and complicated downtown Shanghai that was completely believable.

"Actually, we were in this strange place where we wanted to create the *impression* of downtown Shanghai rather than what it really looked like. So we thought, *Well, we'll just make our own*. We'll take pictures of hundreds of buildings and then piece them together and make something that looks *more* interesting. The shots looked the way I believed Shanghai *should* look even if it didn't really look that way. I loved that. You're creating a completely believable environment, and you're doing it extremely efficiently. And as a tool for a filmmaker, it's amazing because you don't have to travel to Shanghai and you don't have to build a practical model of Shanghai."

Image-based modeling from the photographs was also used to create details, which allowed the director to be in control of a giant set. The city could be "adjusted" and bits of CG added. Roads were made busy and video billboards were added.

CHESAPEAKE BAY BRIDGE ATTACK

As with ILM's creation of a "virtual Shanghai," the team was also responsible for creating a digital environment for the Chesapeake Bay Bridge attack sequence.

Roger Guyett:

"We went to Chesapeake Bay needing to film this incredibly elaborate sequence at the height of the busy tourist season, not to mention that it was also hurricane season. We were told we could close the bridge for an hour at a time, and then we had to let people through. We quickly realized that

shooting it this way would be a hideous experience. Closing the bridge down wouldn't give us much time, and we would be limited in what we could shoot, because we were just a hundred feet off the water. So we started thinking about how else we could do it. Maybe we could re-create the bridge, and we don't need the water. So it was sort of like the Shanghai principle. You can film in a much more controllable and safer environment, but you get the overall impression that you're on a bridge over water."

Ultimately, Guyett's plan involved building a six-hundred-foot bridge outside of Los Angeles. The bridge had hills on one side and an infinite horizon on the other. The hilly side was covered with more than four hundred feet of green screen. The crew designed a truss system that used electric winches to move the green screens up and down. ILM built a library of photographic images from the real bridge in Virginia, showing different views and lighting conditions. The library was used to reconstruct the environment around the bridge. Complex digital matte paintings were also created for this sequence. The damage done to the bridge by the rockets was all visualized in the computer.

WHERE'S THE CUT?

Rather than just showing the results of the "mask process," in which a character takes on the role of another, director J. J. Abrams wanted to let the audience see how the process worked, including how the equipment was used. The sequence shows the Mission: Impossible team turning pictures of Owen Davian (Phillip Seymour Hoffman) into 3-D images, which is a process that, in reality, can be done. The M:I team then uses a process similar to a CAD application, where the mask is milled out of a piece of rubber. Abrams's idea was for the audience to see how things worked and, in the context of the film, not question the process.

J. J. Abrams, director:

"The masks had always been a part of the world of *Mission: Impossible*. But I had never seen them in a way that I could actually believe they exist. How did they get fabricated? In the scene, we see the mask being made and applied to Tom Cruise's character so he transforms into Phil Hoffman's character. We had a million discussions on how to do it.

Ultimately, we decided the best way was to shoot it with a Steadicam, where you go behind a character and it's sort of an invisible wipe. You've just seen Tom Cruise pull the mask over his head, and when you come around the other side, ILM made what was Phil Hoffman's actual head look like a mask. We'd obviously put Tom Cruise's face under the mask, but when his face is patted down to help apply the mask, the transformation was made digitally from the digital mask of Phil Hoffman to the live Phil Hoffman. You think, *Oh, I saw where they hid the cut*, but then the scene continues and you really see this mask and you think it *wasn't* the cut. The fun of it was combining the very old-fashioned technique with ILM's use of modern CG technology."

In fact, the latest scanning technology as well as Maya and RenderMan shaders were used for the mask process sequence.

STUNTS

ILM was responsible for creating all of the major stunts in the film. For the sequence in which Cruise parachutes off a building, the actor was shot in a flying rig on a massive interior green-screen set.

Roger Guyett:

"We built very small pieces of set so Tom Cruise does jump off a building, except he's jumping off a car park in Los Angeles, which is a lot more controllable and a lot safer—and you know what? No one has to go to Shanghai. We went to China for different reasons, but we didn't have to worry about trying to deal with a real person jumping off a thousand-foot skyscraper. We could add all of that later."

Another reason for the jump shot being executed using green screen was that all of the lights in Shanghai are turned off at 10:00 P.M. It would have been impossible to find the required background in the real location.

THE ESTABLISHMENT
OF KERNER OPTICAL (2006)

Miles Perkins, director of marketing and communications, ILM:

"ILM was moving all of the CG operations to the Presidio complex, but kind of leaving the stages behind, and we, as a company, couldn't focus, from a marketing point of view, on Kerner Optical's core interests. So as a result, we had people who didn't work as much. The concept was that by selling Kerner, we could still work together, but Kerner would be able to go after other projects, as well; they could have a concentrated marketing focus on their business of practical effects."

In 2006, a year after the ILM digital effects team moved to the Presidio in San Francisco, Lucasfilm accepted an offer to buy Kerner Optical, the dedicated practical-effects division of ILM. The management-led acquisition created an independent spin-off company, called the Kerner Company. The Kerner Company remained at the original Kerner Campus and included what had previously been ILM's sound stages, Model Shop, camera engineering, and practical-effects departments. The company would carry on a tradition of extraordinary craftsmanship that had been developed at ILM during the preceding thirty years.

Initially, all of the original ILM model crew stayed at the Kerner facility, including Model Shop legends such as Charlie Bailey, Steve Gawley, and Lorne Peterson.

Kerner's production activities were separated from ILM's digital facility in the Presidio, but collaboration continued. At first, most of Kerner's feature-film work came through ILM. At the same time, they were free to also work with other companies.

Poseidon

2006

Boyd Shermis, visual effects supervisor, production:

"There were two fundamental goals: to out-Titanic *Titanic* in terms of the look and behavior of the ship, and to out-Perfect-Storm *The Perfect Storm* in terms of the ocean water and the wave. Wolfgang wanted this to be the most spectacular shipwreck of all time. To create that, we had to raise the bar on the wonderful work that had been done before."

Director: Wolfgang Peterson
Producers: Wolfgang Peterson, Mike Fleiss,
   Akiva Goldsman, Duncan Henderson

ILM Show Leadership:
Visual Effects Supervisor: Kim Libreri
Associate Visual Effects Supervisor: Mohen Leo
Visual Effects Producer: Jeff Olson
Digital Production Supervisor: Patrick Conran
Visual Effects Art Director: Wilson Tang

Academy Award® Nomination:
   Best Achievement in Visual Effects
Boyd Shermis
Kim Libreri (ILM)
Chas Jarrett
John Frazier

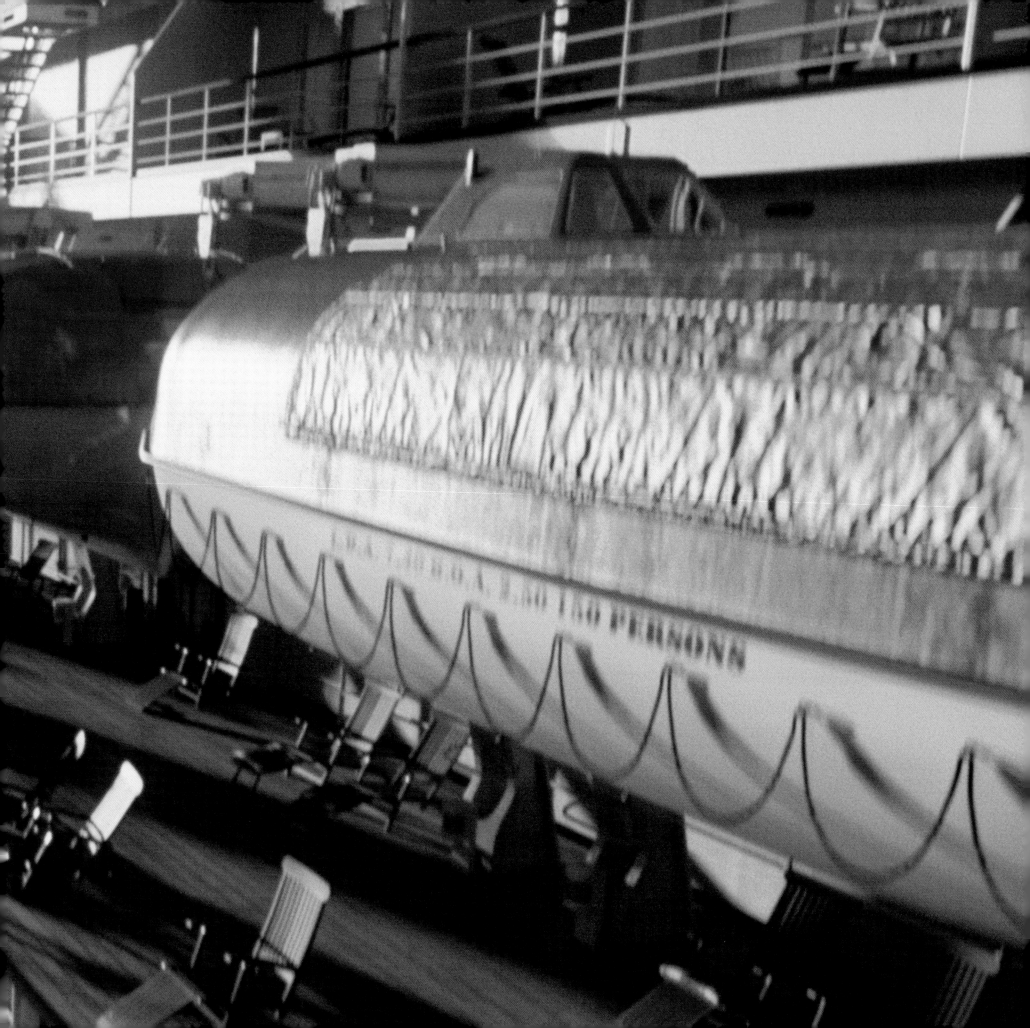

EVEN THOUGH *POSEIDON* was considered a remake, many of the visual effects created for the film can be considered groundbreaking achievements in the field. The shots were exceptionally difficult and used more resources on a per-shot average than any other film ILM had undertaken to date.

ILM was responsible for ninety-six shots. For *Poseidon*, the challenge had more to do with the complexity of the work than volume. The shots required included *Poseidon* exteriors, CG oceans and skies, digital doubles, a rogue wave, a *Poseidon* rollover, a capsized and sinking ship, and a helicopter rescue.

The creation of computer-generated water for *Poseidon* was even more challenging than the effects ILM had achieved in *The Perfect Storm* (see pages 132–139). For *Poseidon*, ILM had to create a huge CG wave that *wraps around* the ship. The ship then rolls in a 3-D volume of water. By contrast, in *The Perfect Storm*, the boat bobs on the top of the water.

ILM produced a dozen shots of the wave breaking on the ship, rolling it 180 degrees. The breaking shots required the most sophisticated fluid dynamics ever applied to a film production—fluid dynamics technology had never been used to create water simulations on this scale. Professor Ron Fedkiw's hydrodynamics team at Stanford University had developed a fluid dynamics engine, which ILM had used on *Terminator 3* (see pages 176–181) to generate the look of liquid chrome and in *Harry Potter and the Goblet of Fire* (2005) to create shots of a ship rising out of the water.

Steve Sullivan, senior technology officer:

"*The Perfect Storm* was the first real water-simulation movie for us, and it used a lot of clever tricks, like a deep-ocean simulator and small simulations composited on top to make it look like a real ocean. But it wasn't built to last. It was built to just

PREVIOUS SPREAD, ABOVE, AND OPPOSITE

The opening shot of *Poseidon* ran 4,329 frames, starting beneath the water, circling the boat while integrating Dylan Johns (Josh Lucas, filmed against green-screen at Supulveda Dam) jogging during a spectacular sunset. Except for the actor, everything was digital. *Poseidon* represented a huge advance in water simulation, with the luxury cruiser also becoming the largest and most complex digital model at that time. Digital deck details, such as chairs, towels, and newspapers, were also added. Ultimately, it took 23 hours per frame to render just the digital boat and water.

get that film out the door, which was a huge undertaking. *The Perfect Storm* showed it could be done, established some key concepts, came up with the prototype, and then when the other movies came along, we realized we needed to invest in this for real.

"When it came time to do the *Pirates* movie and *Poseidon*, we realized that there wasn't a water system that you could just pick up and turn on and use again. We had to reinvent it. But this time, we had a better foundation for our simulations due to our collaboration with Stanford on their simulation system, called PhysBAM. We built the water simulations on that. Both *Poseidon* and the *Pirates* movies collaborated on pushing the technology forward because they were running roughly concurrently. We actually went out and hired some extra R & D staff, just because we knew it was a trend in the industry and we had to make this real."

Ron Fedkiw, research and development:

"*Poseidon* was the second big jump in technology for us on a system that won the Academy Award. The big development was going from modeling something small, like a glass of water or a liquid Terminator, to modeling something big, like a whole ocean. There's tons of CG water in *Poseidon*. We had to get the ocean, the spray, the foam, the waves splashing around, and even match real footage. So the scale of it was much bigger, and we had to come up with a whole host of new ideas to augment the basic level set method so it could be used."

The work was so complex, in fact, that it required a higher level of processing power. Some thirty computers were linked together to undertake the task.

Ron Fedkiw:

"We had to use MPI, a programming-language term for something that allows computers to talk to each other so that they can share effort on the same problem. Before *Poseidon* started, the simulation at Stanford was extremely cutting-edge. We showed that to the people who were making *Poseidon*. ILM's visual effects supervisor on *Poseidon*, Kim Libreri, took our simulation, showed it to the people making *Poseidon*, and said, 'Imagine if we could do this in a movie.' Everyone bit on the idea, and said, 'Let's try it.' We were so excited about doing something like that, nobody thought about what would happen if it failed. There was no real backup plan. You'd have to delete scenes if we didn't come through.

"A lot of times when you do research work, you get lucky and do something spectacular. But in *Poseidon*, we actually planned to do stuff that couldn't be done with current ideas. But if we weren't lucky, we wouldn't be able to finish the film. For example, the ship had to turn over and sink, and they didn't have any turning over, sinking ships. For *Pirates of the Caribbean: Dead Man's Chest*, which was going on at exactly the same time, John Knoll went down to Mexico and shot a whole bunch of water. He also shot practical effects that he could use, and if he had good fluid technology, he could use that to make it better. So *Dead Man's Chest* was being done in a way with water where the movie could have been done without any of the cool technology; but if they had it, it would be better. It's important I think to understand the difference between those two films. *Dead Man's Chest* had a backup plan—but *Poseidon* did not."

For the climactic scene showing the ship sinking, ILM created numerous simulations of waves crashing with simulations below the water, including bubbles and debris.

Ron Fedkiw:

"Everything was simulated; it was a completely CG environment. We built a CG ship, which they wanted to sink in fully CG water. And it became very stressful and very panicked—because we realized we had no plan B, and we were unsure if we were going to be able to pull this off. But once we did pull it off, we almost got arrogant, and we started using the system for everything. For example, the wake behind the ship could easily be done with existing techniques, but we used all of the new fancy techniques for it, because it was easier to do. So it became a really powerful system for the last few weeks of work on the film."

SYNTHETIC SHIP

Director Peterson challenged ILM to create a synthetic *Poseidon* that looked photoreal even in close views. After more than a year of development work, the result was the largest, most detailed and most complex CG model built at ILM to date.

Boyd Shermis:

"We'd say to the cruise lines: 'We'd like to hire your ship for our disaster movie about a ship that sinks. How about it?' They weren't very excited about that concept, obviously. One company briefly entertained the idea, and they allowed us to scout a real cruise ship. We had a day to go in and photograph every corner of this ship, which gave us a lot of great reference material. But ultimately, none of the cruise companies was interested in letting one of their ships represent the *Poseidon* in this movie."

ABOVE
The digital cruise ship at night, when most of the film takes place. Keyed to the model's light fixtures, ILM used 1,200 CG "lights" and then added ambient glows when compositing. Render times were substantially higher than the daytime shots, due to the hundreds of light reflections on the ocean surface.

ABOVE

The sinking of the 1,100-foot CG *Poseidon*. (Insets: the doomed ship at several stages: three-dimensional water volume enveloping the ship as it sinks; the ship itself; fluid sim)

Production didn't build any of the ship exteriors to be photographed by first unit, except approximately twenty feet of deck with a railing and a door. No element of the outside of the boat was photographed. All wakes, horizons, oceans, and exteriors of the ship were created in ILM's computers.

Mohen Leo, associate visual effects supervisor:

"At the beginning of our work on this film, we looked at a model and realized that a cruise ship involves an incredible level of detail. There are signs, towels, doors and door handles, windows, lighting fixtures, tables, deck chairs—a cruise ship is basically a small city. Every part of this model would have to have texture and dirt and bumps to sell that it was real."

Three full-time modelers worked in Maya for more than eight months to develop a kit of 6,500 separate ship set pieces. Ultimately, the modelers produced 181,579 individual pieces to build the ship and dress it with items such as chairs and coffee cups.

Pat Conran, digital production supervisor:

"We had a lot of reference from the *Queen Mary*. And since we're at the Presidio, we had wonderful views of cruise ships in San Francisco Bay. Whenever a cruise ship would pass underneath the Golden Gate Bridge, we'd yell, 'Cruise ship!' and everyone would come running to a window to look at it."

Pirates of the Caribbean: Dead Man's Chest

2006

John Knoll, visual effects supervisor:

"We wanted motion capture that happened on set. And the experiences from the *Star Wars* Prequels through *Pirates II* are what really drove the development of that Imocap process. We got all the benefits that we wanted of being able to let *all* the performers be present on set: The director is able to work with both sides of the performance, the camera operator frames up on somebody who's really there, and then editorial doesn't have to maintain a parallel cut."

Director: Gore Verbinski
Producer: Jerry Bruckheimer

ILM Show Leadership:
Visual Effects Supervisor: John Knoll
Additional Visual Effects Supervisor: Roger Guyett
Visual Effects Producers: Ned Gorman, Jill Brooks
Associate Visual Effects Producer: Lori Arnold
Animation Supervisor: Hal Hickel
Associate Animation Supervisor: Marc Chu
Digital Production Supervisor: David Meny
Visual Effects Art Director: Aaron McBride

Academy Award®: Best Achievement in Visual Effects
John Knoll (ILM)
Hal Hickel (ILM)
Charles Gibson
Allen Hall

BAFTA Film Award: Best Achievement in Special Visual Effects
John Knoll (ILM)
Hal Hickel (ILM)
Charles Gibson
Allen Hall

METHOD MO-CAP

The motion capture technique used for the first *Pirates of the Caribbean* film, *The Curse of the Black Pearl* (see pages 183–189), was acceptable for that production because most of the work involved action scenes, such as characters sword fighting with one another. But for the second *Pirates* film, CG characters had to *act* and carry on dialogue scenes opposite the live-action actors.

Steve Sullivan, research and development:

"On the first *Pirates* movie, they would shoot the scene; then, months later, in a separate location, they would have CG actors try to reenact the parts on a dedicated motion capture stage. It was very disconnected. Neither the live-action side nor the CG-actor side had a feel for who they were acting against. And the director feels very out of the loop because he's never seeing the actual scene take place before him.

PREVIOUS SPREAD

Captain Davy Jones and his cursed, completely CG crew.

ABOVE

Wyvern, a member of Davy Jones's crew, was realized via computer graphics using actor John Boswall's performance as a guide. All of the facial animation was painstakingly keyframe-animated by ILM's animation team.

During principal photography, Bill
Nighy (Davy Jones) and others
were motion captured for animation
reference (above left). Initially ILM
was concerned that they wouldn't
be able to replicate the feeling in
the actors' eyes, so the area around
the eyes was darkened so they could
be retained. However, ILM learned
as shots were finished that artists
could in fact replicate even the actors' eyes, as they created keyframe
hand-animation for the whole crew
(above right), except Bootstrap Bill
(Stellan Skarsgård, in rear), who had
digital prosthetics only.

"The one showcase instance of this was when, in the first
movie, Johnny Depp's character picks up a coin, rolls it in
his fingers, and does a certain flourish with his hand. Gore
Verbinski really loved that. He saw Johnny doing the reference
motion, and he said, 'Great, I want exactly that.' So they went
off to shoot the motion capture, on a separate day. Johnny
looked at the reference footage and tried to do the same thing,
but he never got it exactly the same. This kind of thing drove
Gore crazy, because he said, 'Look, I got this thing I want, I
want that, right there.' And it was just too difficult to match.

"So for *Pirates II*, he wanted to be able to conquer that
and shoot everything in one place. John Knoll and Hal Hickel
were instrumental in pushing this forward. It was very risky
at the time. Nobody knew if they could do it, and there was a
fear that we might slow down shooting. But they said, 'No, we
have to have that, let's invest in it.'"

For *Dead Man's Chest*, ILM developed a new technology, Imocap, which
made it possible to do motion capture on location, at the same time
the director was shooting principal photography.

Hal Hickel, animation supervisor:

"On *Pirates II*, when Bill Nighy as Davy Jones was acting opposite Johnny Depp, whatever acting he did there, we could
extract his motion and apply it to the CG Davy Jones, so our

CG character would have the exact same performance. We
were preserving an acting moment that occurred where it
should occur, which is to say on set with all the other actors,
not on a motion capture stage on a different day."

Roger Guyett, additional visual effects supervisor:

"If I want to see Davy Jones act in a movie, should I get a
hundred different people to animate him and try to animate
him in a way that's consistent across all of the animators?
Or is there a different way of doing it? It's this idea of using
a real actor as a proxy for a CG character. So it was a great
opportunity to cast somebody and just say, 'Be Davy Jones—
just act it all out. And you know what we're going to do?
We're going to paint you out afterward and put the CG Davy
Jones in your place.'

"The great thing was that Gore Verbinski suddenly had
an actor he could just cast as Davy Jones; he could see how
the guy was playing him. He didn't look like Davy Jones, but
he certainly behaved like him. And I think that was one of the
first times that had been done to that extent. Each member of
the pirate crew had a real actor behind them. The Davy Jones
character had incredibly believable eyes. People thought that
we were doing some kind of trick. But the eyes were digital.
Every aspect of that character was digital—the wetness, the
different levels of decayed material."

Hal Hickel:

"Gore's on set, and he's got two characters, and he wants both those actors reacting to each other. He doesn't want some weird hybrid Frankenstein process where one actor is doing *his* part and then two months later we do the other half of the conversation on a motion capture stage while they're playing back the first actor's performance. Plus, it gives the editors both performances to cut to, which made the filmmaking process much more like a regular live-action film."

John Knoll:

"When we started on *Pirates II*, fortunately it was a little bit of a different situation from what we had on *Pirates I*, because we didn't have to do transitions. The actors that were going to be on set were only going to be computer generated—we would never see them as their live-action equivalents. So it didn't really matter what they were wearing; we had this opportunity to dress them in something that would allow for better reproduction of their motion. So our challenge to the R & D department was: 'We want to be able to get motion recovery from the performer, but we need to be able to do this on set and we need to be able to do this with a minimal amount of equipment. We can't have a bunch of cameras, and we can't have any real restrictions on lighting or the environment—it has to be able to go anywhere.' And they scratched their heads about it a little bit and came back with a proposal for Imocap."

The Imocap system tracked actors wearing custom-made marker-striped suits. This provided the underlying skeletal motion, which animators enhanced with facial expressions. To capture Imocap data in the studio, ILM used high-frame-rate, black-and-white commercial security cameras connected to a small portable computer synchronized to the film camera. For location scenes, ILM used non-synchronized battery-powered high-definition camcorders, which provided enough data to record the performers' positions.

Hal Hickel:

"To do the Imocap on set, Bill Nighy had to wear this gray suit with weird checkered bands. I think, early on, he was probably a bit bummed about that. He probably looked around at the

LEFT

One of ILM's first shots for the second *Pirates* film was of the dice game. Originally slated for only four characters, the scene ultimately included around a dozen. The challenge mounted when the ship had to roll, tilt, and have digital and practical smoke. But ILM pulled it off thanks to its new Imocap system, which proved its worth in this sequence.

other guys, like Stellan Skarsgård (Bootstrap Bill) and his really cool makeup, and just thought, 'Wow. I have to wear this weird gray suit with this checkerboard band.'

"But I think about a month into shooting, with the long nights and these crazy sets that were constantly being soaked with rain, he started to figure out how lucky he was—because Stellan was in the makeup chair for four hours every morning, whereas Nighy put on these gray pajamas, and he's ready to go. And I know that he was happy with the results, because at the *Pirates II* premiere, I saw him on the red carpet, and he gave me a big hug and said he thought it was fantastic.

"That really made me happy because I was concerned that here's an actor that's *really* good, and he created a *really* interesting performance—and we had covered him up entirely, head to toe, with a CG character. I was worried that he might feel like, 'Where am I in all of this?' But we had worked really hard. It would probably make him uncomfortable to know how minutely we had studied every movement in his face. We really wanted to kind of milk it for everything we could, because it was such a great performance.

"Indeed, by the time we developed Imocap, people weren't really worrying so much about the stigma of motion capture. Because previously, when an animator did everything themselves, they're making all of the choices about the performance. When they're working with motion capture, some of those choices have already been made for them by the motion capture performer, and then they're kind of working on top of that. It took animators a while to realize that both things are valid as long as they serve the shot and the effects you're trying to create."

DAVY JONES'S MAGICAL LOCKER

Davy Jones and all but one of his crewmembers were entirely computer generated. This allowed ILM to create character effects, such as holes through the figures, which would have been difficult or impossible to accomplish with makeup or prosthetic appliances. The writhing tentacles that made up Davy Jones's "beard," however, presented ILM with one of its greatest technical and artistic challenges.

Jason Smith, creature technical director:

"The tentacles were difficult, because it was a big fleshy group of appendages and those things had to perform. He picks things up with them, they curl over each other and bump into each other. So the creature development artists started by putting in wonderful animation controls that allowed animators to move the tentacles in very specific ways. They bump into each other and then they're stopped, or they hit each other and then bounce over—exactly that kind of stuff that's really impossible to animate."

John Knoll:

"It was obvious that we didn't want the tentacles to be keyframe animated, because there were forty-six of them and it would've taken forever to do. And they needed to move in a way that looked very realistic. You wanted it to be a simulation of some kind, but you couldn't just make them all rigid body segments, because they're also supposed to be alive. So the key thing that was missing was to be able to have joints between our rigid segments that could be animated. A program was written that would drive the individual joints between the segments of the beard with a whole variety of parameters, so you could have high-level control over the behavior. You could dial in different amounts of curling strength and curling speed. And by animating those parameters in different ways, you could get what appeared to be very different emotional states in the behaviors: If you had them writhing very strong and very fast, Davy seemed very agitated."

Miles Perkins, director of marketing and communications:

"Davy Jones reminded me of when I walked into the theater back in 1993 and saw the first T. rex test. It was that stunning. You weren't seeing building blocks leading up to it, it was this huge breakthrough that was just immediate. There's this close-up of Davy Jones filling the screen, something that you wouldn't want to do with an actor in general, but it was so incredibly believable. That was clearly the reason why we were able to get the Academy Award. It was really revolutionary on the scale that *Jurassic Park* was."

Performance Capture

SINCE THE BEGINNING OF CINEMA, one of the most common visual effects was to add something to a shot that wasn't there when it was originally photographed: i.e., adding to the "clean plate." For example, when Ray Harryhausen had an actor battling with sword-fighting skeletons in *Jason and the Argonauts*, the actor was filmed fighting empty space, pretending that the skeletons were there, and afterwards Ray would animate the skeleton to react to the actor's performance.

Prior to the advent of digital technology, removing something from a shot was difficult and expensive, so wherever possible plates were photographed "empty" so that the visual effects task could be limited simply to adding the required items.

It is not surprising then that this methodology was used for the first digital characters: the stained-glass man from *The Young Sherlock Holmes*, the pseudopod from *The Abyss*, the *Jurassic Park* dinosaurs, etc. Acting to an empty space can be difficult and confusing not only for the actors, but for everyone involved. Where should the actor look? How should the shot be framed? When is it the right time to cut to the next angle? So, wherever possible, a performance reference is shot where an actor performs some representation of what the CG character should be doing. This reference allows everyone on set to rehearse the shot, and the director to provide some initial input on what the performance should look like.

Approximately half of all the digital character work on *Pirates of the Caribbean: The Curse of the Black Pearl* was done with performance reference and clean plates. The exceptions to this were the transformation scenes in which the cursed pirates step into the moonlight and reveal their true skeletal form. To accomplish this we filmed the actors, and matched animation to the actors' movements, then digitally removed their images for the frames in which they were to be skeletons. By this time, our paint tools had improved to the point where this quickly became the preferred methodology. And the concept of match-animation, or 'matchimation,' had become a sound methodology for our animators. It meant better

performances, no eyeline problems, no composition problems, less work for the editor, and so on. In short, the shots were just better.

When we began work on *Pirates of the Caribbean: Dead Man's Chest*, we initially planned on employing this new methodology. However, although matchimation produced superior results, it was a tedious and time-consuming manual process. We needed a better solution, a new way to translate the motions of the actors on set to the animation of our CG characters.

An ideal tool for this task would have been motion capture, something we had been using in production since *Star Wars* Episode I. However, for this film we wanted to provide the director, Gore Verbinski, with the freedom to film all of his actors on set, during principal photography and without any technical overhead to slow down production. Being that we were going to be filming on location in the Caribbean and in many conditions—in close quarters, on the decks of rolling

ships, in pouring rain, in blazing sunlight, in the middle of a jungle, and even knee deep in the ocean—existing motion capture techniques were out of the question because they had too many limitations. We had to find a new solution that would accurately capture the actors' performances with the accuracy and fidelity of traditional motion capture and without fail.

It was time for something newer and better. We challenged the R & D department to develop a lightweight, low-footprint, robust, and filmmaker-friendly motion capture system that we could use on location—and the result was Imocap.

Imocap is an image-based motion capture technology comprised of hardware and software that can, if necessary, capture an actor's movement with just the principal camera.

John Knoll

Pirates of the Caribbean: At World's End

2007

John Knoll, visual effects supervisor:

"Having seen how difficult doing computer-generated water had been on the first two *Pirates* pictures, I was trying to avoid doing any CG water. But then for *Pirates III*, we had this climactic battle in a giant storm—at sea. Since there was no big whirlpool, they couldn't shoot live-action plates. And we couldn't really do it as a miniature in a tank. The only real option was computer graphics, so we had to do fluid simulations—for hundreds of shots!"

Director: Gore Verbinski
Producer: Jerry Bruckheimer

ILM Show Leadership:
Visual Effects Supervisors: John Knoll, Roger Guyett
Visual Effects Producer: Jill Brooks
Animation Supervisor: Hal Hickel
Associate Animation Supervisor: Marc Chu
Digital Production Supervisor: David Meny
Visual Effects Art Director: Aaron McBride

Academy Award® Nomination:
 Best Achievement in Visual Effects
John Knoll (ILM)
Hal Hickel (ILM)
Charlie Gibson
John Frazier

BAFTA Film Award Nomination:
 Best Achievement in Special Visual Effects
John Knoll (ILM)
Hal Hickel (ILM)
Charlie Gibson
John Frazier

ABOVE, INSET

ABOVE, INSET

The CG ship and three main simulations were combined to create the final shot.

ABOVE

To realize the maelstrom, ILM had to simulate approximately 15.5 billion gallons of water in order to create a half-mile-wide storm. Existing computer techonology couldn't handle the volume necessary for such a massive undertaking; so instead, a novel approach was taken: The entire volume would be flattened in 3-D space and forces would be redirected so that when the volume was redistorted to the funnel shape, it would yeild the desired effect.

Pirates of the Caribbean: At World's End has more than two thousand visual effects shots, as many as the first two *Pirates* films combined. Because ILM's capacity was approximately 750 shots, seven other vendors were involved in producing the visual effects for the film. Virtually the entire ILM team was working on the film at the same time. It was the first time that this had happened at ILM since *Return of the Jedi* (1982–1983).

In *Dead Man's Chest*, Davy Jones had been the star CG character. For *At World's End* there was a new CG star: the maelstrom. This climactic storm sequence involved more than 650 visual effects shots and approximately twenty minutes of screen time.

To create the maelstrom, ILM undertook research and development based on the company's past experience with digital water from *The Perfect Storm* (see pages 132–139) and *Poseidon* (see pages 252–257).

But the whirlpool required the creation of fluid simulations on a larger scale than had ever been attempted for entertainment purposes: an apocalyptic sea with a nearly unprecedented level of detail.

At World's End pushed the limits of water-simulation technology available at the time, so John Knoll worked with fluid-dynamics engineer Frank Losasso Petterson and CG supervisor Joakim Arnesson to develop the climactic storm.

John Knoll:

"The maelstrom is supposed to be massive—a mile and a half across—and the way you make something look massive in a fluid simulation, since it's done on a three-dimensional volume grid, is that you make that grid as finely divided as you can. But there's an amount of memory associated with

PREVIOUS SPREAD
An all-digital Jack Sparrow (Depp) has a hallucination of himself as one of the first pirate crew.

RIGHT
At Kerner, an old technique of using scale models in water was later supplemented by ILM's digital effects.

every cell on the grid. You have to store all the values in every grid cell. And as soon as you make something that's high resolution in all three dimensions, it takes a vast amount of memory. So we took our biggest-memory computers, which had thirty-two gigabytes of RAM, and we ran the highest resolution simulations that we could afford to run. Of course, they took forever—a full week.

"Then, once you've got the simulations, you have to do a whole series of secondary simulations—the subsurface bubbles and the spray. You have to do foam. And those all take a while to tweak to make sure they look good. So it took several months to get to the point where we had one shot that had all of these looks developed.

"I thought, *All right. Now, we're starting to get somewhere with this*. So I showed this shot to Gore, and he hated it. He hated it because he felt like, 'It just doesn't look big enough. I don't think I'm seeing something that's a mile and a half across. That looks like it's three hundred feet across.' And I had to admit he was right about that, but that was as much detail as we could get out of the simulation. Since Gore had flatly re-

jected that and we were already at our ceiling on the memory and computational limits of our fluid simulation, we had to figure out how we were going to get *four times* this amount of detail out of our simulation.

"It became apparent that we had to take a different approach. We transformed the forces—bent gravity and bent the wind vectors—and then ran our simulation as a *flat disc*, which gave us much more spatial resolution. Then we warped that back into its original space. That was how we managed to achieve a sufficiently high level of detail. And because the character of the maelstrom at the bottom is different than at the top, we needed one simulation for on top and one for down below. Then there were very specific actions that required custom simulations, like when the *Flying Dutchman* finally capsizes and the water swarms over it. We had to do a lot of massive simulations on that film."

Steve Sullivan, head of R & D:

"Both *Poseidon* and the *Pirates* movies pushed the technology forward. We were saying, 'Okay, water's something we're

going to be asked to do over and over and over again. Let's build it to be more reusable, so we have a real water system to depend on.' So that's the thread. *Perfect Storm* showed it could be done, established some key concepts, came up with the prototype, and then when *Poseidon* and the *Pirates* movies came along, we realized we needed to invest in this for real."

WYVERN JACK

In *At World's End*, Jack Sparrow has a vision of himself as Wyvern Jack, embedded and encrusted into the ship like the character Wyvern in *Dead Man's Chest*. Jack has barnacles and corals growing out of his forehead. When he pulls away from the ship, he leaves the top of his head behind.

Hal Hickel:

"It made sense to us to do Wyvern Jack all-CG because of the way his head has to splinter apart and break into pieces of coral. But it had to be very much Johnny Depp. We wanted

people to look at this and say, 'That's Johnny, but how? Look what they did to him!'

"We had great reference of Johnny, because he's there, in the footage, wearing the mocap bands and acting out the part. And we just covered him up completely with our CG version. Then we had to paint out some bits because the whole back of his head is missing and he plucks his own brain out and he licks it, which is really disgusting."

MINIATURES

John Knoll:

"I missed the whole era of the wooden-boat movies from the forties. But this seemed like a really great opportunity to employ some of those great old techniques. You build a big ship model, and you put it in a tank out back. And you start the fans up, you roll camera at high speed, and there you go. But we had the opportunity to fix the things that

ABOVE, INSET

Principal photography recorded three ships for reference and for their water wakes; the two ships on the right were completely replaced with miniatures built by Kerner Optical, while the left ship received only digital sails (final frame, above).

ABOVE

For a secret island, ILM created a
3-D digimatte painting (inset: prep
for the final painting).

didn't work about that. For example, if you look at the old
wooden-boat movies from the forties, there're droplet-size
problems where the scale kind of gets blown. The water
goes out of focus in the foreground, and you never see anybody walking around on deck. The nice thing is that we had
the opportunity to fix all those things digitally, since we
could split in live-action water in the foreground and fix the
out-of-focus problem. Where we have problems with drop-

lets that look like they are out of scale occasionally showing
up in the wakes of the boat, you either paint them out or
you put live-action, larger-scale elements over the top. And
we could put little CG people on deck as needed. So it was
possible to use this old technique, but to then use some of
the newer tools to repair the places where that technique
was unsatisfactory."

Transformers

2007

Scott Farrar, visual effects supervisor:

"This project was completely different from anything that's ever been tried before. The goal was to make our characters look photoreal, and to act, speak, and move in a cool, athletic fashion."

Director: Michael Bay
Producers: Ian Bryce, Tom DeSanto,
   Lorenzo di Bonaventura, Don Murphy

ILM Show Leadership:
Visual Effects Supervisor: Scott Farrar
Associate Visual Effects Supervisor: Russell Earl
Visual Effects Producer: Shari Hanson
Animation Supervisor: Scott Benza
Digital Production Supervisor: Jeff White
Visual Effects Art Director: Alex Jaeger

Academy Award® Nomination:
   Best Achievement in Visual Effects
Scott Farrar (ILM)
Scott Benza (ILM)
Russell Earl (ILM)
John Frazier

ILM WORKED ON *TRANSFORMERS* for a full two years, producing 430 shots. The focus of the work was on the creation of fourteen photorealistic computer-animated hero robot characters.

Scott Benza, animation supervisor:

"A lot of the appeal of *Transformers* was showing the audience something they had never seen before. And a photorealistic vehicle transforming into a completely convincing robot was something new and fresh. Usually, when we start on a project, we look for references of similar work. We were all pretty surprised that almost no work had been done with giant robots. I'm sure there were animated films that had robots, and there was the *Transformers* cartoon series, but as far as very large humanoid-type robots go, we couldn't find any reference. It was on us to set the standard for this type of work."

LIGHTING

Lighting was crucial in creating credible *Transformers* characters. The CG vehicles and their robot forms had to be lit just as creatively as the scenes created by Michael Bay and his director of photography, Mitchell Amundsen. Acquiring lighting environments is standard procedure in visual effects work; for this project, however, ILM had to create a level of detail far beyond what had been attempted in past productions. The standard is 1,000 pixel resolution texture maps; for this film, ILM used 8,000 pixels.

Fortunately, by the time ILM was working on *Transformers*, the company's lighting and rendering tools had advanced to a point where it was possible to light the CG robots so that they were completely integrated with surrounding environments. This visual connection greatly enhanced their realism. But animation also played a significant role.

PREVIOUS SPREAD

A CG transformer—Decepticon Skorponok—attacks a special operations military unit in Qatar (live action was filmed in New Mexico, with a practical Transformer head and tail).

ABOVE

The battle between Megatron and Optimus Prime. The real car between them was actually the Porsche Cayenne used by director Michael Bay as the camera car. It had a camera rig mounted on its roof; while they were removed, the car itself was kept in the shot because it was not out of place.

ANIMATING HUNDREDS OF PARTS

Scott Benza:

"The animation could have easily broken the realism if we'd had the robots move too fast or not follow the rules of physics. And since they were supposed to be living machines, we had quite a challenge in delivering emotional performances with characters whose faces had parts that moved but didn't deform like skin. Much of the facial animation that we're used to doing at ILM is shape-based, so you change the shape of something to help mimic how a human's face would deform. But with robot faces composed of a couple of hundred individual moving parts that don't deform, we had to be innovative with those individual parts."

One of the most important breakthroughs on *Transformers* was the final layer of rigging for the robots. This was called "dynamic rigging," a system of controls that enabled animators to move every piece of geometry on the model, independently and by hand.

Nevertheless, actual transformations presented a challenge for animation rigging. ILM therefore created forty-three distinct transformations from vehicles to robots, each of which required complex animation and rigging, especially given the fact that none of the transformations were locked-off shots. Each transformation had to be designed to a specific camera angle *and* a specific camera movement. A completely different transformation was required every time a Transformer transformed.

THE PARTS LIBRARY

The ILM team built a huge library of automobile parts to support the development of the robot models. The facility of the library greatly increased the complexity of the figures. Each robot model

was composed of thousands of pieces of individually modeled and painted geometry.

Jeff White, digital production supervisor:

"When we first started to get the artwork from the production office, it was immediately clear that we were going to be creating something incredibly complicated. In the *Transformers* animated cartoon series, the characters were pretty simple and boxy. Michael Bay didn't want anything like that. He wanted a lot of exposed car pieces; he wanted them to look photorealistic, complex, and visually interesting, yet still retain details so that you could tell who was who. When we looked at his requirements and the timeline we had to build these characters in, we knew that we were going to have to put together a library of parts.

"The library functioned similarly to the ILM Model Shop, where model-makers would do a lot of kit-bashing; they would get model kits, smash them up, and pick up the pieces they needed. That's the kind of approach we took for *Transformers*, where if you modeled a flywheel or a piston or an axel, we added the new element to the parts library, and then it was there to help build the rest of the characters even faster. What was interesting about that was just how many different kinds of pieces we ended up needing. We spent a lot of time finding references of car parts and looking to see how we can integrate these into the character, to help it feel like the internal mechanics are making the character move.

"It also had to be visually interesting. Because at the end of the day, that mattered more than being physically correct. The challenge there was Michael had shot a lot of car commercials, so he knew how metal is supposed to react and he knew what it's supposed to look like and where it is supposed to have glints and gleams."

LEFT

For a shot in which Megatron and Optimus Prime smash through an office building while the former is in jet form, Kerner Optical built a one-quarter-scale structure that even included tiny office equipment. A mandrel on a mechanical sled stood in for the CG Transformers in the miniature shot to provide the necessary physical action.

KEEPING TWELVE MILLION POLYGONS REAL

All of the *Transformers* together had more than 60,000 moving parts and more than twelve million polygons. These were the densest and most geometry-heavy models ever created at ILM. Each figure featured thousands of articulated, uniquely modeled, and painted parts.

Russell Earl, associate visual effects supervisor:

"At ILM, we get the fastest and the best computers. But the geometry of the robots was so complex, and the data was so huge, that we had problems loading these models. There was the sheer scale of the models, but then there was also the transforming. We started with a dozen or so transformations—and we ended up with almost fifty. And all of the transformations were very hero, right in camera, nothing to hide. It was challenging for us to deliver that level of realism. You see this truck, it's real, and now you see it transform into a robot, and you've got to keep the same level of realism with the materials, how the light reflects off it, how the highlights travel across the surfaces, all of which is visually very complex.

"For one shot, the Optimus Prime truck is driving away from us just before he transforms. In the original photography, we shot the truck by chasing behind it in a camera car. Then, at a certain point, Optimus Prime stands up and transforms. We knew we had to transform from the live vehicle to the CG truck, because the CG truck would then need to transform into Optimus Prime.

"So we decided to just paint out the real truck and use an all CG truck. We figured we could match the look of the real truck more easily than trying to blend from the real truck to the CG truck to the CG robot. But Michael saw the CG truck, and he was instantly on it: 'That's not my truck!' 'Well, no, but it looks just like …' 'That is *not* my truck.'

"Sure enough, our tire was maybe an inch wider, or the trailer hitch was slightly off, or the window was slightly rounder—all of these really small details that you wouldn't notice, but Michael was right on it. He just challenges you and pushes you to get the best. And it's great because you have the opportunity to make that change and put the best image up there."

Integrating the CG robot figures with the live-action environment wasn't always easy.

Russell Earl:

"When we were shooting the plates on set, we had window-washer poles that we could extend to try and help the cameraman visualize where these robots would be. We'd say, 'Bring in the Optimus Prime pole!' And you'd have somebody walking with this giant window-washer pole that's twenty-two feet high. In some cases, it had a big cardboard face on top of it that would help the camera operators to envision the robots in the plates. In many cases, you'd say to Michael, 'So what's going on in this shot? Is Optimus Prime falling over and Bumblebee is next to him?' And Michael would just say, 'I don't know! It just looks cool.' So you're shooting this stuff on faith that when you bring it back to ILM, we'll be able to make it work."

SHOOT IT DIRTY

Russell Earl:

"Some people say Michael Bay is difficult to work with, but he's really just trying to get the best out of everyone. One of the things about this film is that in the past, with CG, we would say, 'Don't put any smoke in there, we have to put in a blue screen.' It was very technical and everything had to be exact. But Michael just doesn't work that way. He likes to blow things up. I remember one shot where we're ready to roll and all of a sudden Michael yells, 'Pop the smoke!' It hadn't been discussed before, but the next thing you know, there's just this massive curtain of smoke between us and it, which makes our work that much more difficult. But for *Transformers*, we said we were going to shoot it dirty, put everything in there, all of the smoke and fire, and we'll rely on the artists at ILM to blend the robots in and match the smoke. It was a lot more work, but I think in the end it gave us a much more successful result."

The visual approach to the CG robots was also "dirty" in terms of the details of the design.

Jeff White:

"Our first version of Bumblebee matched the artwork in form, paint, and color, but it didn't look real. It looked kind of CG. Right away, Michael said, 'Dirty it down, paint in scratches, mud, dirt, rust, weather it, make it feel old.' Even though in their car form, they're shiny and new, the robots themselves are old and battle worn. They've been battling for hundreds of years, so it made sense that they would look beaten up. And that was important in terms of making the CG look a lot more realistic, because any time you can weather something and add scratches and chips, it's just that much more believable. Adding in rust and dirt and all of that made a huge difference."

This approach harked back to the original *Star Wars* trilogy, where George Lucas had instructed ILM to abandon the traditional sleekness of science fiction. He wanted instead to create a "used universe," in which space vehicles and devices looked aged and dirty.

Fluid Sim Overview

AS WELL AS FANTASTIC CREATURES and impossible machines, one of the classes of effects ILM is often called upon to provide is fluid phenomena such as water, fire, clouds, mist, smoke, and explosions. Together with digital creatures delivering dialogue, these can be some of the most challenging effects to pull off convincingly. Fluids have no well-defined shape, they are complex and constantly changing, and yet their appearance and motion are instantly recognizable. They can form beautiful and fascinating shapes, move in compelling ways, subtly enhance a scene without drawing attention to themselves. Or they can shout "fake" and ruin a shot if executed poorly.

There are two main ways we typically meet this challenge. The first is to sculpt the shapes we want and animate them by hand to move in a convincing way. While this gives us ultimate artistic freedom, it can be almost impossible to create something that looks completely natural. The second way is to use the computer to model the physics of the effect we want to create, set up the conditions of the environment, and run a full physical simulation of how the fluid might behave. This gives us a massive data set that we can then use to render an image that looks completely natural because it follows the laws of reality. In working this way, digital artists become almost like live-action special effects technicians—they must use all their ingenuity to build a setup that will give the desired performance, then throw the switch, stand back, and see what nature, or in this case the computer algorithm, delivers.

Until relatively recently, the first option—doing it by hand—was the only one available to us. This changed in 1999, when ILM was tasked with the effects work on *The Perfect Storm*. This movie demanded far more than anything that had ever gone before—stormy oceans and giant waves, massive yet controllable and photorealistic, and forming a major part of the movie, essentially becoming one of the central characters. It was clear that the ad-hoc methods of creating fluid effects up until that point would never meet the challenge, and so, with the help of John Anderson, an academic and expert in the field of computational fluid dynamics, ILM developed its first systems for simulating the physics of ocean water. Under the creative leadership of Stefen Fangmeier, the effects team created something that had never been seen before, and the movie was nominated for an Academy Award for Best Visual Effects in 2000.

effects supervisor Kim Libreri the daunting task of trying to surpass the work done on *The Perfect Storm* five years earlier. To do this, the entire fluid-simulation system was revised and improved, and an all-new effects pipeline built around it. A similar system was used by the team led by John Knoll for the digitally generated ocean in *Pirates of the Caribbean: Dead Man's Chest*, and in 2006 both movies were nominated for the Academy Award for Best Visual Effects, with *Pirates of the Caribbean* eventually winning the Oscar.

In subsequent years, fluid simulation at ILM is near ubiquitous and is used on most movies that the company works on, whether to create invisible effects or huge spectacles. It has been used in many more Oscar-nominated movies, including *Pirates of the Caribbean: At World's End*, *Transformers*, *Iron Man*, *Star Trek* and *Avatar*. In 2008, the ILM fluid-simulation system was awarded an Academy Award in its own right, for the contribution it has made to visual effects. It seems that as computational power increases, fluid simulation will continue to produce results that forever push the envelope, and only imagination limits what we might next use it to create.

Willi Geiger

ABOVE

The Perfect Storm challenged the ILM crew to create a fluid dynamics system that would allow for the creation of everything from still water, to turbulent seas, to waves the height of a 10-story building. For the turbulent seas (main image), separate simulations were run for the "bottom water," essentially the body of the ocean itself, and "top water," wave crests, foam, mist, etc. When skillfully combined with live-action elements (top right), the result (main image) was seamless.

RIGHT

To create the realistic mushroom cloud resulting from the nuclear explosions in *Terminator 3: Rise of the Machines* (large image), the ILM crew came up with a clever solution. They ran numerous extremely high-resolution, two-dimensional simulation slices (top left), which are used to create a velocity field that particles move through (top right). Additional turbulence was added to break up the interpolated velocity field. The rendering of the explosion was extremely taxing computationally, so the contribution of each light was baked into a map, thus allowing compositors to balance the lighting (main image) as necessary.

Anderson continued to work with ILM, helping create more ocean water, huge smoke plumes and explosions for *Pearl Harbor* in 2001, the same year that his work with ILM won him an Academy Award. Effects work using his physical simulation systems was also seen that year in *Jurassic Park III*, this time in a shot where many people might not even realize it was a visual effect—the smoke grenade. It is often at this point—where an effect is used "invisibly," that a technique can be said to have reached maturity, and indeed from that point forward, physically-based fluid simulation became a standard component of the artist's tool kit at ILM.

The next chapter in the story of fluid simulation at ILM came in 2003, with *Terminator 3: Rise of the Machines*. ILM began a long and fruitful collaboration with Stanford University, and in particular with Ron Fedkiw, a professor there and a leading researcher with more than eighty published papers in the field of computational physics and computer graphics. Fedkiw helped ILM take fluid simulation for visual effects to the next level, with artists using his software to create all the shots of the liquid metal T-X Terminator as well as many digital pyrotechnic shots for the first time, including the nuclear blast that is the centerpiece of the opening shot of the movie. *Star Wars*: Episode III *Revenge of the Sith* and *Harry Potter and the Goblet of Fire* followed.

In 2005, it was another movie about rogue conditions at sea that pushed the state of the art forward again—*Poseidon*. *Poseidon* gave ILM

Iron Man

2008

Jon Favreau, director:

"I wanted the effects to be an exciting element of the movie, but I made every effort to integrate the effects into the reality of the story. A lot of super-hero movies lose sight of the fact that they have to keep things photoreal—because the less real the action is, the more you detach yourself emotion-ally from the story … maintaining realism was an overall strategy that we stayed true to throughout the making of this movie."

Director: Jon Favreau
Producers: Kevin Feige, Avi Arad

ILM Show Leadership:
Visual Effects Supervisor: Ben Snow
Visual Effects Producer: Wayne Billheimer
Animation Supervisor: Hal Hickel
Associate Animation Supervisor: Marc Chu
Digital Production Supervisor: Doug Smythe
Visual Effects Art Director: Aaron McBride

Academy Award® Nomination:
    Best Achievement in Visual Effects
John Nelson
Ben Snow (ILM)
Daniel Sudick
Shane Mahan

BAFTA Film Award Nomination:
    Best Special Visual Effects
Hal Hickel (ILM)
Shane Mahan
John Nelson
Ben Snow (ILM)

FOR *IRON MAN*, director Jon Favreau set flawless photorealism as the standard. Once again, the challenge was to integrate seamlessly visual effects into the live-action elements. More than four hundred visual effects shots were awarded to ILM, most of which involved a computer-generated Iron Man suit.

IRON MAN IRON

Using ILM's on-set motion capture technology, Imocap, allowed the team to put lead actor Robert Downey Jr. in environments without him having to wear the entire Iron Man suit, much of which was created in CG. Using a partial practical suit made it possible to achieve a better performance and allowed for more flexible camera work.

Hal Hickel, animation supervisor:

"The group at Stan Winston Studio came up with an awesome suit that an actor could wear that was quite an amazing translation from the comic book's 2-D design to an actual 3-D object. It looked great and was good for heroic static shots, but the actor couldn't move very well in it. So we knew the suit would have to be largely computer-generated. But, because there's supposed to be a human in there, we wanted realistic motion. We figured this was something we'd want to use Imocap for.

"The trick is that on the *Pirates* films, where we used motion capture, you'd have an actor on set doing something that later we were always *completely* covering up with CG. But in *Iron Man*, we had a number of shots where Robert Downey

PREVIOUS SPREAD

The CG Iron Man in action

ABOVE

Robert Downey Jr. (as Tony Stark/Iron Man) was filmed against green-screen (inset) wearing the ILM Imocap suit so artists could outfit him in the digital Iron Man armor.

Jr. would open the visor or take off the helmet—and so in effect we were doing digital costuming. We were putting a CG suit around a live actor. It had to match absolutely perfectly, because there were parts of the real actor that you could still see—either his bare hands or his head poking out of the top of the suit—so the accuracy of our tracking had to be much higher on this film.

"It's this whole thing of trying to fool the audience. The problem with audiences nowadays is they've seen so much 'making of' stuff that even if they don't know exactly how something was done, if you show them something that couldn't possibly be real, like a dinosaur or a tidal wave, nobody ever says anymore, 'How did they do that?' They just go, 'Yeah, they did that with a computer.' The trick to getting an audience to feel the 'wow' of the shot is: one, there have to be great concepts behind it; and two, we have to keep them guessing with the techniques.

"And so with *Iron Man*, we wanted to have shots where people were absolutely certain that it had to be a real suit the actor was wearing, but then you have another shot where he takes off and flies and they think, *Well, okay*, that's *got to be computer generated, right?* But *then* when you have a shot where maybe it starts close on the suit and you can see all the little scratches and dings and you're thinking, 'Okay, that's got to be real.' But when he starts flying, you start to mess with the audience's expectations about technique.

"And that led to all kinds of interesting conversations on whether Robert should be wearing parts of the suit with other parts CG. In fact, Robert started out wearing the real suit, but then he couldn't really move in it. So we began to do shots where he would wear half the suit. Then Robert said, 'Well, I can just wear that gray suit, right? With the little checkerboard bands—that's a lot more comfortable, can I just wear that?' So, over the course of the film, he started wearing the actual armor less and less and wearing our Imocap suit more and more. More and more of the shots therefore became all CG.

"But it was great because we still had a number of shots that were either the all–Stan Winston suit or pieces of it. I know there are shots in the movie that are 100 percent CG that people think are the real suit, and there are shots in the

film that are the real suit where people think it's CG. It's great to keep the audience guessing."

ILM also used CG to create more heroic proportions for the suit, proportions that could not be achieved with a suit that a real person would wear. The final CG suit is three inches taller than the practical suit, which gives additional impact to the image.

ON YOUR MARK . . .

The shiny metallic surface of the Mark II suit presented challenges at every stage of creating the CG version. Of course, ILM had dealt with shiny metallic objects in CG before (T-1000 in *Terminator 2*, spaceships and droids in *Star Wars*, robots and vehicles in *Transformers*), but the CG chrome Mark II suit had to be seen in extreme close-ups, often cutting back to the real suit. This required an exceptionally high level of photorealism for the CG work.

Standard HDRI alone could not be used to model lighting and reflections on the brushed metal suit. The ILM team had to explore technology related to "bidirectional reflectance distribution function" (BRDF), a term that describes the changing appearance of objects when they're illuminated from different angles.

Ben Snow, visual effects supervisor:

"Our challenge was to match the silver suit photographed on set. One of the things we decided to do was to try to derive the BRDF, which is a way of measuring the way a surface reflects light. It involves a big elaborate machine. So Stan Winston Studio painted small cubes with the different materials for the Iron Man suits. We sent these off to a place in Russia, one of the few facilities in the world equipped to derive precise BRDF data. We got BRDFs back for two of the materials, but for the brushed metal suit, they put it on the thing for two days—and the machine broke down. It wasn't able to derive something from a surface like that at the time. But we got enough information from this process that our lead technical director Pat Myers and the show's CG supervisor, Doug Smythe were able to go in and do it by brute force, old school. They worked with our R & D people to change the way we created reflected light off brushed surfaces."

SUIT-UP SEQUENCE

The first time the silver suit is seen, Iron Man is testing his flight surfaces.

Ben Snow:

"As we started to add CG components seamlessly alongside the silver suit components, we wanted more and more of the suit to work. One bit would move, and Jon Favreau said, 'We need more of it to move.' So of course, we go crazy and have everything moving, and before you know it, we've replaced 90 percent of the practical suit. We were then pre-senting footage to the client, and it was clear that everyone

on the client's side had forgotten which bits were CG and which were real. So we ended up replacing the whole suit for the scene, because it meant that we didn't have to lock down the matchmove quite as closely. The studio had become very excited by this scene where he tested all his flying surfaces. It's a scene I like to call 'Hardware Worship.' Gearheads in the audience are really excited by this. So the studio and Jon decided, 'We want more of this Hardware Worship stuff.'"

More "Hardware Worship" came in the form of Iron Man's suit-up sequence, which was added late in the production after Downey was no longer available. Almost the entire sequence was fabricated without the actor.

ABOVE

Stark (Downey), in his garage work-shop, gets into the Iron Man suit with the help of ILM's digital suit-up machines and CG Iron Man armor.

ABOVE, INSET

Downey mimes the action of the suit-up machines pulling his arms and legs, as shot during principal photography.

Obadiah Stane (Jeff Bridges) performed in the "Tea Pot," which consisted of the chest pod of the Iron Monger character on a wheeled rig. ILM would later complete the character digitally, giving it arms and legs and adding paintwork to the practical set piece to better blend the materials.

Ben Snow:

"They came to us and said, 'We've got this sequence we want to do, where Tony puts on the suit in his workshop, but we don't have the workshop any more. Do you think you can create backgrounds for this, based on clean plates we've shot for other material and stills?' We told them we could do it, and then they said, 'Great, we'll give you Brian, Robert Downey Jr.'s stand-in, in a wetsuit on a blue screen, with a floor painted to look like the floor of the workshop.'

"So we went out and filmed a bunch of plates of him standing there in the wetsuit on the middle of this blue screen. Then we talked about concepts for how the suit-up machine would appear. I always loved this scene in *Total Recall* where Schwarzenegger is disguised as a woman, but then her head opens up into these little sliding components. So I thought the floor should open up like this woman's mechanical head, which would mean that we could justify the panels and cover up the background a little bit.

"In the end, we replaced the floor that the guy was standing on. The only real part of that is the stand-in. But they didn't like his wig, so we took stills of Robert Downey Jr. from a texture shoot and replaced the real guy's wig with Robert's real hair. For the last shot in the sequence, we actually did film Robert on a blue screen in an Imocap suit, because we're tracking the whole suit onto his body. For the rest of it, it's Brian, and a lot of CG."

Indiana Jones and the Kingdom of the Crystal Skull

2008

Pablo Helman, visual effects supervisor:

"The aesthetic premise behind *Kingdom of the Crystal Skull* was that it had to match the three other *Indiana Jones* movies. The effort to unify this film with the previous three included Spielberg's decision to shoot on photochemical stock, use as many practical stunts and effects as possible, and to edit on film. In that spirit, we went back to the essence of the action-adventure genre: stunt work, with special effects and visual effects working together to facilitate his vision."

Director: Steven Spielberg
Producers: Kathleen Kennedy, Frank Marshall

ILM Show Leadership:
Visual Effects Supervisor and Aerial Unit Director: Pablo Helman
Associate Visual Effects Supervisor: Marshall Krasser
Visual Effects Producer: Stephanie Hornish
Animation Supervisor: Steve Rawlins
Digital Production Supervisor: Jeff White
Visual Effects Art Director: Christian Alzmann

BAFTA Film Award Nomination:
  Best Special Visual Effects
Pablo Helman
Marshall Krasser
Steve Rawlins

THE STATE OF THE VISUAL EFFECTS industry, and audience expectations, had changed dramatically since 1981's *Raiders of the Lost Ark*. One of the great challenges for ILM on *Crystal Skull* was to create a seamless mixture of processes from an earlier era of filmmaking with digital techniques.

George Lucas, executive producer:

"Steven wanted to do it the old way, and that's fine. It did cost quite a bit more money, and it's more difficult, but he wanted that look. But we also did do quite a bit more digital than was anticipated, because some of the shots just couldn't be done any other way. That's the whole miracle of digital. It allows you *not* to be constrained. Now, you can actually do almost anything you want, so you begin to think that way. Then you forget that you can't really do it the old way, so you have to use digital technology to accomplish that."

The scope of ILM's visual effects work for *Crystal Skull* was broad: fantastic environments and creatures, practical and supernatural effects, ambitious stunt sequences, and the systematic destruction of ancient structures and massive exterior locations. Nearly all of the ILM team for *Crystal Skull* had grown up watching the earlier *Indy* films.

Richard Bluff, digital matte supervisor:

"We were huge *Indiana Jones* fans, so there was a certain anticipation about what we were going to be doing. Spielberg wanted to shoot it in a very similar style to the original *Raiders* picture, so he was going to shoot with the same lenses that he had reconditioned from the original film.

"Wherever possible, we wanted to try to mirror the approach by using old-time visual effects techniques: For example, we shot cotton balls for clouds in the sequence above the Nazca in the cemetery. Paul and a few other artists got a ton of cotton balls and set up a stage shoot. They developed a huge lighting rig that allowed us to shoot multiple passes of the cotton balls with different lighting conditions. Then we moved the cotton balls again, and shot another one, and over the course of a few days, you almost had a time-lapse effect of stormy clouds. Then Paul Huston took the cloud images into

a compositing package and did some color grading and more animation and re-times on that. And, lo and behold, he had animated clouds using a technique very similar to the ones used in the original movies."

DOOM TOWN

Pablo Helman:

"Doom Town was a miniature in its entirety, except for a single house and two full-scale facades. For the latter part of the sequence, when a nuclear explosion reaches the structures, the miniature town was blown up utilizing massive air cannons. This footage was combined with CG particle simulations in an intricately layered composite."

Richard Bluff:

"Doom Town was a particularly challenging sequence because you had a housing estate that was a nuclear test site, and we knew that these buildings had to be blown up on a stage at Kerner. But we also had to reproduce the set for a lot of the wide shots with computer graphics. So we built models of three of the unique houses and set these up on a Lazy Susan outside. We photographed the houses from different angles as they were rotating around. They were huge buildings, and it required three people to rotate the Lazy Susan around. We shot the houses when it was an overcast sky, so we could then add our own sun at any particular angle, and get the right sort of effect.

"In Doom Town, we also had to populate some of the driveways for wide vista shots with old 1950s cars. Normally we would model these cars in CG. But Paul Huston suggested

that the best approach would be simply to buy toy cars of the right era, photograph these from the required angles, and then just put them on cards in the shot. So when you see a lot of the cars on the streets, they're actually photographs of toy cars. That was something Paul used to do in years gone by."

OLD FRIENDS

The warehouse from the final scene of *Raiders of the Lost Ark* was reprised in *Kingdom of the Crystal Skull*. Hangar 51 was an interior environment that had to be fabricated in CG from a much smaller practical set.

Jeff White, digital production supervisor:

"It was an amazing opportunity to revisit some of the locations from the original films, like the crate warehouse from *Raiders*, which originally was an incredible matte painting. For *Crystal Skull*, production actually had built quite a few crates for the foreground, but we were able to extend the space out with CG. I think that was a real thrill for everyone."

KILLER ANTS

ILM created more than 200,000 digital Saifu ants to populate several shots. The ants were rendered and layered in three resolutions and animated through motion cycles and crowd simulations. Those ants closest to camera and hero ants with specific behaviors were keyframe animated.

Jeff White:

"The digitally generated army of ants is a great example of the best laid plans. Production had a big field in which the scene was going to take place. When Pablo Helman showed up, production had covered the field in brown woodchips. And of course, red ants on a really busy field of brown chips are quite difficult to see. So we had that as challenge number one—how do you make sure that our ants are visible on top of this ground? Challenge number two was that there were all of these anthills that had been placed. We went out and actu-

ABOVE

Hungry digital ants devour Dovchenko (Igor Jijikine).

ally did LIDAR scans—we recorded where each of those hills were and what their specific terrain was so that once we got the plates back, our CG ants could be walking down exactly the same terrain. The unfortunate thing was that production had built the mounds to be movable; when we showed up on the second day, the hills had moved to a whole new position.

"So, once we got the footage back to ILM, we cut out all of our ant mounds and then took one, tried to find its match, and then lined it up so our ants had accurate geometry in order to be able to walk down the ant hills.

"Using our particle system, each particle represented an ant that had rules that it could follow and fields that could influence it. The artist could set up curves that would form paths for the ants to group into, or they could set up fields where, as the ants would start to cluster together into groups, they would stack on top of each other. Pablo worked with the artist to make sure that no matter where the sun was in the plate, our ants were backlit—so they had a nice specular highlight and some translucency. They almost look squishy and juicy, which was really part of the idea. But getting them to move in a way where they didn't just follow along a path involved adding hesitation, so they would walk and stop and then start again. When you just run a simulation, it's going to look pretty regular. We wanted to add a lot of organic movement to them."

JUNGLE CHASE ILLUSIONS

Creating elements for the jungle chase sequence was particularly complex. A broad variety of tools and techniques were involved in executing this work, including digimatte paintings and a digital library of 3-D plants.

Richard Bluff:

"The jungle chase was an interesting problem to solve. Steven wanted to shoot the chase and to have the trees and the plants at very close quarters to the actors, which was not physically possible shooting under the constraints that they had. So second unit ended up going to Hawaii and finding a road that went through a jungle. It was ideal in terms of the location, but not ideal in the sense that the jungle was quite a distance away from the cars that were traveling down the road. Also, the jungle had to look pristine, and these vehicles were plowing their own path through the foliage. We ended up having to create numerous types of jungle plants that could be simulated, which in effect means that the cars could run over these plants, they could break them, they could bend them, they

could hit them so the leaves fall off. We had to create plants in the computer that cars interacted with in a believable way."

Jeff White:

"I think there's a lot more digital environment enhancement in the film than people realize. There are a lot of sequences that take place in the jungle that were either shot on blue screen or on set and then augmented by environment work done. For the jungle sequences, we took a similar approach to *Transformers* with the part library (see pages 275–277), but instead of building mechanical parts, we built vegetation. The vehicles driving through the jungle needed to interact with the plants. The plants needed to move and react to that, and the cameras were constantly moving. So we went in and developed this library of all kinds of foliage that was built off of reference shot in Hawaii."

Richard Bluff:

"There were a number of shots where our hero is being chased by the bad guys on a cliff that was a thousand feet

above the ground. The original plate was shot without a cliff. We had to re-create the entire right side of the image with what was actually a huge vista of the Brazilian rainforest. Pablo went out with a second unit cameraman with a VistaVision camera in a helicopter over the jungles of Brazil to shoot plates of rain forests and waterfalls. We were able to place these in the backgrounds of the cliff shots to give the impression of the cliff being over the real Brazilian rainforest. On a number of occasions, however, we weren't able to use the plates because Steven wanted to move the camera in a very dynamic and visual way. That required us to re-create a computer-generated version of the same Brazilian rainforest. We had to have thousands of trees in the computer, so we could capture the correct angle."

CRUMBLING TEMPLE

To create the crumbling temple sequence, digimatte artists built the landscape using photographic textures and projections of scenic material onto 3-D terrain. ILM generated the pyramid as a 3-D simulation, which was animated to tear apart. An innovative tool called Fracture was developed to generate fracturing geometry. Instead of having to model one-by-one all of the pieces of an object that were to fracture, the tool made it possible to procedurally draw lines that represented cracks and ruptures in the geometry, and let the simulation break out the assets.

Richard Bluff:

"In the climax, our heroes find their way into a valley that has a huge ancient temple. So in order to prepare the artists

working on this sequence, and to gain the right sort of reference images, Paul Huston went to Machu Picchu in Peru to photograph the monuments and the beautiful vistas."

"We knew the temple had to be destroyed at the end of the movie, but we also knew there were numerous shots of the temple where it was just sitting off in the distance looking majestic. So we needed a computer-generated version that could be destroyed. We could also use a miniature model and photograph it outside with the sun on it, to ensure it looked as real as possible. So we had the old-school miniature models in shots (and as reference), and we had the CG version for the destruction. Kerner Optical built us a tenth-scale miniature pyramid, and because, obviously, a pyramid is four-sided, and is almost identical on all four sides, we had them only build two sides, with the back side being bare wood and support structures. We had this pyramid on a huge Lazy Susan, and a couple of matte department photographers took shots of it under different lighting conditions that we knew were going to be reproduced in the movie."

Indiana Jones and the Kingdom of the Crystal Skull was released nineteen years after the previous film in the series, *Indiana Jones and the Last Crusade* (1989). Paul Huston was one of the ILM team members who had worked on the original Indy films.

Paul Huston:

"*Last Crusade* was one of the last films that ILM did using all traditional techniques. All of the models and matte paintings for that film were physical. A lot of what we did for *Crystal Skull* was digital. It did rely on photographs of real places and

ABOVE

Extras were filmed on a partial
temple set built on the studio lot.
Digital matte artists then extended
the temple using photography of a
purpose-built miniature, and added
the surrounding environment.

Kerner Optical built a miniature temple that I photographed
for some of the shots. So we were still using some of the same
approaches to miniatures and locations, but all of the matte
painting was done in Photoshop and all of the shots were
composited digitally, so it was totally different. During *Last
Crusade*, we were at Kerner in the studio. We had our matte
cameras on the stage. We had a loft for a painting studio with
easels and oil paints and a ventilator fan to blow the fumes
away. We used tungsten halogen stage lights to light the
paintings, and we used 35mm Mitchell cameras to photograph them. After we photographed the paintings, they were
composited with the live action with optical printers.

"Now, everyone is at a workstation, and we're in an office environment. You go to see digital dailies. Back on *Last
Crusade*, we'd have dailies in the screening room, and you
could see your shot only once. Maybe if you were lucky, they'd
wind the film back and go through it a couple of times, but
anything more than that was kind of excessive. Now you can
loop your shot in a player and look at it a thousand times if
you want. And people do.

"Working on *Crystal Skull*, I thought that I might fall over
dead before it was finished—because it was just too cool to
have worked on all of the *Star Wars* and *Indiana Jones* movies.
Indy IV had been rumored to be a project in motion for such a
long time that when they finally did actually produce it, it just
seemed too good to be true. It was a big milestone to have
been able to work on all of them."

Terminator Salvation

2009

Ben Snow, visual effects supervisor:

"Suddenly, rather than two or three shots of a very dimly lit Terminator that may or may not be Schwarzenegger, we had more than ten shots of a fully visible Arnold, including some super close-ups. Instead of tracking the endoskeleton to a body-builder's face, we were going to have to track a fully digital Schwarzenegger to his body."

Director: McG
Producers: Derek Anderson, Moritz Borman,
Victor Kubicek, Jeffrey Silver

ILM Show Leadership:
Visual Effects Supervisor: Ben Snow
Visual Effects Producer: Susan Greenhow
Animation Supervisor: Marc Chu
Digital Production Supervisor: Philippe Rebours
Visual Effects Art Director: Christian Alzmann

THE BULK OF THE VISUAL EFFECTS work for *Terminator Salvation* was assigned to ILM. The company, after all, had created groundbreaking work for the last two installments of the Terminator franchise. For this fourth Terminator film, ILM created the iconic T-800 endoskeleton using computer graphics. *Terminator Salvation* was an opportunity to show the endoskeleton as it had never been seen before. In the first two Terminator films, the audience didn't have a clear look at it. In *Terminator 3*, the endoskeleton was shown only in flashbacks. For *Terminator Salvation*, ILM had the challenge of working on a sequence that was completely built around the endoskeleton. This time, the audience would see the figure moving in a way it hadn't before. Moreover, the endoskeleton was given a real personality, existing as a substantial villain.

But even though computer animation would facilitate endoskeleton movement that was more complex and dynamic than ever before, the animators were also aware that, for the sake of continuity, the endoskeleton behavior could not differ too much from those achieved with the puppets in earlier films.

ARNOLD IS BACK

Given the *Terminator* legacy, a pressing question had been whether Arnold Schwarzenegger would reprise his role in some capacity. Schwarzenegger-inspired bodybuilder Roland Kickinger was chosen

PREVIOUS SPREAD

Pyrotechnics and two riders on cycles were recorded live action; ILM then replaced the bikes and stuntmen with CG moto-Terminators.

ABOVE

The T-800, redesigned by ILM to be bulked up and more complex; the CG model was integrated seamlessly into the complex background thanks in large part to a new energy-conserving lighting approach.

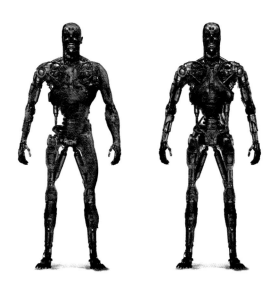

ABOVE

Concept art of the Terminator
T-800's damage levels as it goes
from full-flesh form to endoskeleton.

to stand in for the T-800, assuming the role that Schwarzenegger would have otherwise filled.

Ben Snow:

"As we were shooting, McG gave a talk at the San Diego Comic-Con or some similar event, and the fans were so enthusiastic about the idea that there might be some representation of Schwarzenegger in the film that, afterward, McG came to us and said, 'We have to find a way to get Arnold in the film.'"

Under normal circumstances, a facility would require a year or more to match an actor and develop a human performance in CG. In this case, because the decision from McG came relatively late, ILM was left with less than six months to create Schwarzenegger's "performance."

Ben Snow:

"We had a bit of digital-human work prior to this, pushing our digital-double technology. But once these fully lit close-ups of the Arnold T-800 were added, our digital-double project suddenly became a digital-human project. But we didn't have the advantage of Schwarzenegger driving a mocap session, and we couldn't have Roland drive the mocap sessions, because, although he resembles Schwarzenegger, he doesn't look enough like him, facially, to make that really work."

Snow decided to use a technique that had been employed on *King Kong* (2005). On that film, director Peter Jackson had reviewed extensive foot-

age of gorillas to select specific actions and behaviors; Snow suggested to McG that a similar approach be taken for *Terminator Salvation*. Footage of Schwarzenegger from *Commando*, *The Terminator*, and other films he'd made around that time were reviewed to find scenes in which Schwarzenegger was performing actions appropriate to the T-800 performance. These scenes were then used as a guide to animating the Schwarzenegger head.

Mark Chu, animation supervisor:

"We searched for the particular emotion we needed for the shot *and* from the same camera angle. Our animators would put the reference right up there on their monitors not only for performance cues, but also to make sure our CG Arnold was staying on-model from each specific camera angle. We also used reference for lighting cues and rendering."

The digital Schwarzenegger head was created from photographs of the actor from the 1980s, as well as from a scan of a Schwarzenegger head lifecast Stan Winston Studio had produced during the production of *The Terminator*. A library of facial shapes for animation was also built. The facial performance of the digital Schwarzenegger was keyframe animated. Texture maps for the digital human head, synthetic skin, and digital hair were also created. Finally, all of these elements were composited together to create a digital Arnold.

SKYNET "HARVESTER"

In a dramatic sequence, survivors are seized by a massive Skynet "harvester" robot that smashes through store walls. A reference plate of the intact gas-station interior was shot. The actors then departed, and two cross-shaped metal rings were pulled through the set to simulate the harvester claws.

Ben Snow:

"Then we cleared those metal shapes out and filmed just the holes that were left. We went to lunch at that point, so that the stunt people could rig what they needed for the people being pulled out through the holes; when we got back from lunch, we discovered that, to make it safer for the stunt people, they had cut square holes in the set, ruining the beautiful

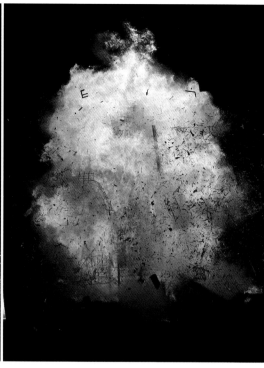

holes that had been created with the metal shapes! They shot their practical elements of the stunt people being lifted out, with mortars blowing harmless debris to help with the interaction of the visual elements that would be composited. Then we reassembled all those separate passes and combined them with our CG claws.

"But it took a lot of hand-paint work to put the interesting-looking holes back in over the bland square holes."

The production art department had created designs for the harvester, but as ILM began building it, the filmmakers thought it looked a bit too much like something from *Transformers*.

Ben Snow:

"So visual effects art director Christian Alzmann and his team at ILM redesigned the harvester to make it a little less humanoid and less like an anime-style giant robot. We got rid of its head and added some of the features we all loved from the ED-209 in *Robocop*. This was McG's monster, so it had to be somewhat anthropomorphic, but he also wanted it to have a retro look, like a World War II battleship—filthy and pumping black smoke into the atmosphere."

ALL TOGETHER NOW

Terminator Salvation provided an excellent opportunity for ILM and Kerner Optical to work together once again, with Kerner creating miniatures for the film.

ILM designed and created four shots for the Skynet destruction sequence, integrating miniatures into background matte paintings. For the first shot, Kerner built a one-twenty-fourth-scale Serena's tower, with its surrounding structures. The twenty-foot-tall tower was mounted onto a twenty-five-square-foot elevated deck. A steel structure was built, and the whole tower was then clad in "slide glass," usually used for microscopes. The structure was pre-scored so it would blow apart in a predicable manner when hit by production's pyrotechnics. The miniature had to perform on the first take; after the explosion, there would be little left in the way of usable material for a subsequent take.

A second one-forty-eighth-scale set, measuring approximately fifty feet squared, was used to create views of the shock wave traveling over a larger expanse of the city, after the tower explosion. Ultimately, ILM extended the miniature sets with background matte paintings that included the Golden Gate Bridge and the Transamerica Pyramid. The image was enhanced with CG destruction and debris.

ABOVE

Kerner Optical built a 20-foot-tall model on a 25-foot deck of Serena's tower at the Skynet compound. The entire tower was laced with pyrotechnics by Geoff Heron and his team, with different events for different floors at different times. It was then filmed in one take with three cameras.

OPPOSITE

The gas station and 7-Eleven were practical; the on-location practical explosion was augmented digitally by ILM, which also added the CG ecologically unsound harvester robot.

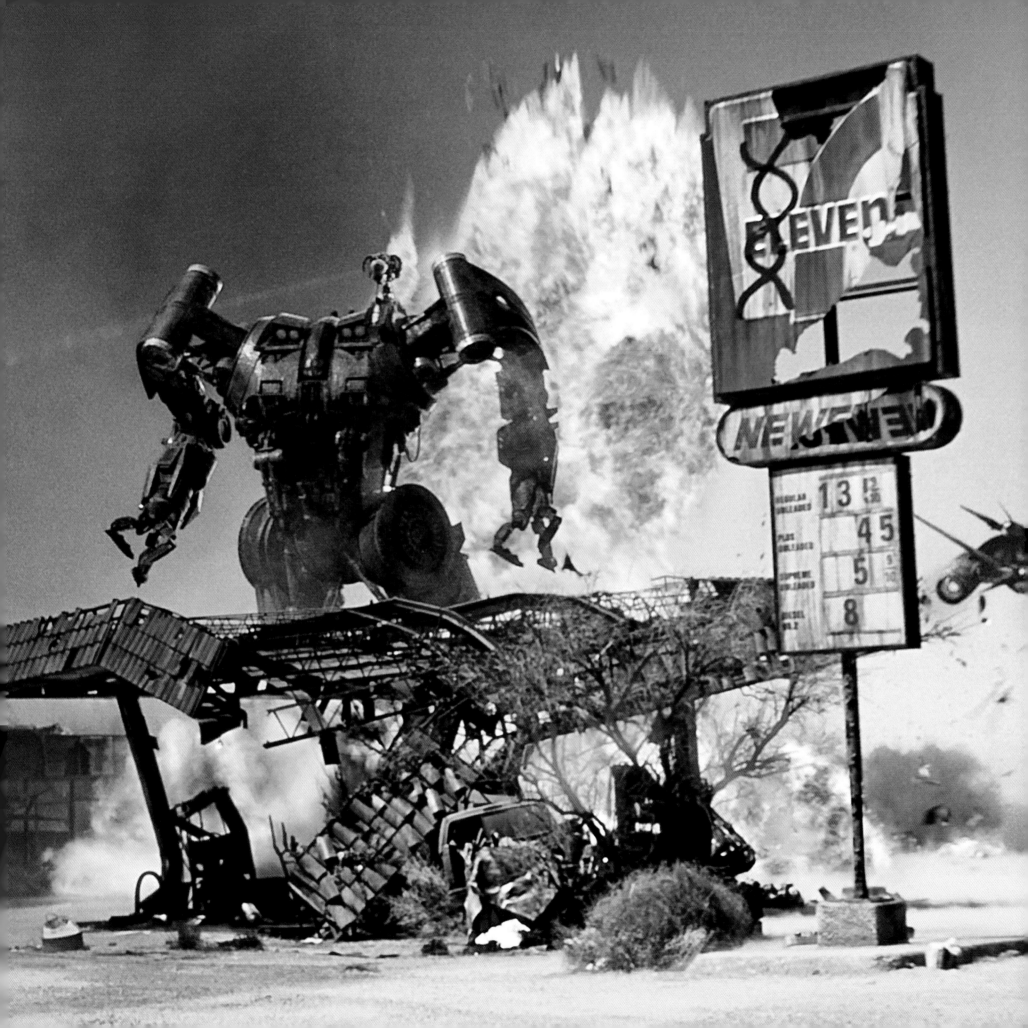

Star Trek

2009

Roger Guyett, visual effects supervisor:

"We create effects for all kinds of films, but, in a funny way, the thing that I'm most proud of is the way that the images look; just like *Star Wars*, doing a movie like *Star Trek*, you have a lot of opportunity to create the frames from scratch."

Director: J. J. Abrams
Producers: J. J. Abrams, Damon Lindelof

ILM Show Leadership:
Visual Effects Supervisors: Roger Guyett and Russell Earl
Associate Visual Effects Supervisor: Eddie Pasquarello
Visual Effects Producers: Jeff Olson, Jill Brooks
Animation Supervisor: Paul Kavanagh
Digital Production Supervisor: Michael DiComo
Visual Effects Art Director: Yanick Dusseault

Academy Award® Nomination:
Best Achievement in Visual Effects
Roger Guyett (ILM)
Russell Earl (ILM)
Paul Kavanagh (ILM)
Burt Dalton

BAFTA Film Award Nomination:
Best Special Visual Effects
Roger Guyett (ILM)
Russell Earl (ILM)
Paul Kavanagh (ILM)
Burt Dalton

IN THE DAYS WHEN *STAR TREK* FIRST APPEARED on the big screen, a simple shot of the *Enterprise* moving across camera was anything *but* simple in terms of process.

Roger Guyett:

"Back in the eighties, it was quite complicated. The *Enterprise* would have been a huge miniature, and that would be a day-long shoot to try to program a motion control rig. Then they would have to paint things out of the shot and composite the ship over other elements. Now, it would take someone ten minutes to program or animate an *Enterprise* traveling across frame. That increased ease allows you to spend more time on the creative aspects."

J. J. Abrams, director:

"I still own the first Cinefex with images of the *Enterprise* in drydock. I loved those models, and the idea of being on a set filled with atmosphere and little fiber-optic floodlights was

so romantic. But the reality of what is possible now digitally would have made that a vanity choice. We would have been doing something for the wrong reasons."

ILM's work on *Star Trek* involved more than 250 artists handling 860 shots. Many members of the ILM team were lifelong *Star Trek* fans.

Roger Guyett:

"I watched reruns of the original TV series in the early 1970s when I was growing up, and I think this movie kept true to that spirit. Of course, the classic elements have all changed over the various films, but we took inspiration from them and gave them a fresh look. When I first came to Industrial Light & Magic, John Knoll was supervising *Star Trek: First Contact*. Back then, we were just entering the digital age, but they did some amazing work. In fact, the original series had an incredible history in visual effects—in this latest *Star Trek*, I wanted to honor that, while at the same time adding new energy."

PREVIOUS SPREAD

Final frame of the new/old *Enterprise* from *Star Trek* (2009), larger in scale than the original and realized entirely in CG (director J. J. Abrams liked this image, as the negative space created the *Star Trek* insignia).

ABOVE

Principal photography for this scene took place at California State University's Northridge campus which ILM then modified with futuristic buildings and the drilling "ray" plunging into San Francisco Bay.

FOLLOW THE DIRECTOR

As always, ILM was sensitive to the director's particular vision. In this case, in the spirit of the original *Star Trek* series, much of Abrams's focus was on the story's characters and realism.

Russell Earl, visual effects supervisor:

"J. J. is a writer, so he wants you, as an audience member, to care about the characters. He wanted to make sure that when you're watching this movie, you're connecting to what's going on inside of the ship, and when you cut to the exterior, he didn't want it to take you out of the film—where you're looking at it and going, 'Oh, that looks CG.' He wanted to blend character and visual effects seamlessly.

"In the opening sequence of the film, with the USS *Kelvin*, you're with the characters on the inside. The drama is unfolding as they're attacked by the *Narada*. Then, we're cutting back and forth from the external to internal, and we're really trying to keep the audience engaged by making sure it's the best CG space and CG spaceships we can create."

J. J. Abrams:

"One of the things that I have always been very conscious of was having visual effects shots feel as if they were being filmed by a live camera operator, not by a perfect, prescient computer. That's a really important element to the work that Roger Guyett and ILM did. They elevated scenes by incorporating our shooting style into really cool shots that blended perfectly with the live action. It was very exciting to see them incorporate the look of the movie into the visual effects."

In fact, ILM developed animation tools to replicate Abrams's style of photography on the set. Animators applied camera shake via a small rotational motion capture sensor on a tripod at their workstations.

Paul Kavanagh, animation supervisor:

"We noticed that J. J. liked handheld camera shake effects. He would sit behind the camera and rhythmically tap his hand on the back of the film magazine. When we cut our exteriors with that live action, we felt that we should try to emulate what J. J.

was doing on set, so we came up with techniques to do that. We hooked the sensor up to the CG camera on our animation inside Zeno. As we tapped our desk in the same way that J. J. had tapped on his camera magazine, the motion sensor on the tripod picked up the vibration and translated that motion to our smooth camera moves in the computer."

J. J. Abrams:

"*Star Wars* made it impossible to do anything new in space. There's not a weather system, an environment, a character color, a number of arms or legs, there's nothing. I mean George did everything. So when we were doing *Star Trek*, the challenge was, well, 'How are we going to do aliens in the movie beyond the obvious? How many are there? Does it become *Star Wars*? Does it feel like a whole *Star Wars* Cantina scene rip-off?

"Every once in a while, someone would whisper, 'Remember, *Star Trek* came before *Star Wars*.' And I was like, 'Yeah, that doesn't help me, because George outdid it.' I had a meeting with George before I did the movie and I said, 'Listen, I'm doing the *Star Trek* movie, do you have any advice?' And he said, 'Just put lightsabers in it!' I was like, 'George, you could not be less helpful.' But I did give Sulu a sword, so I sort of listened to him. But I'm such a *Star Wars* fan—so much was done so brilliantly—that I wanted to do the best job we could, knowing that I could never compete with it."

BLACK HOLE

The black-hole sequence was one of several in the film that combined various visual effects techniques: CG space, elements shot on partial sets on stages at Paramount Studios, and extensive digital set extensions.

Russell Earl:

"I read the script, and it was a fun read. But there's the other part of your brain saying, *Spock beams down to the planet and Vulcan gets destroyed—how are we going to do that?* Luckily, one of the greatest things about ILM is knowing that there's a huge talent pool of artists, technical people, and scientists. You can talk about these things and figure out how you are going to do it.

"The black hole is a perfect example. We sat down with a couple of people who were our black-hole experts, employees who have a fascination with black holes, or science. We would say, 'What is a black hole? What does it really mean?' J. J. wanted it to have a sense of reality, but the reality is that you can't really get that close to a black hole.

"So you take the science, you think about it, you find the interesting bits, and then you try to adapt those to a film. But how do you visualize something that no one has really seen before? So we do quick iterations for the director where we provided a variety of choices. Then we'd go back and refine and say, 'Okay, let's combine the things you do like and get rid of what you don't like.'"

On top of the imagery of the black hole itself, the ILM team built layer upon layer of detail into the shots, including the Vulcan planetary destruction, which required extensive use of ILM's simulation software.

In the film's finale, Kirk takes command to rescue Pike and to stop the Romulans from attacking earth. The sequence begins with the *Enterprise* warping into the atmosphere of Saturn's moon, Titan. ILM worked with planetary scientist Carolyn Porco to create digimatte representations of the ringed gas giant and its moon. Porco had been head of NASA's Cassini-Huygens project, so she was very familiar with that part of the solar system. She provided insight into how the process might work and where things were located geographically. The ILM team then mapped, moved, and reorganized real space imagery to suit their needs.

ABOVE

The newly launched pride of the fleet, the USS *Enterprise*, departs a sprawling Federation space station, based on production concept designer Ryan Church's initial design, fleshed out by visual effects art director Alex Jaeger, and built by the digital Model Shop team.

RIGHT

Concept art by visual effects art director Alex Jaeger depicting a vista of Vulcan prior to its destruction

BOTTOM LEFT

Constructed in the parking lot of Dodger stadium, a 1:1 segment of the *Narada* drill platform was constructed to shoot the climactic fight sequence. The remainder of the platform was created with the help of CG. In the background is the Delta Vega ice planet set where scenes of a marooned Kirk were filmed.

BOTTOM RIGHT

A police officer on a hover cycle attempts to apprehend young Kirk in his Corvette, which was towed by the stunt department. The special effects team articulated the hover cycle on a parallelogram rig that extended from a Padelford camera car and connected to a mini-gimbal within the cycle.

The final shot in the film, which shows the *Enterprise* flying off into warp paid homage to the way the original television series closed. Artists at ILM tried to match the style and color palette of the old show.

Russell Earl:

"There's such a huge history to the *Star Trek* franchise, and people are very connected to it. And Paramount was trying to reinvigorate the franchise and make new fans. Because if you're appealing only to *Star Trek* fans, then I just don't think that it would be as successful of a film."

Roger Guyett:

"*Star Trek* touches on such a wide range of work, really on everything we do these days: very complicated creatures, organic environments, water, ice, and snow, ships firing at each other, and virtual pyrotechnics. Lots of people can do that kind of work, but more often than not, they can't do it to that level of ability that the artists at ILM can. It's like getting a great handmade suit. There are only a few people in the world that can make a great handmade suit. And ILM is kind of the Savile Row of the suit-making experience. We bring not only the ability to create those images, but we also do it extremely well. I think we do it in an elegant way and with a degree of panache and class. *Star Trek* is one of the movies that shows off the caliber of what we do. We really collaborated with the director and helped him make his movie."

Transformers:
Revenge of the Fallen

2009

Scott Farrar, visual effects supervisor:

"This movie was *much* bigger in scope and scale, overall, than the first one."

Director: Michael Bay
Producers: Ian Bryce, Tom DeSanto,
   Lorenzo di Bonaventura, Don Murphy

ILM Show Leadership:
Visual Effects Supervisor: Scott Farrar
Associate Visual Effects Supervisor: Jeff White
Visual Effects Producer: Wayne Billheimer
Animation Supervisor: Scott Benza
Associate Animation Supervisor: Rick O'Connor
Digital Production Supervisor: Jason Smith
Visual Effects Art Director: Alex Jaeger

THE VISUAL EFFECTS WORK for *Transformers: Revenge of the Fallen* was undertaken by ILM and Digital Domain. ILM, however, was responsible for the majority of the show's 1,600 effects shots.

The easiest shots on *Revenge of the Fallen* were equivalent to the hardest shots on the first *Transformers* film. The first film had eleven robots, while *Revenge of the Fallen* had a total of sixty robots, forty-six of which were created by ILM. Each robot took twelve to fifteen weeks to build, and then at least that or more to RIG, so overall a robot required more than twenty-five weeks of work before it was ready to be put into a shot. The second *Transformers* film therefore had a team of fifty-four animators, nearly three times the number on the original film.

FIRING UP JETFIRE

In *Revenge of the Fallen*, Jetfire was the robot with the most dialogue and close-ups. Work on this character thus required some of the most delicate animation ILM created for the film. Animators studied performances and characterizations in iconic live-action films to inspire the development of the Jetfire character.

Scott Benza, animation supervisor:

"The most helpful actor reference was Burgess Meredith in the *Rocky* movies. He talked out of the side of his mouth, and one side of his face was squinted up. We used that asymmetry for Jetfire, to sell the fact that he was a weathered veteran. We also compiled scenes from other films with older actors delivering lines that the Jetfire character could, conceivably, have delivered himself. These included Max von Sydow in *Snow Falling on Cedars*, Nick Nolte in *Tropic Thunder*, and Christopher Lloyd in *Back to the Future Part III*.

"Jetfire had to be rickety in his movement. He's been kind of resurrected after fifty years of being in this hibernated state, so he has stiff joints; Michael described him as being geriatric. At the same time, he's very bitter about being woken up and thrust back into this war between Autobots and the Decepticons. So finding acting reference of somebody who is geriatric and stiff at the same time as being bitter was extremely difficult. We had to combine aspects of those multiple performances for the animated character."

PREVIOUS SPREAD

Optimus Prime fires a projectile in a battle with Megatron.

ABOVE

Actor Shia LaBeouf was painstakingly rotoscoped out of the plate and composited atop a computer-generated Bumblebee, who delivers a nuanced performance that highlights the close interaction ILM's digital performers had to achieve and create with the principal actors.

HARD FACIAL EXPRESSIONS

As in the first *Transformers* film, a key challenge in creating facial expressions for the robots was that the characters are made of hard surfaces. There is no expressive skin to support the communication of emotion. As a result, the robot's eyes were an important element in creating compelling performances.

Scott Benza:

"When you watch an actor deliver lines, you're looking at their eyes more than anything else. They're the most expressive part of the face, so it was very important to have a high level of detail and control built into that area of the robot faces. Each of their eyeballs was made up of almost a hundred pieces, so we would find different ways to dilate the eyes to help show anger and other emotions. In the end, the process became very similar to how we would animate a traditional organic character. The challenge was how we were able to derive those facial expressions from a bunch of rigid pieces on the face."

Close-ups were more numerous and more lingering than in the first film. It was necessary for the model-and-paint team to create finer details on the facial areas of the robot models. The faces were built of hundreds of small movable parts, which gave animators the flexibility they needed.

Scott Benza:

"It's very challenging to engineer how the hundreds of individual moving parts will move in ways that mimic human facial expressions. The robot designs typically would have elements built into them that would mimic facial features on humans, so there would be mechanical parts for the eyebrows and eyelids. We had to make do with what the robot designs called for. So, for example, if a character had a helmet built into their forehead area but didn't have much of a representation of eyebrows, we would pull that helmet down to almost the eyebrow level at certain points in the performance to serve, essentially, as eyebrows. If the character had to make a scowling face or be angry, we would drag that helmet down into the forehead area, and due to the nature of the way it is swept up on either side of the face, it would feel like the character was scowling."

A LIBRARY OF REAL-WORLD PARTS

One of the lessons the ILM team learned on the first *Transformers* film was that director Bay preferred robots that looked like they were made of real-world, relatively low-tech mechanical parts, rather than futuristic mechanisms. For the second film, the model department built an even more extensive library of real-world parts, from which modelers assembled their CG robots.

LEFT
The Decepticon Transformer Ravage, one of the only animalistic Transformers in the film, was animated to mimic the movements of a large feline.

OPPOSITE
In the first *Transformers* film, Optimus Prime was the largest and most complicated model ILM had ever done up to that time. In *Revenge of the Fallen*, Devastator was essentially six Optimus Primes, made up of six huge construction vehicles. This was the largest computer model ever built at ILM. The completed Devastator model was made up of more than 52,000 pieces of individual, "animatable" geometry, which broke down to 12.5 million polygons. First, the ILM crew modeled and painted the robots and construction vehicles that comprised Devastator. All of the data was then pumped into the parts library system, which was used to assemble the model. Thousands of parts were then textured with Viewpainting software.

David Fogler, modeling and texturing supervisor:

"I come from the ILM Model Shop, where there was a long tradition of kit-bashing. This was the same idea. We wound up with easily a thousand parts—every little screw and gear and spring—all textured and plugged into this library. Our first robot took a long time to make, because we were building everything from scratch; but as work on the film went on, we were able to work faster, because everybody had access to everything that had been built. That's not to say that the later robots built themselves. There was a lot of custom work for every robot."

VIRTUAL DESTROYER SYSTEM

ILM's motion capture crew developed a new virtual-camera system, which was used for the underwater and *Nemesis* sequences in the film. The system allowed Michael Bay to compose all-CG shots as if he were in a live-action environment with actors.

Scott Benza:

"Bay is used to being behind the camera, so he's very specific about camera work. But in shots with all-digital environments, all he could do was *describe* the camera to us. We had to interpret what he said. So we made use of a virtual camera that had a display on it that allowed Michael to look into a CG environment. We'd load our 3-D environment into Zeno, our proprietary environment package, and he could operate the virtual camera to create camera moves within that environment on the fly. As he moved this device, it would move like a camera through the 3-D environment. Using controls on the virtual camera, it could simulate Steadicam moves, handheld, whatever; focal lengths could be adjusted, a small move could be made into a large crane move. He just strapped this thing on and started running around doing shots within minutes. All of those moves were recorded, so we could plug them into our shots. It was great to know that we had exactly the move he wanted to start from."

ILM's most challenging work on *Revenge of the Fallen* was the creation of a sequence that took nine months to complete. The Fallen returns to earth to lead a full-scale attack on the planet and to extract information regarding the location of a vital energy source from Sam's brain. These villains arrive on earth in what looks like a meteor shower, destroying an aircraft carrier at sea. The shots for the sequence featured many digital assets in addition to the robots. An ILM crew accompanied Bay aboard the USS *John C. Stennis* on a sea run, to capture authentic textures. ILM then used these reference photographs to build everything on the ship's deck in CG, including Blackhawk helicopters, missile carts, F-18 Hornets, and deck debris. ILM crewmembers were shot on ILM's motion capture stage, in costumes, portraying deck soldiers. Explosions were photographed on a one-twentieth-scale model of the ship's damaged interior hull at Kerner Optical. And hundreds of rigid simulations were run for the elaborate exploding hardware and falling debris.

On numerous fronts, *Revenge of the Fallen* broke ILM's records for size of models, complexity of simulations, and many other aspects of CG shot production.

ANOTHER ROAD TO ILM, OR "SO, HOW DID I GET HERE?"

Scott Benza, animation supervisor:

"I was a senior in high school, and I went to see *Terminator 2*. At the time, I wanted to be a dentist. I walked out of that theater knowing exactly what I wanted to do: I wanted a career in computer graphics and to work for ILM specifically.

"Everything that I did from that point onward was to work at ILM. I taught myself computer graphics. I saved up as much as I could and got a personal loan for 3-D Studio version 2.0—about $1,500, which is a lot for somebody still living at home and working at McDonald's. I created a portfolio of my work and found that there was a company in the Tampa Bay area, where I lived at the time, which did news graphics for the local stations using this very high-end piece of software called Soft Image. Soft Image was what I had found out ILM was using, so I saw that as a stepping-stone.

"I volunteered my time. I ran errands in return for time to learn the software on the computers there. After two or three months of learning the software, I was able to build enough of an experience base to get a job at Microsoft in Redmond Washington, doing 3-D computer graphics. During my time at Microsoft, we created this short film called *Robit* that was made to help create a branded character, a mascot for the Microsoft Network.

"It got into the SIGGRAPH electronic theatre. A couple of weeks after SIGGRAPH, I got two calls: one from Pixar and the other from ILM. That was a very big day for me. I had to decide which one I wanted to go work for. It was a pretty easy decision for me. I opted for ILM, and I'm going on twelve years now. It's like going to a theme park for me every day. I have so much fun."

RIGHT

In White Sands, New Mexico, unit photography worked on a half-destroyed-town set built on location. A helicopter on a rig would become a mechanical effect on a plate to which ILM would add blades, Transformers, and myriad details.

FOLLOWING SPREAD

That same set seen after ILM had worked its magic.

Harry Potter
and the Half-Blood Prince

2009

Tim Alexander, visual effects supervisor:

"If you look at the live-action elements we have, it's basically Harry and Dumbledore standing on an eight-foot-by-four-foot piece of crystal, with green screen all the way around that. Basically, everything else is fabricated by ILM."

Director: David Yates
Producers: David Barron, David Heyman

ILM Show Leadership:
Visual Effects Supervisor: Tim Alexander
Associate Visual Effects Supervisor: Robert Weaver
Visual Effects Producer: Jill Brooks
Animation Supervisor: Marc Chu
Digital Production Supervisor: Robert Weaver
Visual Effects Art Director: Aaron McBride

BAFTA Film Award Nomination:
Best Special Visual Effects
John Richardson
Tim Burke
Tim Alexander (ILM)
Nicholas Aithadi

THE VISUAL EFFECTS WORK for *Harry Potter and the Half-Blood Prince* was shared by several companies: Double Negative, the Moving Picture Company, Rising Sun Pictures, Cinesite, Framestore, Luma Pictures, and ILM.

ILM was responsible for the greenhouse sequence, as well as one in which Harry and Dumbledore attempt to get one of the Horcruxes out of a cave. The work on the cave sequence, however, proved to be extremely diverse and complex.

Director David Yates wanted the gigantic cave to look like a salt mine, so the environment was filled with large crystals. On set, a small section of the cave was built, where Harry and Dumbledore could be photographed. ILM extended the set digitally to create an enormous cave and water environment surrounding the actors.

Tim Alexander:

"The cave is supposed to be at least a mile long, and it had to have crystals and gigantic columns, like stalactites and stalagmites. There's a small island in the middle of the cave, and that little island was a set piece that production built. They created little chunks of the environment where Harry and Dumbledore had to interact with the set, and then we extended all the way around that."

The firestorm tailored by ILM to satisfy director David Yates.

ABOVE

Harry Potter (Daniel Radcliffe) and Professor Albus Dumbledore (Michael Gambon) are inside Horcrux Cave; the only real part of the cave was the little crystal island built for the actors to stand on.

ABOVE

Particle blocking, an intermediate stage. The orange color and yellow color determined where the CG "fuel" was for the fire simulation; yellow was the hottest; darker red was smokier and cooler. This method allowed ILM to control the behavior of the firestorm as requested by director Yates (the final frame is on pages 318–319).

A RIVER STYX

In the cave, Dumbledore and Harry travel in a boat across a lake that surrounds the small island where the Horcrux lies in a crystal basin. On set, the actors were shot riding a mechanical rig that gently rocked the boat as it moved on a rail toward the island. ILM built a matchmove model of the boat to simulate interactions with a digital water-plane. The lake was generated as a two-dimensional fluid simulation with depth refractions.

Tim Alexander:

"We mainly used the water simulation tool that had been developed for the maelstrom sequence in *Pirates of the Caribbean: At World's End*. That tool's previous generations were based on our work on *The Perfect Storm*. A lot of these techniques are pretty much the same."

INFERNAL INFERI

In the film, the Inferi are humans who were trapped in the cave by Voldemort. They are tortured souls that rise out of the lake. The characters were designed to be emaciated beyond anything that could have been portrayed by an actor. The look of the Inferi was based on images of dead bodies from concentration camps. ILM's creature team and animation supervisor worked from production artwork and a full-size maquette to develop the digital Inferi.

Tim Alexander:

"The Inferi have been sitting in this water for a very long time, so they're extremely emaciated and water-logged. Production's design process began by pulling a lot of artwork of Dante's *Inferno*. They were looking for a tortured souls idea. Once they had some references, they started producing their own artwork—what the cave might look like with Inferi in it and what the Inferi actually

looked like. Then they sculpted a full-scale Inferi out of clay that we could photograph and walk around, so we could understand the proportions and just how skinny these people were.

"At that point, the design was handed off to us and we built the creatures in the computer. Because the Inferi are so emaciated, the skin had to slide across them as they bended or twisted. So we started by creating a full skeleton underneath so we could slide the skin over it. We needed thousands of Inferi, so we had to create variations. We had a variety of heads we could put onto the figures so they would look different. Then we started doing some investigation into different types of skin. We went onto Google or Flickr and looked at photos of waterlogged bodies. We pulled up movies. We even went out to the store to pick up a chicken to see what its skin looks like."

To create the unusual way the Inferi moved, ILM used limited performer reference and avoided using motion capture entirely.

Tim Alexander:

"When we do a humanoid-like creature, often the question we have to ask ourselves is whether we are going to use motion capture or keyframe animation.

"For the Inferi, our animation director, Marc Chu, felt we should keyframe them, so that we could get some interesting motion that we might not be able to find in a performance. So early on, Marc did a lot of tests to explore how the Inferi could move. But the director also wanted you to feel sorry for the Inferi. He wanted you to feel like these were souls that were trapped in the cave against their will by Voldemort, so ultimately, we went for a much more realistic human type of movement.

"They did actually cast a few people in England to perform some of the Inferi's actions, so we could use it as reference. But we never directly used it, because Yates was primarily casting people to give us facial reactions—so we could see the emotion that he was going for."

ABOVE

Radcliffe was filmed with a stunt performer in an Imocap suit for underwater sequences and replaced with a digital being created by ILM in post. Underwater fireballs were a challenge, while the walls were made of writhing CG creatures, the Inferi.

Creating the crowds of Inferi swarming on the island involved hand-animating eighty to ninety characters into a writhing mass. When Harry gets pulled under the water, ILM created an underwater version of the cave that had thousands of Inferi bodies covering the walls.

FIRE IN THE HOLE

The biggest technical hurdle was a large firestorm, which ILM created entirely digitally.

Tim Alexander:

"We talked about shooting elements for it, which is the typical thing to do with fire, but in this case the type of fire that the director wanted was going to be extremely difficult, if not impossible, to shoot. He needed to be able to say where the fire was going to go and what it was going to do.

Because he wanted the level of control with the realism, we knew that we had to come up with a digital solution to do the fire."

To create the firestorm, a fire-simulation engine was developed by ILM's digital effects supervisor, Chris Horvath.

Tim Alexander:

"We knew the simulation engine had to be directable. We also knew we wanted it to be fast, so we could turn takes around as quickly as possible. You need iterations on these things to start a dialogue with the director, so that you know that you're all on the same page. It also takes iterations to get things right. Most of the time when you run the simulation, it's not quite what you want, and you have to do it again and adjust parameters to make it look good. So the faster those simulations can run, the better off you are."

Avatar

2009

Steve Sullivan, research and development:

"We did the test for *Avatar* around 2005, which really pushed the tech forward and helped to get the film green-lit. But ultimately, the production ended up working with Weta, so we didn't have an opportunity to use that technology. Often we have a major innovation happening, interesting stuff that for one reason or another doesn't get used in a film at the time the technology is developed. There are things around here that take a long time to gestate because we're waiting for the right film to use it."

Director: James Cameron
Producers: James Cameron, Jon Landau
Co-Producers: Brooke Breton, Josh McLaglen

ILM Show Leadership:
Visual Effects Supervisor: John Knoll
Visual Effects Producer: Jill Brooks
Animation Supervisor: Paul Kavanagh
Digital Production Supervisor: Michael DiComo
Visual Effects Art Director: Alex Jaeger

ILM HAD PREVIOUSLY DISCOVERED, in its work on *Casper* (see pages 32–37), just how difficult it was to create believable emotions and attitudes in a CG character. If creating expressions for a CG ghost was challenging, doing the same for a flesh-and-blood character would be even more demanding.

Dennis Muren:

"It's much more difficult with a person, because you've got so many more clues as to what somebody's thinking. Just look at a good friend of yours. If you're sitting down to coffee and you look at them between words, you've got a feeling of what that person is thinking. How much they're maybe squinting with their eye a tiny bit. Or how they do a little something with their mouth or cock their head. Well, that's what human beings are attuned to recognize and respond to since we're about three days old. All of those little micro-movements that the human face does had to come through in *Avatar*. Because Jim's goal was not to make an animated film, it was to make something that retained the complexity of actors' performances. And that had not really been done to the extent that it ultimately was in *Avatar*.

"So Jim had the idea that we do motion capture and we shoot with multiple cameras. He thought, at the time we did the test, that he was going to be able to mix different takes and then put them together for one whole performance. Well, that proved to be not very successful; you could see the hand of the keyframe animator interfering with the performance, because the muscles transitioned in

PREVIOUS SPREAD

The climactic battle scene from *Avatar*

ABOVE

ILM had to match visual effects work being done by WETA, but couldn't actually use their assets for the floating mountain sequence, which meant a lot of expert work in a hurry. In this final frame, even face masks are digital to avoid stage-lighting reflections.

ABOVE

In a view from Colonel Miles Quaritch's (Stephen Lang) ship, only the
air-copter's window frame and the
actors are real—all else is digtial,
including the HUD screens.

different ways in each performance. It became clear that the
eyes, the nose, the mouth, the muscles, every little nuance
of the human face had to be right, because we're so attuned
to understanding people's faces. So Jim learned, I think,
that he needed to be more rigid when he did his mocap
shoot and be satisfied pretty much with what he got in a
single take.

"For the original test, we took all of Jim's data, along
with the mocap information, and tried to make the scene
when the guy and girl first meet in the jungle. I don't know
if Jim did it to show the studio. He says he did, and that
it green-lit the film, though I'm sure it would have gotten green-lit anyway. But he learned a lot from the test.
Originally, he was doing it with a girl whose face was very

different from the final one. Theoretically, you should be
able to take anybody's expressions and, once you get those
movements into the computer, change the shape of them
so the face is more like what you want—but it never worked
out right. So from that, Jim discovered he had to cast actors
for motion capture that looked like the characters he wanted
the figures to look like.

"Overall, the test was a proof of concept: You *can* get a
CG character who performs like a human. Cameron came
away from the test knowing what he needed to do to get the
performances he wanted. That's when they came up with the
idea of keeping one camera on the actor's head so you always
have a good close up of their face. They weren't doing that for
the initial test."

ABOVE

Scorpions and Dragons escort the *Valkyrie* on a mission to destroy the Home Tree.

But if ILM created the ghostly facial expressions for Casper in 1995, why did it take more than a decade to create successful facial expressions using CG? It took a project like *Avatar*, and the influence of James Cameron, to make it finally happen.

Dennis Muren:

"Creating nuanced facial expressions with CG had been tried in the past, and it wasn't very successful. But Jim was just in your face with hundreds of those shots, so it had to be right. And we've never had a project that had quite so much money. Who's going to be able to raise that much money? You've got to have the gumption of a Jim Cameron and the support of the studio to do this thing that's never been done before. Maybe the tools were there five years ago, but there wasn't

anybody who could put it together. Most filmmakers work within a budget. Jim works within a budget, but he's also prepared, if he feels that this is going to be something really big, to push for more money, and the studio is really good to let him do that. Some directors won't do it, and they can't do it. George had done this on *Star Wars*, but most directors won't do this."

After ILM completed the test for Cameron, it was clear that the scope of work for *Avatar* was going to be exceptional. The company realized that being involved with this one production could take over the entire facility for up to more than two years, preventing ILM from working on films such as *Pirates of the Caribbean: At World's End*, *Transformers*, and *Iron Man*.

Richard Bluff, digital matte supervisor:

"The decision was made that we didn't want to tie up the facility with one movie for that long. So ILM's proposal to Lightstorm Entertainment [Cameron's production company] was that we simply work on a certain portion of the movie. Jim was unwilling to do that, as he wanted only one facility to work on the entire film. As it later turned out, of course, more than ten visual effects studios ended up working on the movie in a fashion very similar to what ILM was predicting."

About a year into the production of *Avatar*, it became apparent that production on the film was running longer than originally anticipated. Given the complexity of the visual effects work, the main facility assigned to the film, Weta, was reaching its capacity.

John Knoll, visual effects supervisor:

"They needed a company that could come in at that level to help take the burden off, so that the film could be completed on time and they wouldn't have to push the release date. We explored a number of different scenarios in terms of how ILM would be able to help in the most effective way. As you can imagine, there were a lot of CG models that needed to be brought into parity with what Weta was doing, so we were trying to limit those types of assets and to minimize duplication of effort. That way we could spend more of our time working on shots."

The scope of ILM's work on *Avatar* included several types of helicopters, the AMP suits, a handful of digital doubles, a couple of creatures, floating mountains, and, as described by Knoll, "a lot of terrain-type things." Much of ILM's work on the film was vehicle- and landscape-oriented. Sequences included the shuttle landing at Hell's Gate at the beginning of the film. For the end battle, ILM created a number of shots that focused on the cockpits and helicopters firing missiles, including elements of the showdown between Trudy and Quaritch, and the crash of Quaritch's ship.

QUARITCH EXPLOSION

John Knoll:

"One of the most significant things was the work we did on computer-generated explosions. When Quaritch's ship blows up, it occurs fairly close to camera, so it's featured large in the frame. We played with different scenarios of how we'd do these shots. We looked at shooting elements, but it was an unattractive option for a variety of reasons. We'd have to shoot stereo, because of the film being in 3-D. We'd have to play back a very specific camera move that Jim was set on preserving at high speed. And it looked like that was going to be very difficult and expensive. So it seemed, if there were a way to do these explosions as a simulation, that the kind of control that you'd get was very attractive. We therefore put a big effort into trying to make good-looking computer-generated explosions, and they turned out extremely well."

MAKING MOUNTAINS

Richard Bluff:

"We created close to two hundred shots of either establishing views of the planet Pandora or of the inner sanctum of the planet, an area that was nicknamed the 'floating mountains.' This area features heavily in the final battle of the movie. It's a location that feels very much like Thailand or Vietnam, with the spectacular pitons—except that these pitons are floating, and they move around.

"So the challenge for us was to create these floating mountains. We decided to experiment with a number of different techniques. First, we went to the local builder's yard and purchased several large rocks similar to the sort you would use in the garden for decorative landscaping. We scanned the rocks, and we photographed them in order to reproduce them in the computer. The photographs of the rocks became the texture and the scan became the geometry. Although the technique actually didn't work very well, we did use the photographs to create bump-and-displacement maps, which is a technique that develops relief on an object, so a smooth surface becomes a rough surface.

"We ended up creating very low-resolution, potato-shaped objects that would represent the finished mountain. We took that mountain into Z-brush, a sculpting software tool that works as if you were sculpting with clay on a table-top. We sculpted rock cracks and fissures into these potato shapes and we sculpted the mountains out of them. We also used photographs of Thailand and Vietnam. We went on location to shoot these images specifically for the film.

"So by the end of the development process, we had several types of rocks. When we were developing the actual shots, we could push these rocks into themselves and create numerous differently shaped rocks. (This technique harked back to the days when ILM created miniatures by kit-bashing shapes together to create something that looks a little different, but with the same characteristics of the traditional shapes.) Then, we needed to be able to spray plants and trees over a large surface of these rocks very quickly. The trees were created and stored in a database, and the spraying technique would randomly choose which trees it was going to put over the top of the rock. Very quickly, in the space of a few minutes, you could get a generic looking rock, smash a few more pieces together to make it look very different from anything else you'd created, and then spray trees and plants all over the top. Moments later, you could have that rock structure lit and rendered in the actual shot and have a very convincing set piece for the world that James Cameron was creating."

THREE QUARTERS OF A BILLION POLYGONS

Richard Bluff was responsible for landmark digital matte elements that were an important part of the opening and closing shots of the film.

Richard Bluff:

"For the opening shot, I created every single tree, did the lighting, created the atmosphere, and finished the composite. When I volunteered to do the shot, I didn't know at the time it was the opening shot, or that it would be one of the most important shots for Jim, as it established the planet Pandora.

"It was a shot that Jim knew he could go to the Amazon and shoot himself for real, but he felt he could get far more control if it was all done in the computer. So he was very hands-on with the development of the shot. I would speak to him about which particular tree he wanted in what particular location, the color of the bark, how many leaves were meant to be on a particular branch—he went down to the detail of leaves and branches on trees—bearing in mind the actual shot had over 200,000 trees in it. It was the largest polygon count on any shot ILM has ever developed—three quarters of a billion polygons for all of these trees.

"What we created was a forest shot very similar to what you see in the BBC's *Planet Earth* documentaries. In fact, Sigourney Weaver, one of the actresses in the film, even did a promotion piece in which she used a similar voice-over to her narration in the Planet Earth series, where our opening shot featured with a number of other ILM shots, as if she were doing a nature documentary for the planet of Pandora.

"The software I chose to develop the opening shot in was 3-D Studio Max and rendering in Brazil. These are tools that we used very heavily on *Revenge of the Sith*. Now, for Episode III, which was one of the biggest-environment films we had in production at the time, we had a render farm with thirty processors running twenty-four hours a day, specifically for this particular piece of software, so everyone could render their buildings out in good time. On *Avatar*, for this one particular shot, those thirty render processors were increased to *eight hundred* render processors, just for this one shot. The actual shot itself took twenty-four days to render nonstop, from beginning to end. And it was 28,000 frames due to the number of different passes. There was one pass for the jungle, three more passes for some of the hero trees, another pass for the mountains in the distance and for the sky, and fourteen separate passes for all of the different cloud and fog layers, for a grand total of 28,000 for a shot that lasted twenty-two seconds.

"It was hugely rewarding once the shot was complete. A week or so later, we found out not only was it the first shot in the movie, but it would also be the last shot in the movie, as the end credits play over that shot not once but three times. So despite the fact that ILM came to the party late, we actually sandwiched all of our work for the movie at the beginning and the end."

OPPOSITE

Quaritch in an AMP Suit, a nearly 100-percent synthetic shot

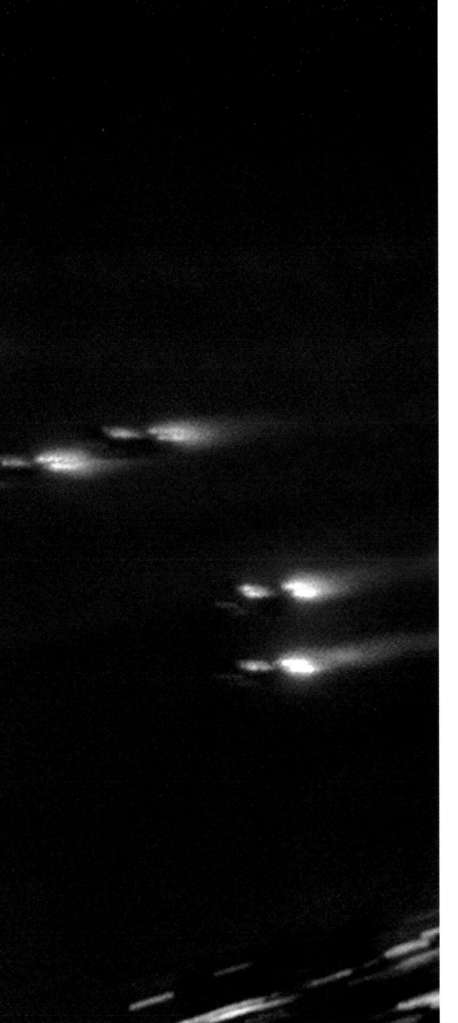

Iron Man 2

2010

Jon Favreau, director:

"*Iron Man 2* is more than 1,400 visual effects, so it's arguably half an animated film. You're working almost as an animation director would over the course of years on the film, and to me, honestly, the most fun I have in filmmaking is working with the visual effects houses. ILM and I have had a great run with these last two *Iron Man* movies."

Director: Jon Favreau
Producer: Kevin Feige

ILM Show Leadership:
Visual Effects Supervisor: Ben Snow
Visual Effects Producer: Wayne Billheimer
Animation Supervisor: Marc Chu
Associate Animation Supervisor: Rick O'Connor
Digital Production Supervisor: Doug Smyth
Visual Effects Art Director: Aaron McBride

Academy Award® Nomination:
  Best Visual Effects
Janek Sirrs
Ben Snow (ILM)
Ged Wright
Daniel Suddick

THE VISUAL EFFECTS FOR *IRON MAN 2* required a much greater variety, quantity and complexity of work than what ILM had faced with the first Iron Man. For its 535 shots, ILM pushed digital costuming and armor beyond what had been achieved before. Artists also created and used large environments and new levels of destruction combining practical, computer graphics, and miniature effects. For each challenge they worked with Janek Sirrs and Dan Sudick to find the best tools to try and up the spectacle while retaining the realism that was very important to director Jon Favreau on both films.

Ben Snow, visual effects supervisor:

"On *Iron Man 2* every shot of Iron Man's Mark 5 and 6 suits, the final War Machine costume, the Hammer Drones and the Mickey Rourke battle suit was entirely digital. To accommodate tracking multiple actors interacting plus dealing with stunt performers playing the background robotic Drones in the same shots (who, unlike the principals were to be tracked mostly for action reference) we had to beef up our Imocap on-set capture software."

ABOVE

Tony Stark/Iron Man (Robert Downey Jr.) and James Rhodes/War Machine (Don Cheadle) discuss strategy in the Japanese Garden Pavilion. ILM suited both characters with completely digital armor.

ABOVE, INSET

Downey and Cheadle as shot on set.

PREVIOUS SPREAD

The CG War Machine chases Iron Man in a climatic dogfight.

RIGHT

The Stark Expo stage was enlarged with digital set extensions and ILM created a large, running digital cyc with outside buildings, running fountains, and light shows, as well as the columns of the expo pavilion itself, all layered in 3-D space using the 3-D compositing abilities of nuke. Crowds created using ILM's proprietary crowd pipeline completed the shots.

BOTTOM RIGHT

A CG Iron Man in Mark III armor, seen in the aftermath of the kitchen fight sequence.

BOTTOM FAR RIGHT

One of the larger set pieces for the film was constructed on a soundstage on the Sony lot in Los Angeles. The set, a serene Japanese Tea Garden, was built complete with running creek and hundreds of pounds of pyrotechnics, which would be unleashed by the special effects department during filming. Due to changes in the storyline late in production, ILM's Digimatte department would have to re-create virtually the entire environment to set the scene for the film's elaborate end battle.

Rango

2011

Gore Verbinski, director:

> "I witnessed the birth of a really elite team of story-tellers. We took a team of people who were very good at making shots and made them partners in a very different process—the process of telling a story from beginning to end."

Director: Gore Verbinski
Producers: Gore Verbinski, John B. Carls, Graham King

ILM Show Leadership:
Visual Effects Supervisors: Tim Alexander, John Knoll
Visual Effects Senior Producer: Jacqueline M. Lopez
Visual Effects Producer: Katie Lynch
Animation Director: Hal Hickel
Digital Production Supervisor: Michael Bauer
Art Directors: John Bell, Aaron McBride

PREVIOUS SPREAD
In ILM's first animated movie, Rango leads a charge of eclectic characters.

LEFT
Bad Bill confronts Rango in the saloon.

OPPOSITE
Rango portrays a dramatic role in a play of his own making in his terrarium.

RANGO WAS ILM'S FIRST FULL-LENGTH feature animated film. The director is Gore Verbinski, with whom ILM worked on the three *Pirates of the Caribbean* films. ILM's work on the film took place over a period of three years.

This was a very different type of project for the company: *Rango* was ILM's first opportunity to work on an animated feature. Of course, ILM had created thousands of CG shots before, but the company had never made a full-length feature film where absolutely every element—environments, characters, and sets—had to be created inside the computer.

Hal Hickel, animation director:

"ILM's work on *Rango* comprised everything from layout to final render. Verbinski had his own story team in L.A. at his Blind Wink Productions offices, and they created the 2-D (drawn) story reels in the typical fashion for animated features. While ILM was involved from day one, it was really once the story reels were done that the main part of the company's work began. First, our layout group transformed the 2-D animatics into 3-D CG scenes, working closely with Gore on the camera work. When a sequence had been approved in layout (basic blocking of characters, camera position, etc.), it was then handed off to animation where the character animators bring the scene to life. When a sequence was completed in animation, it moved on down the line to cloth simulation, effects (smoke, fire, blowing dust, etc.), lighting, and rendering."

A PHOTOGRAPHIC STYLE

The look of *Rango* is unique. It's a collaborative creation between ILM and a live-action director. The look isn't photoreal, it's photographic. And that's an interesting distinction.

Tim Alexander, visual effects supervisor:

"When someone looks at a photoreal image, they absolutely believe what they see can happen in the real world. It's something they would be able to go out and take a photograph of and not need to digitally enhance it. A photographic look, like we used on *Rango*, has the *qualities* of photography. When you take a photograph, if you're exposing for the shadows, the sky will blow out and be very bright. There's lens distortion. There's vignetting. There's film grain. These are qualities you get from photography and film that you can add to CG images to make them feel more photographic. Really looking at lighting and staying true to how photography works gives you a photographic look, versus what I consider to be more of a typical feature-animation look, where everything is saturated and at the same level. We went for more of a photography look."

One of the key challenges for ILM on *Rango* was the scale of the project. A very large visual effects film at ILM may have one thousand or more shots, with six hundred or so having character animation

ABOVE

A panoramic rendering of the town of Dirt

in them. But for *Rango*, ILM had to create character animation for an entire film.

Hal Hickel:

"*Rango* has approximately 1,600 shots, and virtually *all* of them involved character animation. Of course, this is what studios like Pixar do all the time, but it was a new experience for ILM. Typically, we're working with background footage that has been shot on location or on a set, into which we are placing digital elements (set extensions, digital creatures, explosions, etc.), so quite a lot of the scenery in the frame exists already. In an animated feature, you're creating everything from the ground up: every stone, every blade of grass. Just keeping track of all the thousands of assets needed to create this virtual world is a task in itself. Fortunately, ILM has a long history of tackling very big, very complex visual effects projects."

ANIMATED PIPELINE

Coping with the scale of the project caused ILM to develop a new pipeline that was tailored to the needs of an animated feature.

Hal Hickel:

"We really couldn't just plow ahead with our regular visual effects methodologies that were designed for live-action films. We had to design a new pipeline from the ground up, and even schedule the work differently, using an approach that was more sequence based, rather than focusing on the individual shots.

"One of the breakthroughs that came out of that is 'sequence based lighting.' It's a way to take a whole series of shots that share a similar lighting setup and work on them as one big group, rather than each shot being its own individual little project. Changes that globally affect all the shots can be pushed out more easily, while we still have the ability to go into each separate shot and tweak them at that level, too. It's all about 'efficiencies of scale' where you start to see savings—in both time and dollars—when you're working in a smart way with very large amounts of footage. The more efficient you can be, the more time the artists have to put their effort where it's really going to be seen, on screen, rather than in chores that have to do with managing all the work, but have nothing to do with making creative decisions."

ABOVE
An ILM lighting test featuring most of the main characters, in the bank environment

NINETY UNIQUE CHARACTERS

ILM developed ninety unique characters for the film. Each one is filled with an impressive amount of detail.

Tim Alexander:

"Every one of our characters can really act. We've never built that many characters on any one film, and to build that many at the detail level that we did, and then wrangling them all, is a significant accomplishment."

Hal Hickel:

"We've had projects from time to time where the focus is on acting rather than action: Yoda in *Star Wars*: Episodes II and III, Davy Jones in *Pirates of the Caribbean II* and *III*, to name a couple, but on *Rango*, it was 'all acting, all the time.' That was very exciting for the animators—and quite a challenge for us all."

ILM COMPLETE CREDITS

ABOVE, FROM LEFT TO RIGHT

ILM crew photos, themed to the show: *Indiana Jones and the Kingdom of the Crystal Skull* (2008); *The Perfect Storm* (2000); *Star Tours* (1987); *Twister* (1996); *XXX: State of the Union* (2005).

FOLLOWING SPREAD

A hidden cable catapult system rapidly accelerated quarter-scale models of both the DeLorean (3-feet long) and the steam locomotive (13-feet long, and 1,300 pounds) to a speed of twenty-two miles per hour past quarter-scale props and scenery. The action was captured from a camera platform atop a car driven by Dick Dova; key camera operator Pat Turner operates a camera on sticks mounted to the platform.

1977

Star Wars
20th Century Fox/Lucasfilm Ltd.
Academy Award®: Best Visual Effects

1980

Star Wars: Episode V
The Empire Strikes Back
20th Century Fox/Lucasfilm Ltd.
Academy Award®: Best Visual Effects

1981

Dragonslayer
Paramount
Academy Award® Nomination: Best Visual Effects

Raiders of the Lost Ark
Paramount/Lucasfilm Ltd.
Academy Award®: Best Visual Effects

1982

The Dark Crystal
Henson Productions

E.T.: The Extra-Terrestrial
Universal
Academy Award®: Best Visual Effects

Star Trek II: The Wrath of Khan
Paramount

Poltergeist
MGM/UA
Academy Award® Nomination: Best Visual Effects
BAFTA Award: Best Visual Effects

1983

Twice Upon a Time
Korty/Lucasfilm Ltd.

Star Wars: Episode VI Return of the Jedi
20th Century Fox/Lucasfilm Ltd.
Academy Award®: Best Visual Effects
BAFTA Award: Best Visual Effects

1984

Starman
Columbia

The Ewok Adventure
20th Century Fox Television/Lucasfilm Ltd.
Emmy Award: Best Visual Effects

The Neverending Story
Bavaria Studios

Star Trek III: The Search for Spock
Paramount

Indiana Jones and the Temple of Doom
Paramount/Lucasfilm Ltd.
Academy Award®: Best Visual Effects
BAFTA Award: Best Visual Effects

1985

Out of Africa
Universal

Enemy Mine
20th Century Fox

Young Sherlock Holmes
Paramount/Amblin
Academy Award® Nomination: Best Visual Effects

Ewoks: The Battle for Endor
20th Century Fox Television/Lucasfilm Ltd.
Emmy Award: Best Visual Effects

Amazing Stories
Universal Television/Amblin

Mishima
Warner Bros.

Explorers
Paramount

Back to the Future
Universal/Amblin
BAFTA Nomination: Best Visual Effects

Cocoon
20th Century Fox
Academy Award®: Best Visual Effects

The Goonies
Warner Bros./Amblin

1986

The Golden Child
Paramount

Star Trek IV: The Voyage Home
Paramount

Captain Eo—3-D Film for Disneyland
Disney

Howard the Duck
Universal

Labyrinth
Tristar/Hanson Prod.

General Cinema Trailer
General Cinema Corp.

The Money Pit
Universal/Amblin

1987

Empire of the Sun
Warner Bros./Amblin

Star Trek: The Next Generation
  Journey to Farpoint
    Paramount Television

*Batteries Not Included
  Universal/Amblin

Innerspace
  Warner Bros./Amblin
  Academy Award®: Best Visual Effects

Harry and the Hendersons
  Universal/Amblin

The Witches of Eastwick
  Warner Bros.
  BAFTA Award: Best Visual Effects

Star Tours—Simulator Ride for Disneyland
  Disney/Lucasfilm Ltd.

1988

The Last Temptation of Christ
  Universal

Cocoon, the Return
  20th Century Fox

Caddyshack II
  Warner Bros.

Who Framed Roger Rabbit?
  Touchstone Pictures/Amblin
  Academy Award®: Best Visual Effects
  BAFTA Award: Best Visual Effects

Tucker: A Man and His Dream
  Lucasfilm Ltd.

Star Trek Attraction—
  Universal Studios Tour
    Universal/Paramount

Willow
  MGM/Lucasfilm Ltd.
  Academy Award® Nomination: Best Visual Effects

1989

Always
  Amblin/Universal

Back to the Future, Part II
  Amblin/Universal
  Academy Award® Nomination: Best Visual Effects
  BAFTA Award: Best Visual Effects

The Abyss
  GJP Productions/ 20th Century Fox
  Academy Award®: Best Visual Effects

Ghostbusters II
  Columbia

Indiana Jones and the Last Crusade
  Lucasfilm Ltd./Paramount

Field of Dreams
  Universal

Tummy Trouble
  Disney

Mickey—Eisner Spot
  Disney

Body Wars—Simulator Ride for Disneyworld's
  Epcot Center
    Disney

Skin Deep
  Blake Edwards Co.

The 'Burbs
  Renfield Productions/Universal

1990

Die Hard 2
  20th Century Fox

Back to the Future, Part III
  Amblin/Universal

The Hunt for Red October
  Paramount

Ghost
  Paramount

The Godfather, Part III
  Paramount

Joe Versus the Volcano
  Warner Bros.

Akira Kurosawa's Dreams
  Kurosawa Prods./Warner Bros.

Roller Coaster Rabbit
  Disney

1991

Hook
  Tristar/Amblin
  Academy Award® Nomination: Best Visual Effects

Star Trek VI
  Paramount

Space Race Simulator Ride
  Showscan

Terminator 2: Judgment Day
  Carolco/Tristar
  Academy Award®: Best Visual Effects
  BAFTA Award: Best Visual Effects

The Rocketeer
  Disney

Backdraft
  Universal Pictures
  Academy Award® Nomination: Best Visual Effects

Hudson Hawk
  Tristar Pictures

The Doors
  Tristar Pictures

Arachniphobia
  Amblin/Universal

Switch
  HBO Films

Mickey's Audition
  Disney

1992

Death Becomes Her
  Universal
  Academy Award®: Best Visual Effects
  BAFTA Award: Best Visual Effects

Alive
  Disney/Paramount

Alien Encounter Simulator Ride
  Showscan

Memoirs of an Invisible Man
  Warner Bros.

The Young Indiana Jones Chronicles
  Lucasfilm Ltd.

1993

Schindler's List
  Amblin/Universal

Jurassic Park
Amblin/Universal
Academy Award®: Best Visual Effects
BAFTA Award: Best Visual Effects

Fire in the Sky
Paramount

Rising Sun
20th Century Fox

Malice
Castle Rock/Warner Bros.

Meteorman
MGM

Last Action Hero
Columbia Pictures

Manhattan Murder Mystery
Tristar Pictures

The Nutcracker
Warner Bros.

1994

Disclosure
Warner Bros.

Star Trek Generations
Paramount

Radioland Murders
Lucasfilm Ltd./Universal

ABOVE, FROM LEFT TO RIGHT

*Master and Commander: The Far
Side of the World* (2003); *Peter Pan*
(2003); *A.I. Artificial Intelligence*
(2001); *Dragonslayer* (1981); *Jurassic
Park* (1993); *Rango* (2011).

The Mask
New Line Cinema
Academy Award® Nomination: Best Visual Effects
BAFTA Award Nomination: Best Visual Effects

Forrest Gump
Paramount
Academy Award®: Best Visual Effects
BAFTA Award: Best Visual Effects

Baby's Day Out
20th Century Fox

Wolf
Columbia

Maverick
Warner Bros.

The Flintstones
Amblin/Universal

The Hudsucker Proxy
Warner Bros.

1995

Jumanji
Tristar

The American President
Columbia/Castle Rock

Sabrina
Paramount

The Indian in the Cupboard
Paramount

Congo
Paramount

Casper
Amblin/Universal

Village of the Damned
Universal

In the Mouth of Madness
New Line Cinema

1996

Mars Attacks!
Warner Bros.

Star Trek: First Contact
Paramount

101 Dalmatians
Disney

Daylight
Universal

Sleepers
Warner Bros.

Trigger Effect
Universal

Eraser
Warner Bros.

DragonHeart
Universal
Academy Award® Nomination: Best Visual Effects

Twister
Warner Bros./Universal
Academy Award® Nomination: Best Visual Effects
BAFTA Award: Best Visual Effects

Mission: Impossible
Paramount

Special Effects (An Imax Film)
WGBH

1997

Deconstructing Harry
Fine Line Features

Amistad
DreamWorks SKG

Titanic
20th Century Fox/Paramount

Flubber
Disney

Midnight In the Garden of Good and Evil
Warner Bros.

Starship Troopers
Tristar/Touchstone

Spawn
New Line Cinema

Contact
Warner Bros.

Men in Black
Columbia
BAFTA Award: Best Visual Effects

Speed 2: Cruise Control
20th Century Fox

The Lost World: Jurassic Park
Amblin/Universal
Academy Award® Nomination: Best Visual Effects

Star Wars Trilogy Special Edition
20th Century Fox/Lucasfilm Ltd.

1998

The Last Days
October Films

Mighty Joe Young
  Disney
  Academy Award® Nomination: Best Visual Effects

Jack Frost
  Warner Bros.

Celebrity
  Miramax

Meet Joe Black
  Universal

Reach the Rock
  Gramercy Pictures

Snake Eyes
  Paramount/Disney

Saving Private Ryan
  DreamWorks SKG
  BAFTA Award: Best Visual Effects

Small Soldiers
  DreamWorks SKG

Deep Impact
  DreamWorks SKG/Paramount

Mercury Rising
  Universal/Imagine Films

Deep Rising
  Disney

1999

Sweet and Lowdown
  Sony Pictures Classics

Snow Falling on Cedars
  Universal

Magnolia
  New Line Cinema

Galaxy Quest
  DreamWorks SKG

Deep Blue Sea
  Warner Bros.

The Green Mile
  Warner Bros.

Sleepy Hollow
  Paramount
  BAFTA Nomination: Best Visual Effects

Bringing Out the Dead
  Paramount/Disney

The Haunting
  DreamWorks SKG

Wild Wild West
  Warner Bros.

Star Wars: Episode I The Phantom Menace
  Lucasfilm Ltd.
  Academy Award® Nomination: Best Visual Effects
  BAFTA Nomination: Best Visual Effects

The Mummy
  Universal
  BAFTA Nomination: Best Visual Effects

October Sky
  Universal

2000

Pollock
  Sony Pictures Classics

Pay It Forward
  Miramax

Space Cowboys
  Warner Bros.

The Perfect Storm
  Warner Bros.
  Academy Award® Nomination: Best Visual Effects
  BAFTA Award: Best Visual Effects

The Adventures of Rocky and Bullwinkle
  Universal

Mission to Mars
  Disney

2001

The Majestic
  Warner Bros.

Harry Potter and the Sorcerer's Stone
  Warner Bros.

Planet of the Apes
  20th Century Fox

Jurassic Park III
  Universal

A.I. Artificial Intelligence
  Warner Bros./DreamWorks SKG
  Academy Award® Nomination: Best Visual Effects
  BAFTA Nomination: Best Visual Effects

Pearl Harbor
  Disney
  Academy Award® Nomination: Best Visual Effects

The Mummy Returns
  Universal

Sweet November
  Warner Bros.

The Pledge
  Warner Bros.

2002

Gangs of New York
  Miramax
  BAFTA Nomination: Best Visual Effects

Harry Potter and the Chamber of Secrets
  Warner Bros.
  BAFTA Nomination: Best Visual Effects

Star Wars Bounty Hunter
  Lucasarts Entertainment

Punch-Drunk Love
  Columbia/New Line Cinema

Blood Work
  Warner Bros.

Signs
  Disney

K-19: The Widowmaker
  Paramount

Men in Black 2
  Sony Pictures

Minority Report
  DreamWorks SKG
  BAFTA Nomination: Best Visual Effects

The Bourne Identity
  Universal

Star Wars: Episode II Attack of the Clones
  Lucasfilm Ltd.
  Academy Award® Nomination: Best Visual Effects

Big Trouble
  Disney

E.T.: The Extra-Terrestrial: 20th Anniversary
  Universal

The Time Machine
Warner Bros./DreamWorks SKG

Impostor
Miramax/Dimension

2003

Peter Pan
Universal/Columbia/Revolution

Stuck On You
20th Century Fox

Timeline
Paramount

PREVIOUS SPREAD
Visual effects supervisor John Knoll
discusses the USS Enterprise-E
shooting miniature with model project supervisor John Goodson and
chief model maker Kim Smith. The
Enterprise-E was the last complete
physical model of the Enterprise
constructed for filming. Prior to First
Contact, ILM had constructed eight
Starfleet ships of varying scales for
the film franchise and the various
Star Trek television series.

ABOVE, FROM LEFT TO RIGHT
Pirates of the Caribbean: Dead
Man's Chest (2006); Harry Potter
and the Half-Blood Prince (2009);
Young Sherlock Holmes (1985);
Back to the Future, Part III (1990);
DragonHeart (1996); Avatar (2009)

Master and Commander:
The Far Side of the World
20th Century Fox
Academy Award® Nomination: Best Visual Effects
BAFTA Nomination: Best Visual Effects

Once Upon a Time in Mexico
Miramax

11'9"01—September 11 (Segment USA)
Empire Pictures

The League of Extraordinary Gentlemen
20th Century Fox

Pirates of the Caribbean:
The Curse of the Black Pearl
Disney
Academy Award® Nomination: Best Visual Effects
BAFTA Nomination: Best Visual Effects

Terminator 3: Rise of the Machines
Warner Bros.

The Hulk
Universal

Dreamcatcher
Warner Bros.

Tears of the Sun
Revolution Studios

The Hunted
Paramount

2004

Lemony Snicket's
A Series of Unfortunate Events
Paramount

Sky Captain and the World of Tomorrow
Paramount

The Village
Disney

The Bourne Supremacy
Universal

The Chronicles of Riddick
Universal

Harry Potter and the Prisoner of Azkaban
Warner Bros.
Academy Award® Nomination: Best Visual Effects
BAFTA Nomination: Best Visual Effects

The Day After Tomorrow
20th Century Fox

Van Helsing
Universal

Hidalgo
Disney

Twisted
Paramount

Along Came Polly
Universal

2005

Munich
DreamWorks SKG

The Chronicles of Narnia: The Lion, the Witch and
the Wardrobe
Disney
Academy Award® Nomination: Best Visual Effects
BAFTA Nomination: Best Visual Effects

Rent
Revolution

Cheaper by the Dozen 2
20th Century Fox

Harry Potter and the Goblet of Fire
Warner Bros.

Jarhead
Universal

Chicken Little
Disney

The Island
DreamWorks SKG/Warner Bros.

War of the Worlds
Paramount/DreamWorks SKG
Academy Award® Nomination: Best Visual Effects

Herbie: Fully Loaded
Disney

The Adventures of Shark Boy and Lava Girl
Dimension Films

Star Wars: Episode III Revenge of the Sith
Lucasfilm Ltd.

XXX: State of the Union
Revolution

The Amityville Horror
MGM

Eros
Masti

The Pacifier
Disney

Son of the Mask
New Line Cinema

Are We There Yet?
Revolution

2006

Eragon
20th Century Fox

The Nightmare Before Christmas 3-D
Disney

Lady in the Water
Warner Bros.

Pirates of the Caribbean: Dead Man's Chest
Disney
Academy Award®: Best Visual Effects
BAFTA: Best Visual Effects

Poseidon
Warner Bros.
Academy Award® Nomination: Best Visual Effects

The Fast and the Furious: Tokyo Drift
Universal

Mission: Impossible III
Paramount

Eight Below
Disney

2007

National Treasure: Book of Secrets
Disney

Touching Home
Independent

Lions for Lambs
United Artists

There Will Be Blood
Paramount Vantage

Rush Hour 3
New Line Cinema

Harry Potter and the Order of the Phoenix
Warner Bros.

Evan Almighty
Universal Pictures

Transformers
Paramount/DreamWorks
Academy Award® Nomination: Best Visual Effects

Pirates of the Caribbean: At World's End
Disney
Academy Award® Nomination: Best Visual Effects
BAFTA Nomination: Best Visual Effects

2008

The Tale of Despereaux
Universal Pictures

Twilight
Summit Entertainment

Miracle at St. Anna
Disney

*Wall*E*
Disney/Pixar

The Happening
20th Century Fox

The Love Guru
Paramount

Indiana Jones and the Kingdom of the Crystal Skull
Lucasfilm/Paramount
BAFTA Nomination: Best Visual Effects

Speed Racer
Warner Bros.

Iron Man
Marvel Studios/Paramount
Academy Award® Nomination: Best Visual Effects
BAFTA Nomination: Best Visual Effects

The Spiderwick Chronicles
Paramount

2009

Avatar
20th Century Fox

Surrogates
Touchstone Pictures

Jonas Brothers: The 3-D Concert Experience
Disney

Harry Potter and the Half-Blood Prince
Warner Bros.
BAFTA Nomination: Best Visual Effects

Transformers: Revenge of the Fallen
Paramount/DreamWorks

Terminator: Salvation
Warner Bros./Sony Pictures

Star Trek
Paramount
Academy Award® Nomination: Best Visual Effects

Confessions of a Shopaholic
Disney

2010

The Last Airbender
Paramount

Iron Man 2
Marvel Studios/Paramount
Academy Award® Nomination: Best Visual Effects

2011

Transformers Theme Park Ride
Creative Park Productions

Mission: Impossible—Ghost Protocol
Paramount

Cowboys & Aliens
Universal

Transformers: Dark of the Moon
Paramount/DreamWorks

Super 8
Paramount

Pirates of the Caribbean: On Stranger Tides
Disney

Star Tours II Theme Park Ride
Disney

Rango
Paramount/Nickelodeon

I Am Number Four
Disney

2012

Battleship
Universal Pictures

The Avengers
Disney

Red Tails
Lucasfilm Ltd.

AWARDS

Academy Awards® for Scientific and Technical Achievement

The Academy's Scientific and Technical Awards honor the men, women, and companies whose discoveries and innovations have contributed in significant, outstanding, and lasting ways to motion pictures. Each year's honorees are celebrated at a formal dinner held two weeks prior to the Oscar ceremony. As of 2011, ILM has received 24 Academy Awards.

1981

Technical Achievement Award
Motion Picture Figure Mover
Recipients: Dennis Muren and Stuart Ziff

Scientific and Engineering Award
Beam Splitter Optical Composite Printer
Recipients: Richard Edlund and Industrial Light & Magic

Scientific and Engineering Award
Empire Camera
Recipients: Richard Edlund and Industrial Light & Magic

1987

Technical Achievement Award
Wire Rig Model Support System
Recipient: Tadeuz Krzanowski

1992

Technical Achievement Award
The Morf System
Recipients: Tom Brigham and Doug Smythe

1993

Scientific and Engineering Award
Digital Motion Retouching
Recipients: Mark Leather, Les Dittert, Doug Smythe, and George Joblove

1994

Scientific and Engineering Award
ILM Trilinear High Resolution CCD Digital Input Scanning System
Recipients: Lincoln Hu, Michael Mackenzie, and Glenn Kennel and Mike Davis of Eastman Kodak

1995

Technical Achievement Award
Digital Film Compositing
Recipients: Doug Smythe, Lincoln Hu, Douglas Kay, and Industrial Light & Magic

1996

Scientific and Engineering Award
Viewpaint
Recipients: Zoran Kacic-Alecic, John Schlag, Brian Knep, and Tomas Williams

Scientific and Engineering Award
Dynamation
Recipient: Jim Hourihan

Technical Achievement Award
Direct Input Device (D.I.D.)
Recipients: Brian Knep, Craig Hayes, Rick Sayre, and Thomas Williams

Technical Achievement Award
Computer Generated Fur
Recipients: Jeffrey Yost, Christian Roulet, David Benson, and Florian Kainz

1998

Technical Achievement Award
Motion-Controlled Silent Camera Dollies
Recipients: Michael MacKenzie, Mike Bolles, Udo Pampel, and Joseph Fulmer

Technical Achievement Award
"Caricature" Animation System
Recipient: Cary Phillips

2002

Technical Achievement Award
Motion and Structure Recovery System (MARS)
Recipients: Steve Sullivan and Eric Schafer

Technical Achievement Award
Creature Dynamics System
Recipients: Cary Phillips and Sebastian Marino

2003

Technical Achievement Award
Subsurface Scattering Render Technology
Recipient: Christophe Hery

2006

Technical Achievement Award
OpenEXR
Recipient: Florian Kainz

Scientific and Engineering Award
Image-based Modeling System
Recipients: Steve Sullivan, Colin Davidson, Max Chen, and Francesco Callari

Scientific and Engineering Award
Fluid Simulation System
Recipients: Nick Rasmussen, Ron Fedkiw, and Frank Losasso Petterson

2010

Technical Achievement Award
Imocap
Recipients: Steve Sullivan, Kevin Wooley, Brett Allen, and Colin Davidson

Technical Achievement Award
Ambient Occlusion
Recipients: Hayden Landis, Ken McGaugh, and Hilmar Koch

Scientific and Engineering Achievement Award
Point-based Rendering
Recipients: Christophe Hery, Per Christensen, and Michael Bunnell

2011

Technical Achievement Award (Certificate)
ObaQ Render Queue Management System
Recipient: Florian Kainz

BIBLIOGRAPHY

Books

The Art of Star Wars: The Empire Strikes Back
        by Deborah Call, 1997
Creating the Worlds of Star Wars: 365 Days
        by John Knoll and J. W. Rinzler, 2005
Sculpting a Galaxy by Lorne Peterson, 2006
Industrial Light & Magic: The Art of Special Effects
        by Thomas G. Smith, 1988
Industrial Light & Magic: Into the Digital Realm
        by Mark Cotta Vaz, 1996

Documents provided by ILM

Document by Habib Zargarpour on *Twister*
Document by Henry LaBounta on *Twister*
Document by James Straus on *DragonHeart*
Document by Scott Squires on *DragonHeart*
Document by Dennis Muren on *The Lost World:*
        Jurassic Park
Document by Eric Brevig on *Men in Black*
Document by Daniel Jeannette on *The Mummy*
Document by Ben Snow on *The Mummy*
Document by Stefen Fangmeier on *The Perfect Storm*
Document by Eric Brevig on *Pearl Harbor*
Document by Dennis Muren on *A.I. Artificial Intelligence*
Document by Scott Farrar on *Minority Report*
Document by Robert Stromberg on *Master and Commander*
Document by Roger Guyett on *Harry Potter and the Prisoner*
        of Azkaban
Document by Bill George on *Harry Potter and the Prisoner*
        of Azkaban
Document by Dennis Muren on *War of the Worlds*
Document by Pablo Helman on *Terminator 3:*
        Rise of the Machines
Document by ILM, *Architecture at LDAC*

Articles

Cinefex, issue 63, *The Ghost and Mr. Muren* by Jody Duncan
        (*Casper*)
Cinefex, issue 66, *Heart and Soul* by Jody Duncan
        (*DragonHeart*)
Cinefex, issue 66, *Riders on the Storm* by Jonathan Luskin
        (*Twister*)
Cinefex, issue 68, *Martial Art* by Mark Cotta Vaz
        (*Mars Attacks!*)
Cinefex, issue 69, *Everything Old Is New Again* by Mark
        Cotta Vaz (*Star Wars Special Edition*)
Cinefex, issue 70, *Basic Black* by Janine Pourroy
        (*Men in Black*)
Cinefex, issue 70, *On the Shoulders of Giants* by Jody Duncan
        (*Jurassic Park: The Lost World*)
Cinefex, issue 72, *Titanic Aftermath* by Jody Duncan (*Titanic*)
Cinefex, issue 78, *Heroes' Journey* by Jody Duncan, Kevin
        H. Martin, Mark Cotta Vaz (*Star Wars*: Episode I)
Cinefex, issue 85, *Warrior Kings* by Joe Fordham
        (*The Mummy Returns*)
Cinefex, issue 86, *More War* by Jody Duncan (*Pearl Harbor*)
Cinefex, issue 87, *Mecha Odyssey* by Joe Fordham
        (*A.I. Artificial Intelligence*)
Cinefex, issue 91, *Future Reality* by Joe Fordham
        (*Minority Report*)
Cinefex, issue 95, *Winds of War* by Joe Fordham
        (*Terminator III*)
Cinefex , issue 98, *Freeze Frames* by Jody Duncan
        (*The Day After Tomorrow*)
Cinefex, issue 102, *Toward a New Hope* by Jody Duncan
        (*Star Wars* Episode III)
Cinefex issue 106, *Wipeout* by Jody Duncan (*Poseidon*)
Cinefex, issue 111, *Bots & Bayhem* by Jody Duncan
        (*Transformers*)
Cinefex, issue 114, *The Man in the Iron Mask* by Jody Duncan
        (*Iron Man*)
Cinefex, issue 118, *A New Enterprise* by Joe Fordham
        (*Star Trek*)
Cinefex, issue 118, *Rage Against the Machines* by Jody Duncan
        (*Terminator Salvation*)
Cinefex, issue 119, *Heavy Metal* by Jody Duncan
        (*Transformers: Revenge of the Fallen*)
Film & Video, December 2005, *Building the War Zone with*
        Invisible FX by Barbara Robertson (*Jarhead*)
Millimeter, November 2005, *Jarhead: Playing with Fire*
        by Ellen Wolff (*Jarhead*)

OPPOSITE

Concept art of Surak statue by ILM
artist Alex Jaeger for *Star Trek* (2009)

Interview transcripts

George Lucas, May 6, 2010

George Lucas, May 16, 2003

Dennis Muren, February 18, 2003

Dennis Muren, February 10, 2010

Scott Farrar, December 16, 2009

Jeff White, December 8, 2009

Roger Guyett, January 25, 2010

Jim Morris, January 8, 2010

Jim Morris, August 20, 2002

Curt Miyashiro, December 17, 2009

Stefen Fangmeier, June 27, 2002

Fangmeier, December 14, 2009

Habib Zargarpour, January 27, 2010

Ken Ralston, February 4, 2010

Fangmeier, June 27, 2002

Scott Squires, June 25, 2002

Rob Coleman, October 28, 2002

Rob Coleman, February 28, 2007

Cary Philips, December 8, 2009

Yusei Uesugi, December 16, 2009

Rick McCallum, January 8, 2004

Hal Hickel, December 9, 2009

David Nakabayashi, January 14, 2010

Lorne Peterson, April 12, 2010

Bill George, December 11, 2009

Roger Guyett, January 25, 2010

Paul Huston, December 10, 2009

Pablo Helman, February 18, 2003

Pablo Helman, January 24, 2010

Steve Sullivan, December 8, 2009

Nigel Sumner, December 10, 2009

Scott Benza, December 17, 2009

Ron Fedkiw, December 17, 2009

Jason Smith, December 18, 2009

Tim Alexander, January 26, 2010

Russell Earl, December 21, 2009

Craig Hammack, January 6, 2010

Richard Bluff, December 9, 2009

John Knoll, April 20, 2010

ILM interview with Rob Coleman, January 13, 2005

ILM interview with Rob Coleman, February 18, 2007

Interview with Ben Snow, conducted by ILM, questions by Glintenkamp, July 28, 2009

Interview with John Knoll, conducted by ILM, questions by Glintenkamp, July 1, 2009

Interview with Miles Perkins, conducted by ILM, questions by Glintenkamp, October 15, 2009

Interview with Lynwen Brennan, transcript provided by ILM does not indicate date or who conducted interview

Interview with Chrissie England conducted by Leslie Iwerks, transcript provided by ILM does not indicate date

Interview with J. J. Abrams, conducted by Leslie Iwerks, April 28, 2010

INDEX

ABRAMS
Editor: Eric Klopfer
Designer: Liam Flanagan and J. W. Rinzler
Production Manager: Ankur Ghosh

LUCASFILM
Executive Editor: J. W. Rinzler
Art Director: Troy Alders
Image Archives: Tina Mills, Shahana Alam, Stacey Leong, Matthew Azeveda

ILM
Director of Marketing and Communications: Miles Perkins
Technical Publicist: Greg Grusby
Cover Design: Kelly H. Smith

Photographers: Matthew Azeveda, Brent Bowers, Sean Casey, Terry Chostner, Greg Grusby, Keith Hamshere, Miki Herman, Alex Ivanov, Stacey Leong, Jay Maidment, Tina Mills, David Owen, and Allyson Wiley

Library of Congress Cataloging-in-Publication Data:

Glintenkamp, Pamela.
 Industrial Light & Magic : the art of innovation / Pamela Glintenkamp.
   p. cm.
 Summary: "Industrial Light & Magic tells the story, through the words of filmmakers, artists, and technicians, of the visual effects house, Industrial Light & Magic, which was founded by George Lucas in 1975"—Provided by publisher.
 ISBN 978-0-8109-9802-5 (hardback)
 1. Cinematography—Special effects. 2. Industrial Light and Magic
(Studio) 3. Cinematographers—United States--Interviews. I. Title.
 TR858.G64 2011
 778.5'345—dc22
          2011007169

Printed and bound in China
10 9 8 7 6 5 4 3

Abrams books are available at special discounts when purchased in quantity for premiums and promotions as well as fundraising or educational use. Special editions can also be created to specification. For details, contact specialsales@abramsbooks.com or the address below.

ABRAMS
THE ART OF BOOKS SINCE 1949
115 West 18th Street
New York, NY 10011
www.abramsbooks.com

Visit the official *Star Wars* website: www.starwars.com

Dedication: For my father, Rik, with memories of our weekly trips to the cinema bookshop after school.   —Pamela Glintenkamp

Author's Acknowledgments

George Lucas, for setting ILM its greatest challenges, and thereby making its history all the more fascinating.

J. W. Rinzler, executive editor at LucasBooks, for the invitation to undertake this project and his support throughout the process.

Miles Perkins, Marcy Ginsburg, and Greg Grusby of ILM, for providing mountains of useful research material.

Tina Mills for her fantastic work managing the images.

Lynne Hale, senior director, public relations at Lucasfilm, for providing the original opportunity for me to produce the Lucasfilm History Project, and conduct the first ILM interviews that fueled the conceptualization of this book.

Cindy Young Russell for her tremendous assistance and enthusiasm during the History Project interviews.

Eric Klopfer, associate editor at Abrams, for his enthusiasm for the project and appreciation of the work involved, and Eric Himmel, editor in chief at Abrams, for his initial support for and belief in the project.

Peter Falkner, for providing encouragement and an ever-attentive ear during the two-year gestation period for this book.

Don Shay and *Cinefex*, for their years of dedication to the art of visual effects and for being the ultimate resource for chronicling the industry.

Rik Glintenkamp, for inspiring my passion for film from a very young age.

Adele Glintenkamp, for her pride, even if in silence.

Bramwell Glintenkamp, for her companionship and patience.

Jo Donaldson, Robyn E. Stanley, and Carol Moen Wing of the Skywalker Ranch Library, for being there to respond to the occasional query.

The individuals who agreed to be interviewed especially for this book: Tim Alexander, Scott Benza, Richard Bluff, Lynwen Brennan, Russell Earl, Chrissie England, Stefen Fangmeier, Scott Farrar, Ron Fedkiw, Bill George, Roger Guyett, Craig Hammack, Pablo Helman, Hal Hickel, Paul Huston, John Knoll, George Lucas, Curt Miyashiro, Jim Morris, Dennis Muren, David Nakabayashi, Miles Perkins, Lorne Peterson, Cary Phillips, Ken Ralston, Jason Smith, Ben Snow, Steve Sullivan, Nigel Sumner, Yusei Uesugi, Jeff White, and Habib Zargarpour.